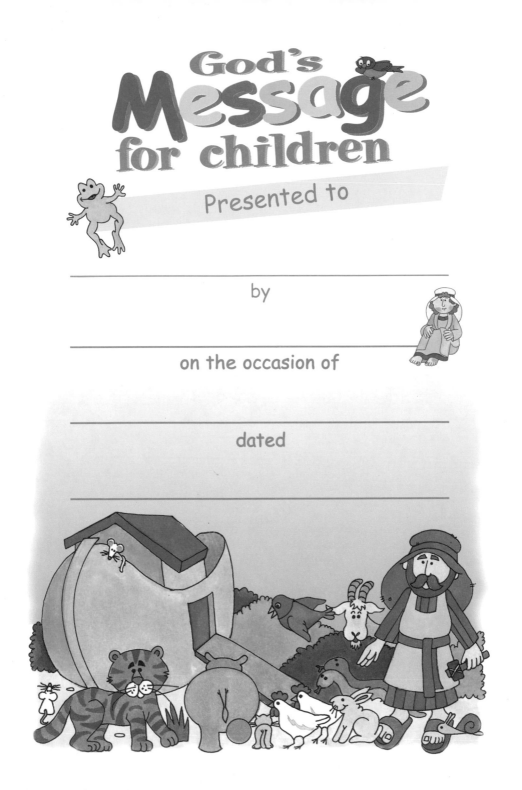

God's Message for children

Presented to

by

on the occasion of

dated

God's Message for children

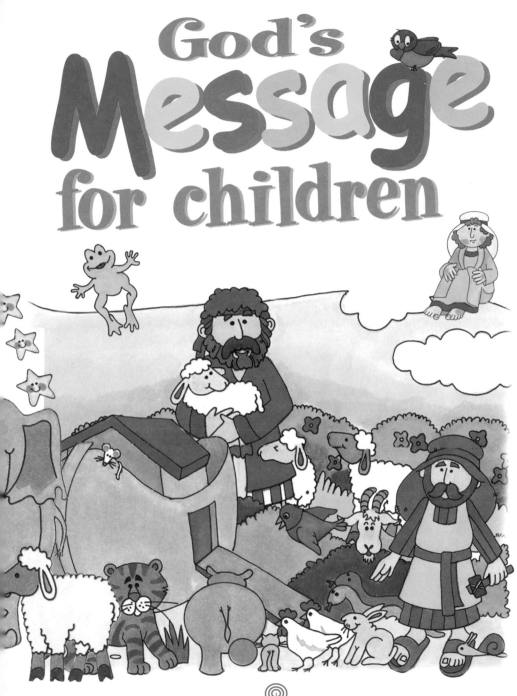

CANDLE
BOOKS

Copyright © 1999
CHRISTIAN ART PUBLISHERS
P O Box 1599, Vereeniging, 1930

Illustrations by Theresa Hills

Published in the UK by Candle Books 2001
Reprinted 2002
Distributed by
STL, P O Box 300,
Carlisle CA3 0QS

Scripture quotations taken and adapted from
the Holy Bible, New International Version
Copyright © 1973, 1978, 1984 by
International Bible Society

ISBN 1 85985 332 3

Worldwide co-edition arranged by Angus Hudson Ltd,
Concorde House, Mill Hill, London NW7 3SA, England.
Tel: +44 20 8959 3668
Fax: 44 20 8959 3678

Printed in Hong Kong

God's Message for children

God never forsakes his
children. He has been
there since the beginning.
Adam and Eve knew this,
Moses saw it when the
Red Sea parted before
him, Jesus came to show it and Paul told everybody about
it. That's why there are so many stories about God's
presence and help. In God's Message for children every
child is invited to join in on the journey through the Bible.
With a story for each day of the year God's love and care
become evident. Children needn't be afraid, because the
Lord is with them.

God's Message for children tries to
convey the principles of the Bible in
easily understood, everyday English.
The passages are short, but long
enough to be more than a mere
thought, and help children to discover Christ's love in a
simple, true-to-Scripture way.

When it all started ...

Genesis 1

In the beginning God created the heavens and the earth. (Gen 1:1)

God made heaven and the earth a very long time ago. Everything was pitch-dark. There were no people or animals, only water. Then God said, 'Let there be light!' and suddenly everything was bright. God was happy with the light.

The next day God decided to make the sky that we see above us every day. On the third day God gathered all the water together into one place and called it the 'sea'. The dry ground He named 'land'. On that same day God also made all the plants and trees.

At the start of the fourth day, God decided to make the sun so it could shine during the day. He also made the moon and the stars to shine at night. On the fifth day God made all the sea creatures and fish and every kind of bird.

On the sixth day God said, 'Let there be animals on earth.' The next moment there were animals as far as the eye could see. The whole earth was now full of life. It was very beautiful.

Remember: Our God is a powerful God. He created everything.

The Lord makes people

Genesis 1

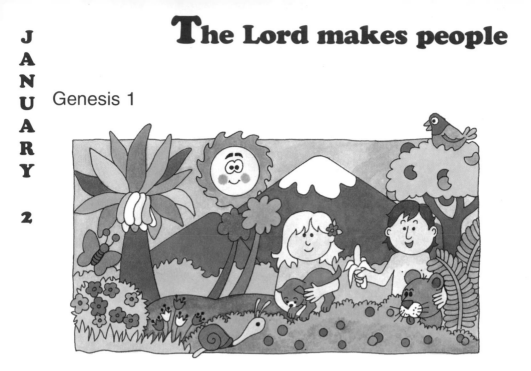

'Let's make people to take care of the earth for Us.' (Gen 1:26)

It took God six days to make the world. There were all sorts of plants, fish and animals but no people, so, on the sixth day, God decided to make people. The first man and woman God made were His most important creation. God was so proud of Adam and Eve that He put them in charge of everything on earth. They were God's representatives and the world was in their hands.

God told Adam and Eve to look after the world and to have children so that, in time, there would be people all over the world. God made sure there was enough food for them to eat. They ate the grain and fruit which grew on the plants and trees. The animals and birds ate grass and leafy plants.

Everything started off well. The first people were more important to God than anything else He had created. God wanted them to take good care of the earth and we need to do the same. Every single part of the world belongs to God, including all the animals and plants. That's why we should not spoil His world by being greedy and wasteful. We should work with nature and protect what God has given us.

Remember: Man is God's most important creation.

God rests

Genesis 2

On the seventh day God had finished with everything He made. Then He rested after all the hard work. (Gen 2:2)

In six days God made all that we see around us as well as everything we don't see. God is so mighty and powerful that He holds the whole world in His hand. His Name is written on the whole universe.

When God finished making everything, He decided to rest and He told the people to rest from their work every seventh day. This was to be a special day.

Today we Christians have our day of rest on Sundays because this is the day when Jesus rose from the dead. It's a day when we can be together with our families and when we can go to church and give thanks for all the wonderful things that the Lord has made. And, on Sundays just as on any other day, we must help others and pray for people who are suffering or in trouble.

 Remember: We serve God seven days a week.

The Lord gives Adam a wife

Genesis 2

'At last!' Adam exclaimed. 'The Lord has made someone just like me. She will be called "woman."' (Gen 2:23)

The story of how God made the world is so awesome that it is told twice, in the first two chapters of Genesis. In Genesis 2 we read about the beautiful Garden of Eden, and how God told Adam, the first human being, that he could live there and take care of the garden.

One day God decided that it was not good for Adam to be all alone. So He made animals and birds and Adam had to choose names for them. But Adam was still the only human being.

So the Lord put Adam to sleep. Then He took one of Adam's ribs and made a woman from it. The Lord brought the woman to Adam. Adam was pleased to have someone like him on earth. From now on the woman would help him and he wouldn't be on his own any more.

The very first wedding took place in Eden. Before there was any sin or death in the world, God brought the first man and woman together. Adam said something very important about marriage. He said grown-ups who get married should love each other for ever and stay together for the rest of their lives. They should love each other for ever.

💡 **Remember:** We must love other people and help them.

Adam and Eve make the Lord very sad

Genesis 3

'It's only the fruit from the tree in the middle of the garden that we are not allowed to eat. God says we must not eat it or even touch it, or we will die.' (Gen 3:3)

The snake wanted to get Eve into trouble. He asked her, 'Did God really say you mustn't eat any of the fruit in the garden?' She told him they could eat all the fruit except the fruit from the tree in the middle of the garden. 'You won't die if you eat it!' the snake hissed. He told Eve that she and Adam should eat the fruit because then they would become like God.

Without thinking twice, Adam and Eve started eating the forbidden fruit. Instantly their eyes were opened. They saw for the first time that they had no clothes on. That evening Adam and Eve tried to hide away from God in the garden when He came looking for them. God asked them what they had done. Adam said it was all Eve's fault. Eve blamed the snake.

The Lord was very sad. He put a curse on the snake. He told Eve that she would suffer a lot of pain when she had babies. Adam's punishment was that he would have to work very hard to make a living. The first people on earth really landed themselves in a mess and to this day we pay a price for it. Fortunately God still cares for us.

 Remember: God's children must obey God.

A second chance

Genesis 3-4

The Lord told Adam and his wife to get out of the Garden of Eden. They had to work the land outside Eden from now on. (Gen 3:23)

The first human beings had the chance of a lifetime and they let it slip through their fingers. They had to live outside Eden because they had disobeyed God, but God gave them another chance. He did not destroy the world, and Adam and Eve were still alive, even if they were not allowed in Eden.

Sadly, they still hadn't learnt their lesson. One day Cain and Abel, Adam and Eve's sons, each brought the Lord an offering. The Lord accepted Abel's offering, but not Cain's. This made Cain so angry that he attacked and killed his brother. They were barely out of Eden, and already someone had been murdered!

We all do wrong things which hurt the Lord, but our God is a good God. He doesn't give up on us when we have done something wrong. He gives us another chance. He even sent His son, Jesus, to die on the cross for us. We can take all our sins to Him and ask for forgiveness. In the Bible it says Jesus promises to forgive us if we are really sorry for what we have done.

🔅 **Remember:** God loves all His children.

Noah builds an ark

Genesis 6-7

Noah was a man who did what God said. There was no one like him on earth at the time. He was very close to God. (Gen 6:9)

The world had become a rotten and violent place because of the people's sins and it broke God's heart. He almost wished He hadn't made people. God decided He was going to wipe them all from the face of the earth. But there was one man who obeyed God – Noah. So God decided to spare the lives of Noah and his family. As for the rest of the world – a flood would destroy every creature on earth.

The Lord told Noah to build a big boat from wood. We call it an ark. Noah had to take a pair of every kind of animal – a male and a female – into the ark with him. This was to make sure that there would be animals and birds on earth again after the flood. God reminded Noah to take enough food for his family and the animals.

It rained for forty days and forty nights. The waters rose higher and higher until they covered even the highest mountains. The flood lasted another one hundred and fifty days. Every living thing died. Only Noah, and those he took with him in the ark, were left alive and God took good care of them.

Remember: We must obey God every day.

The waters start going down

Genesis 8

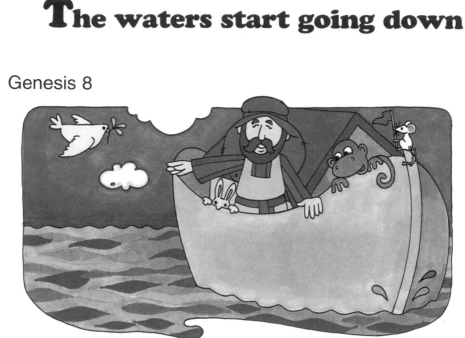

The Lord was pleased with Noah's offering. He said to Himself, 'I will never again send something as bad as this flood. Not even if people do wicked things.' (Gen 8:21)

Slowly but surely the water was receding. One day Noah opened the window in the ark and released a raven. Then he sent a dove out to see if it could find dry ground. It couldn't so it flew back to the ark. Seven days later Noah sent the dove out again. Towards evening, the dove came back with an olive leaf in its beak and Noah knew that the water was almost gone. A week later he sent out the dove once more. This time it didn't return so Noah opened up the ark.

Noah was happy that the Lord had spared their lives. He brought the Lord an offering to thank Him. This pleased the Lord and He promised that the world would never be struck by such a disaster again.

God is such a good God. He loves each one of us so much and He is happy when we listen to Him every day.

Remember: We must look after what God has made.

God's rainbow is meant for all of us

Genesis 9

'I will not break the agreement I make with you. I promise never to send another flood to kill all people and animals and destroy the earth. Never again will there be so much water in one place on earth.' (Gen 9:11)

God blessed Noah and his family. It showed how much He loved them. He gave them plants, animals, birds and fish for food but warned them never to kill another human being.

Then God made an agreement with Noah and his sons. It is called a covenant. He promised never to send a flood to destroy the whole world again. God gave them a sign to prove that He would keep his promise. The sign was a rainbow. To this day we still see a rainbow in the sky after rain and God's promise to Noah still stands. Since the flood in Noah's time there has never been so much water at one time in any place on earth. After a shower of rain, look for a rainbow. It reminds us of how much God still cares for us all.

God doesn't spy on us or try to catch us out. He wants us to be close to Him. We must put our hand in His every day because He loves us.

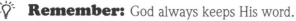

Remember: God always keeps His word.

People aren't as great as they think

Genesis 11

'Come, let's go down and give them different languages. Then they won't be able to understand each other.' (Gen 11:7)

Long ago people all over the world spoke the same language so they all understood one another. One day, to show how clever and important they were, they decided to build a huge city with a tower that would reach to the sky. The Lord came down to see the city and the tower that was being built and He was not impressed. He didn't like the way the people were showing off so He decided to mix up their words. Suddenly everyone started speaking different languages. They were unable to understand one another and that ended their building operations. The city where they built the tower was called Babel.

People moved away from Babel to different places across the world. There was no sense in staying together if they couldn't understand each other. This was God's way of punishing them for thinking too highly of themselves.

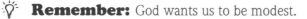 **Remember:** God wants us to be modest.

God's new hero: Abram

Genesis 12-13

'Leave your country, your people and your family. Go to the land I will show you.' (Gen 12:1)

One day the Lord went to the land Ur to tell Abram that He wanted him to move away. Abram didn't have to think twice. He did as the Lord told him, and finally arrived in Canaan. There God told him that this land would one day belong to his offspring. He also said, 'I will bless you and make you famous.' Abram built an altar to thank and worship the Lord.

Later on Abram and his wife Sarai went down to Egypt. Sarai was very beautiful and the Egyptian king took her for a wife. He thought she was Abram's sister but the Lord punished the king for what he did. The king was angry and asked Abram why he hadn't told him Sarai was his wife. Then he told them to leave Egypt straight away.

Yet again God told Abram that he would have very many grandchildren and so would they, and the family line would go on and on. Wherever Abram went, the Lord was with him.

We who believe in the Lord are also Abram's offspring and proof of how God kept His promise to Abram. God is our Father who cares for us.

🔆 **Remember:** We have a Father in heaven who loves us.

Abram will have a big family

Genesis 15

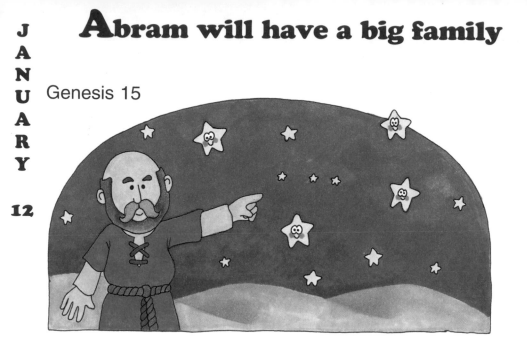

The Lord brought Abram outside beneath the night sky and told him, 'Look up into the heavens and count the stars if you can. Your descendants will be like that – too many to count!' (Gen 15:5)

One day the Lord spoke to Abram again. He told him again that he would be the father of a great nation. But Abram and his wife were childless and he reminded God of this fact. Still the Lord made him look up at the sky and promised Abram that his descendants would be as countless as the stars. Abram believed Him and this pleased the Lord.

That day the Lord made another covenant with Abram to prove that He would keep His promise. Abram had to kill a ram, a goat and a heifer and cut each one open, in two halves. Then, as the sun was going down, Abram fell asleep.

After the sun had set, Abram saw a smoking firepot and a flaming torch pass between the pieces of meat. This was the sign that God would one day give Abram his own country and many descendants.

God never lies. Sometimes it takes a while for His promises to work out, but we must be patient. We should not doubt God even when times are hard. He sees everything and cares for us. As long as we hold on to His hand, He won't let us down.

💡 **Remember:** God will never stop loving us.

The Lord speaks to Abram again

Genesis 17

Then God said to Abram, 'This is my covenant with you: you will be the father of many nations.' (Gen 17:4)

When Abram was ninety-nine years old, the Lord spoke to him. He told Abram, once again, that he would have many descendants. But by this time Abram had given up hope. He and his wife were already very old. As Abram bowed down, he laughed softly to himself. How on earth would it be possible for him and Sarai to have a child at this age? So Abram asked the Lord to bless Ishmael, the son he had by the slave girl, Hagar.

But the Lord had His own plans. He replied that soon Sarai would have a son and that they were to name him Isaac. The name means 'he laughs'. That would always remind Abram that he doubted God's word.

God then changed Abram's name to Abraham because he would be the father of many nations. Sarai's name was changed to Sarah because she would soon give birth to Isaac. The Lord also told Abraham that from now on every baby boy had to be circumcised on the eighth day after his birth, including the baby boys of slaves who lived in their homes. This would be the sign of God's covenant with Abraham.

 Remember: We must not make fun of God.

Abraham prays for Sodom

Genesis 18-19

Finally Abraham said, 'Lord, please do not get angry! May I speak one more time? Suppose there are ten good people in Sodom?' The Lord answered, 'If there are ten good people I will not destroy the city.' (Gen 18:32)

One day the Lord told Abraham He had heard that the people of Sodom and Gomorrah were evil. He had decided to destroy the two cities.

Abraham's nephew Lot and his family lived there so he pleaded with the Lord, 'Suppose You find fifty good people in the city – will You still destroy it?' The Lord promised to spare the whole city if He found fifty good people in Sodom.

Abraham went on, 'Suppose there are only forty-five?' The Lord was prepared to spare Sodom for the sake of forty-five good people. But Abraham still didn't give up. Would the Lord spare Sodom if there were only ten good people in it? Again the Lord's answer was 'yes'.

Eventually the Lord did destroy Sodom and Gomorrah in a mighty fire. But first He sent His angels to tell Lot and his family to run for their lives. The angel also warned them not to look back at the city while it was burning. Lot's wife didn't listen and so she was punished. She was turned into a pillar of salt.

Remember: God must come first in our lives.

Abraham is willing to sacrifice Isaac

Genesis 22

Then God said, 'Put down the knife. Don't kill your son, because now I know that you truly serve Me. You were even willing to sacrifice your only son for Me.' (Gen 22:12)

One day God told Abraham to go and sacrifice Isaac on a mountain in the land of Moriah. Early the next morning Abraham and Isaac set off. It took them three days to reach the mountain.

On the way there Isaac asked his father, 'We have the wood and the fire, but where is the lamb for the sacrifice?' Abraham told him not to worry, the Lord would see to it.

When they arrived at the place for the sacrifice Abraham tied Isaac up and laid him on the altar over the wood. Abraham took his knife and was about to kill his son when an angel of the Lord spoke to him from heaven, telling him to put down the knife and not to kill the boy. Then the Lord sent a ram to sacrifice instead of Isaac.

Abraham proved that he was willing to do anything the Lord said – even to sacrifice his son. We must also give our whole lives to the Lord. We must love the Lord best of all because He loves us so much.

 Remember: The Lord must be the most important in our lives.

Isaac finds a wife

Genesis 24

'O Lord, God of my master Abraham, please give me a miracle today.' (Gen 24:12)

When Abraham was a very old man he called his servant and told him to go to Mesopotamia to find Isaac a wife.

The servant went to the village Nahor, where some of Abraham's relations lived. Standing beside a spring where the young girls of the village came to draw water, he prayed for a miracle. He asked the Lord to show him a girl who would be the right wife for Isaac. He would ask for a drink and the girl who said, 'Yes certainly, and I will water your camels too', would be the one. As he was still praying he saw a girl named Rebekah arrive with a water jug on her shoulder. He went over to her and asked for a drink of water.

She gave the right answer so the servant knew she was the girl. He gave her some expensive jewellery and she took him to her brother Laban's house. When he told Laban and his mother how the Lord had guided him in a special way, they were very happy.

They allowed Rebekah to go back with him.

Rebekah went to live with Sarah. Later on she and Isaac got married. Isaac loved Rebekah very much.

☼ **Remember:** The Lord looks after His children.

Jacob is blessed instead of Esau

Genesis 27

God gives you plenty of dew for healthy crops and good harvests; you will always have enough to eat. (Gen 27:28)

After Abraham's death, Isaac his son and Rebekah had twins. They called them Esau and Jacob. By the time they were grown up Isaac was almost blind. One day Isaac told Esau to hunt some wild game for him. He asked his son to cook it the way he liked it. Afterwards he would bless Esau.

Rebekah heard what Isaac said. She wanted their younger son, Jacob, to be blessed. So she made a plan. She sent Jacob to fetch a goat so she could cook Isaac's favourite dish. Jacob would take the food to his father and pretend to be Esau. Then Isaac would bless him instead.

Rebekah told Jacob to wear Esau's clothes and draped the goat's skin on his arms and neck because Esau was very hairy. Her plan worked! Esau's father couldn't bless him now, because the blessing was meant for only one son.

Esau was furious with Jacob. He wanted to kill him. Rebekah told Jacob to run away so Jacob went to live with his uncle, Laban. In the end, the Lord's promise to Abraham came true.

 Remember: We should always be honest.

Jacob's dream

Genesis 28

At the top of the stairway stood the Lord, and He said, 'I am the Lord, the God of your grandfather Abraham and the God of your father, Isaac. The ground you are lying on belongs to you. I will give it to you and your descendants.' (Gen 28:13)

Jacob was on his way to his uncle Laban. At sundown he arrived at a good place to set up camp and spend the night. As he slept he dreamt of a stairway that reached from the earth to heaven. The angels of God were going up and down the stairs. The Lord stood at the top af the stairway and spoke to Jacob. God promised to be his God as well. Everything He had promised his grandparents would also come true for Jacob. Jacob's descendants would get the land the Lord had promised them.

The Lord also promised Jacob in his dream that he would never be alone again. God would be with him all the time.

When Jacob woke up, he was afraid. He said, 'What an awesome place this is!' To think the Lord was there and he didn't even know it! Early the next morning Jacob named the place Bethel. This means 'house of God'. There Jacob made a vow that he would serve God.

The Lord is with us every day of our lives. We are never alone. He sees everything we do, and hears everything we say.

💡 **Remember:** The Lord knows everything about us.

The dreamer is sold

Joseph had a dream and told his brothers, 'Listen to this dream. We were out in the field tying up bundles of grain. My bundle stood up, and then your bundles all gathered around and bowed low before it!' (Gen 37:6-7)

Jacob had many sons but he loved Joseph more than the others. This made Joseph's brothers jealous of him. One night Joseph dreamt that his brothers' sheaves of corn bowed down to his sheaf of corn. In another dream, the sun, moon and eleven stars bowed low before him. He described these dreams to his brothers in detail and they liked him even less.

Soon after this, Joseph's brothers were looking after the flocks. Jacob sent Joseph to see how they were getting on. When his brothers saw Joseph coming, they decided to kill him. But, thanks to Reuben, they threw him into a pit instead. A while later some traders came by. Joseph's brothers dragged him out of the pit and sold him to them.

Then Joseph's brothers dipped his clothes in goat's blood and told their father a wild animal must have eaten him. Meanwhile the traders sold Joseph to Potiphar. Potiphar was captain of the Egyptian king's palace guard.

Remember: The Lord loves everybody in our family.

Joseph lands up in prison

Genesis 39-40

While Joseph was in prison, the Lord was with him all the time. The Lord was good to Joseph. After a while even the chief jailer liked him. (Gen 39:20-21)

In Egypt, Joseph worked in Potiphar's house. Potiphar's wife took a liking to him. She even wanted them to cheat on her husband but Joseph refused. Eventually she became so angry that she told her husband lies about Joseph. Potiphar believed his wife. He threw Joseph into prison.

The lesson we learn from Joseph is never to listen to friends or anybody who tries to talk us into doing something wrong, even if it means being punished for something we didn't do. We must listen only to the Lord.

God was with Joseph in prison. Some time later, Pharaoh's cup-bearer and chief baker were put in the same prison as Joseph. One morning the two of them told Joseph about the weird dream each had had the night before. Joseph explained the meaning of their dreams to them. He told the cup-bearer he would be back in the palace within three days, pouring Pharaoh's wine again but the baker's news was not so good. He would be dead in three days' time! Everything happened exactly as Joseph had said.

-ᗴ- **Remember:** The Lord is proud of those who obey Him.

Joseph explains Pharaoh's dreams

'I had a dream last night,' Pharaoh told Joseph, 'and nobody can tell me what it means. I hear that you can explain dreams.' Joseph said to Pharaoh, 'I can't do it. God gives me the answers.' (Gen 41:15-16)

One night Pharaoh had a dream. In his dream, seven fat, healthy-looking cows came up from the river and started grazing. Then seven ugly, skinny cows came along and ate the fat ones. Later that night he dreamed about seven full heads of grain on one stalk. Then seven shrivelled-up heads of grain swallowed up the healthy ones.

Pharaoh wondered what these dreams could mean. The man who poured Pharaoh's wine in the palace remembered Joseph in prison. Pharaoh sent for Joseph at once. The dreams meant that there would be seven good years in Egypt with plenty of rain and more than enough food, followed by seven years of famine. Pharaoh was so pleased with Joseph that he gave him a very important job. Only Pharaoh had a higher rank than Joseph.

Joseph's story tells us that the Lord uses people anywhere, even in prison. We must believe in Him no matter where we are.

Remember: The Lord is with us everywhere we go.

Joseph's brothers come to buy food in Egypt

Genesis 42-43

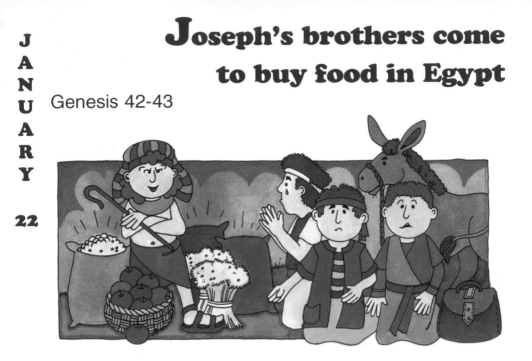

Joseph put his brothers in prison for three days. On the third day Joseph said to them, 'I serve God. If you do as I say, you will live. One of you must stay behind in prison. The rest of you may go on home with grain for your families.' (Gen 42:17, 19)

When the seven years of famine and suffering began, Joseph started selling grain. One day Joseph's brothers arrived from Canaan to buy food. Joseph recognized them immediately, but they didn't recognize him at all. Joseph pretended that he thought they had come to spy on the land to make war against Egypt and he put them in prison.

Three days later Joseph allowed all but one of his brothers to go home. They had to fetch their younger brother, Benjamin, and bring him to Joseph. Then they would be spared.

Meanwhile Joseph secretly put the money his brothers had paid for the grain back in the top of their sacks of grain. They were terrified when they discovered the money. Back home in Canaan they told their father what had happened. At first Jacob refused to send Benjamin to Egypt but his sons pleaded with him and eventually he gave way.

Joseph was very happy to see Benjamin. He invited his brothers to a grand meal in the palace but he still didn't tell them who he really was.

💡 **Remember:** The Lord cares about even the smallest child.

Joseph helps his brothers

Genesis 44-45

'I am Joseph!' he said to his brothers. (Gen 45:3)

Joseph's brothers were ready to leave for Canaan with the grain. This time Joseph secretly had his own silver cup hidden in Benjamin's sack. The brothers were barely out of the city when Joseph's household manager caught up with them and stopped them: 'What do you mean by stealing my master's silver drinking cup?' the man said. Whoever had stolen it would have to stay behind in Egypt as a slave.

The cup was found in Benjamin's sack. The brothers were devastated. Judah told Joseph how heartbroken their father would be if they returned without Benjamin.

Eventually Joseph could stand it no longer. He decided to tell them who he was. His brothers were stunned and afraid. Joseph told them to relax. He wasn't angry with them anymore. His going to Egypt had been part of God's plan. He told them to hurry home and fetch their father so they could live together in Egypt.

God has a plan for each of us. If we listen to Him, He will do great things in our lives.

💡 **Remember:** God never stops working in people.

Joseph meets Jacob

Genesis 46-47

24

Then Jacob said to Joseph, 'Now I can die, because I have seen you with my own eyes and know you are still alive.' (Gen 46:30)

Back home in Canaan Joseph's brothers told their father what had happened. Jacob couldn't wait to see Joseph again.

Jacob and his whole family left for Egypt. Joseph was so happy when he saw his father that he gave him a big hug and cried with joy. Later on Joseph brought his father to Pharaoh so they could meet.

Pharaoh gave them the land Goshen and they lived there happily for many years. When Jacob was very old and it was time for him to die, he called for all his sons and blessed them. After Jacob's death Joseph buried him in Canaan. Then he went back to Egypt.

Joseph's life wasn't always easy but it shows us how great the Lord is. He used Joseph in a truly wonderful way. God showed His great power through the life of one man who loved Him!

Remember: God cares for the young and the old.

Another hero is born

Exodus 2

The princess named him Moses, because 'I took him out of the water.'
(Ex 2:10)

After Joseph's death there was a new king in Egypt. He knew nothing about Joseph and he didn't like the Israelites one bit. There were too many of them for his liking so Pharaoh decided they had to work as slaves. On top of that, all baby boys born to the Israelites had to be thrown into the River Nile.

During this time an Israelite mother made a plan to save her baby son's life. She made a basket of reeds and waterproofed it with tar and pitch. Then she put her baby in the basket, among the reeds on the riverbank.

Shortly afterwards, one of Pharaoh's daughters went for a swim in the river. She saw the basket with the baby inside and decided to keep him. Just then the baby's sister ran up to the princess and said, 'I can fetch someone to take care of the baby until he is older.' The princess was pleased. So the baby was taken to his own mother who looked after him until he was old enough to live in the palace.

Pharaoh's daughter decided to call the baby Moses.

-ᡅ́- **Remember:** God can save us from the greatest danger.

Moses kills an Egyptian and makes a getaway

Exodus 2

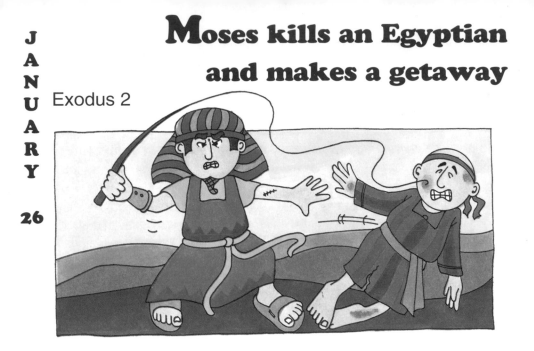

The man said to Moses, 'Do you plan to kill me as you killed that Egyptian yesterday?' (Ex 2:14)

Moses was raised in Pharaoh's palace. One day, when he was already grown up, he walked among the Israelites and saw how hard they were forced to work. The next moment he saw an Egyptian beating an Israelite. Moses was so angry that he killed the Egyptian. Hurriedly, he buried him in the sand.

The following day Moses paid another visit to his people. This time he saw two Israelites fighting. He told them to stop. 'Who do you think you are?' one of the men asked Moses. 'Do you plan to kill me as you killed that Egyptian yesterday?'

When Moses realized people knew what he had done, he was worried. His life was in danger. And sure enough, when Pharaoh heard about it he gave orders for Moses to be killed. So Moses fled to the land of Midian.

One day Moses helped some girls draw water from a well for their flocks. When they told their dad about this, he invited Moses to come and stay with them. Later on, Moses married one of his daughters, Zipporah.

We can't get away with doing wrong. Even if nobody sees us, God sees everything. We can hide nothing from Him.

💡 **Remember:** We should not fight with our friends.

God calls Moses

Exodus 3

'Do not come any closer,' God told him. 'Take off your sandals because you are standing on holy ground.' (Ex 3:5)

Moses looked after the flock of his father-in-law, Jethro. One day a strange thing happened. At Mount Horeb he saw a burning bush. But it did not burn up. Moses went closer to see what was going on. Suddenly a voice called to him from the bush, 'Moses! Moses!'

He answered straight away, 'Here I am.'

Then God told him not to come any closer – he was on holy ground.

God told Moses how sorry He felt for the people of Israel. He had decided to send Moses to go and set them free. This scared Moses. 'I can't do this,' Moses said. 'I am not important enough.'

God said, 'I will be with you.'

Moses asked God His Name. 'I am who I am,' was God's answer.

That day, at the burning bush, Moses heard that God's Name is 'Lord'. This Name is so important that we must be careful how we use it. His Name is holy. Only people who believe in Him and really love Him, are allowed to call Him by His Name.

Remember: God's Name is a holy Name.

The Lord shows Moses that He will help him

Exodus 4

The Lord said to Moses, 'Go now, and do as I have told you. I will help you speak well, and I will tell you what to say.' (Ex 4:12)

Moses was frightened when the Lord spoke to him from the burning bush. He asked the Lord, 'If I go to the people of Israel and tell them You sent me, they won't believe me. Then what should I tell them?'

So God gave Moses three signs to show that He was with him. These were the signs: when Moses threw his shepherd's staff onto the ground it changed into a snake; when Moses put his hand inside his clothes and took it out again, it was white with leprosy; when Moses poured water from the Nile onto the ground it changed into blood.

But Moses was still worried, 'O Lord, I'm just not a good speaker. I'm clumsy with words.' The Lord answered, 'I will help you speak well, and I will tell you what to say.' The Lord also told Moses to fetch his brother, Aaron. He would go to Egypt with Moses. Aaron would speak for him.

Moses and Aaron set off on their journey to the Israelites. When Moses performed the miracles God had given him, they believed him. They accepted him as their leader.

💡 **Remember:** The Lord loves us just as we are.

Moses spoke to Pharaoh

Exodus 5-6

'Now you will see what I will do to Pharaoh,' the Lord told Moses. 'I will force him to let the people go.' (Ex 6:1)

Moses and Aaron went to see the king of Egypt. They told him that the Lord **29** wanted the people of Israel to move out. They had to hold a religious festival in the desert in the Lord's honour.

Pharaoh's answer was, 'And who is the Lord that I should listen to him and let Israel go? I don't know the Lord, and I will not let Israel go.'

Moses tried again, but Pharaoh was stubborn. He decided to make the Israelites work even harder. So Pharaoh told his foremen, 'Don't give the people straw for making bricks anymore. Let them get it themselves!' And they had to make just as many bricks as before.

The poor Israelites had to work harder than ever. They became angry with Moses and Aaron. They blamed Moses. They wouldn't even listen when Moses told them that the Lord would help them.

Sometimes, when bad things happen to us, it is not easy to believe in the Lord. At such times we must not think that God has forgotten about us. He is with His children all the time.

-�523- **Remember:** We must never stop believing in the Lord.

Moses and Pharaoh's magicians

Exodus 7

When I show the Egyptians my power and force them to let the Israelites go, they will realize that I am the Lord. (Ex 7:5)

Once again the Lord sent Moses and Aaron to Pharaoh. Because Moses did not speak well, Aaron spoke for him. Moses was eighty and Aaron eighty-three. The Lord told them beforehand that Pharaoh would not listen to them. He was too stubborn. That's why the Lord would punish him. Later on he would give in and allow the Israelites to leave.

Moses and Aaron went to Pharaoh's palace. Aaron threw Moses' staff on the ground before Pharaoh and it changed into a snake. Pharaoh's magicians did the same thing. Their staffs became snakes too! But then Aaron's snake swallowed up their snakes.

Pharaoh would not listen to Moses, not even after seeing this sign. So Moses and Aaron left.

Just like Pharaoh, there are many people today who don't believe in God. Even if they see miracles, they couldn't care less. We need to pray for them. We must ask the Lord to change their lives so that they will also believe in Him. Otherwise they are going to be punished one day. God doesn't want people to be punished, but to belong to Him forever.

Remember: God wants to change bad people into His children.

The Lord sends plagues to punish Pharaoh

Exodus 7-9

Suddenly gnats were all over the place, covering the Egyptians and their animals. 'This is the finger of God!' Pharaoh's magicians told him. (Ex 8:17)

Pharaoh didn't want to listen to Moses and Aaron so the Lord sent ten plagues over Egypt. The first plague struck the River Nile. The water turned to blood. Nobody could drink it but still Pharaoh would not listen.

Then the Lord sent a plague of frogs. Pharaoh asked Moses to pray that the frogs would go away and then he would let the people go. But he lied!

Then the Lord sent a plague of gnats. Everybody was covered with gnats! But Pharaoh was still stubborn.

Next came a plague of flies. Eventually Pharaoh said it was all right for the Israelites to offer sacrifices to God, but they had to do it in Egypt. But Moses replied, 'That won't do! We must take a three day trip into the wilderness.' Pharaoh agreed, but he didn't mean it.

The Lord sent yet another plague which affected the livestock. All the Egyptians' animals died. But still Pharaoh had a heart of stone.

Remember: Sinners make the Lord unhappy.

More plagues

Exodus 9-10

God said to Pharaoh, 'There is only one reason why I have let you live. Through you I will show my strength. Then all the world will see how great I am.' (Ex 9:16)

The first five plagues were not enough to make Pharaoh listen so God sent five more. The sixth was a plague of boils that broke out on all the people and animals in Egypt. But once again, Pharaoh hardened his heart.

Then a seventh plague struck – a tremendous hailstorm. Pharaoh urgently sent for Moses and said the Israelites could go at once. But he was lying once more!

Moses asked Pharaoh how long he was going to carry on refusing to listen to the Lord. So Pharaoh said the men could go, but the women and children had to stay behind. Moses was not happy with this, but Pharaoh just shouted, 'Get out of here!'

Moses raised his staff over the land of Egypt. Then a plague of locusts swarmed over the land. There were so many of them you couldn't see the ground. This was the eighth plague. Once again Pharaoh asked Moses to pray that the locusts go away.

The ninth plague was three days of darkness. The people scarcely moved because they could not see. After this plague Pharaoh said the Israelites could go. But their flocks and herds had to stay. Moses refused.

-ʼϙ́- **Remember:** Pray for sinners to believe in the Lord.

The tenth plague

Exodus 11-12

And at midnight the Lord killed all the eldest sons in Egypt, from Pharaoh's son to those in prison. Even the eldest of their livestock were killed. (Ex 12:29)

Not even the ninth plague softened Pharaoh's heart. He shouted at Moses, 'Don't ever let me see you again! The day I do, you will die!' Then the Lord told Moses He would send one more plague – at midnight all the eldest children in every family would die. The Egyptians would be heartbroken and their crying and wailing would be heard throughout the land. Not a single Israelite child would die. Then Pharaoh would allow the Israelites to move out. Moses went and told Pharaoh all this but still Pharaoh would not listen and Moses walked out, burning with anger.

At midnight, the tenth plague struck Egypt. Every eldest son, in the richest to the poorest family, died. Even the eldest male animals died.

The Lord showed the Egyptians his power with all the plagues He sent. He did this to save the people He loved so much.

To this day, God watches over us. He cares for us. He takes us by the hand. God will never punish us the way he did the bad Egyptian king.

Remember: The Lord cares a lot about His children.

The first Passover

Exodus 12

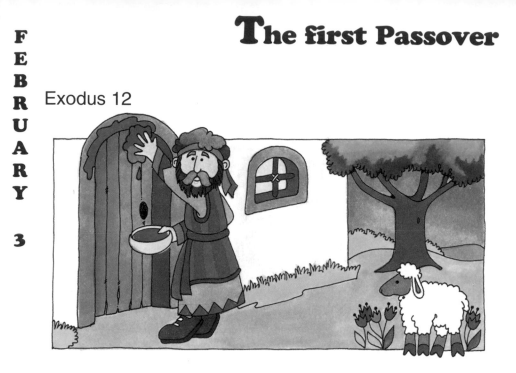

'The blood you have smeared on your doorframes will be a sign. When I see the blood I will pass over you. This plague of death will not touch you when I strike the land of Egypt.' (Ex 12:13)

The day before the Lord struck Egypt with the tenth plague, He told the Israelites to celebrate this day as a special festival. Every family had to slaughter a lamb. That evening everyone would eat roast lamb with herbs and bread made without yeast. This was the feast of the Passover.

That night in Egypt, the Israelites were to take some of the lambs' blood and smear it on the doorframes of their houses. This was the sign to show the Lord that Israelites lived there. No-one in that house would die.

The Israelites celebrated the Passover feast in Egypt and the Lord told them to do so every year from that time onwards. This festival would remind them of the night the Lord freed them from the Egyptians. They also had to explain the meaning of the ceremony to their children. Then they would always remember how the Lord saved their lives the night God sent the tenth plague over Egypt.

The Israelites were very happy. They bowed their heads and worshipped the Lord. Then they celebrated the Passover feast.

🔆 **Remember:** Religious feasts tell us about God's salvation.

The Israelites move out of Egypt

Exodus 13

So God led them along a route through the wilderness toward the Red Sea, and the Israelites left Egypt like a marching army. (Ex 13:18)

The tenth plague was just too much for Pharaoh. He couldn't stand it any longer. So he sent for Moses and Aaron during the night. 'Leave us!' he cried. 'Go away, all of you! Go and serve the Lord. Take your flocks and herds and be gone.'

The Egyptians even gave the Israelites expensive clothes and jewellery to take with them! There were almost six hundred thousand men, not counting the women and children. They took all their livestock with them. After four hundred and thirty years the Israelites were finally moving out of Egypt!

God led the Israelites along a route through the wilderness towards the Red Sea. It was not the shortest way, but the safest. Because it was so hot, the Lord sent a big cloud to give them shade during the day. At night God sent a mighty ball of fire so they could see where they were going. God keeps his promises. Even if we sometimes get impatient, we just need to keep on trusting Him.

 Remember: Even if it takes a long time, God always keeps His promises.

Pharaoh drowns in the sea

Exodus 14

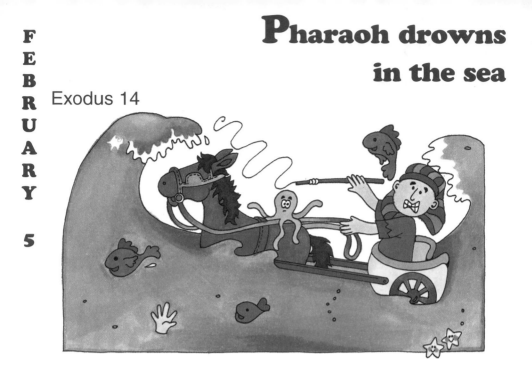

Then Moses raised his hand over the sea, and the Lord opened up a path through the water with a strong east wind. (Ex 14:21)

When Pharaoh realized the Israelites were not coming back he was sorry he had let them go. 'What have we done, letting all these slaves get away?' So Pharaoh called out his troops and a mighty Egyptian army chased after the Israelites. But the Lord watched over his people. An angel moved in behind the Israelites and so did the cloud. Everything in front of the Egyptians was dark.

Moses and the Israelites arrived at the Red Sea. Then Moses raised his hand over the sea and a miracle happened. The sea opened up before them so they could walk through on dry ground with water on each side! The Egyptians followed them but their chariot wheels got stuck. Then the Lord told Moses to raise his hand over the sea again. The water flooded back and all the Egyptians drowned. It was another miracle.

The Lord can do anything. He can even dry up the sea if He wants to. If we look around us we will see plenty of miracles. We can trust the Lord to perform miracles in our lives too!

💡 **Remember:** The Lord still does great things today.

The Israelites thank the Lord

Exodus 15

Then Moses said, 'I want to sing a song to the Lord. He is mighty! He can throw horses and chariots into the sea.' (Ex 15:1)

The Israelites walked through the sea without even getting wet but all the Egyptians died. The Israelites could hardly believe that the Lord had been so good to them. They actually saw Him perform a miracle before their very eyes. He saved them from the mighty Egyptian army and they hadn't even had to fight. The Lord did this for them!

On the other side of the Red Sea, Moses and the people sang a song to thank the Lord for saving them. In the song they sang about God's greatness and His power. His hand dashes the enemy to pieces. Just one word from Him and the wind blows them over and the sea swallows them up.

There is nobody like the Lord. He is the strongest and the best! He is our God too. He cares for us. God is the most important Person there is. He is our heavenly Father. He is never too busy to listen to us. All we have to do, is kneel down before Him. Then He hears every word we say to Him.

 Remember: We should ask the Lord every day to look after our families.

Bitter water made sweet

Exodus 15

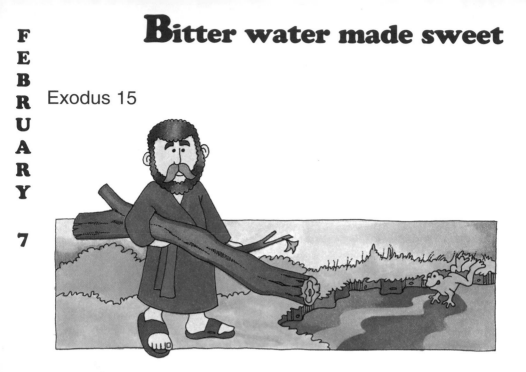

Moses prayed to the Lord and the Lord showed him a branch. Moses took the branch and threw it into the water. This made the water taste good. (Ex 15:25)

The Israelites travelled in the desert for three days without water. When they came to a place called Marah they finally found water. But they couldn't drink it because it had a bitter taste. So they complained. 'What are we going to drink?' they asked Moses.

Moses asked the Lord's advice and the Lord showed him a branch. Moses took it and threw it in the water. Suddenly the water tasted sweet!

It was there at Marah that the Lord told the Israelites to listen carefully to His voice, and to obey Him. If they did this He would look after them. They would not suffer from any of the terrible diseases the Egyptians had. From Marah they went to Elim where there were twelve springs and seventy palm trees.

Often we want to do our own thing and not think about what the Lord wants us to do. God doesn't like this. He wants us to listen to Him. He tells us in the Bible exactly how to please Him. We must believe in Jesus and obey Him.

Remember: Listen to Jesus' voice every day.

Manna and quail from heaven

Exodus 16

Then the Lord said to Moses, 'Look, I'm going to rain down food from heaven for you. The people can go out each day and pick up as much food as they need for that day.' (Ex 16:4)

After two months the Israelites started complaining. 'Oh, if only we were back in Egypt,' they moaned. 'At least there we had plenty to eat. But now you have brought us into this desert to die of hunger.'

So the Lord promised to send them food from heaven every day. At night he sent a kind of bird, called quail. The people could catch these and eat them. Every morning thin flakes, almost like bread, covered the ground. It was called manna. Each family had to gather just enough food for one day. If they gathered too much the leftovers went bad. On the sixth day they could gather food for two days. That was because the seventh day was the holy Sabbath, a day of rest.

It made God angry that the Israelites kept on complaining. By moaning all the time, they showed that they didn't really believe the Lord would take care of them. The Lord wants us to be satisfied with what we have. He will see to it that we get what we need.

💡 **Remember:** The Lord knows our needs.

Water from a rock

Exodus 17

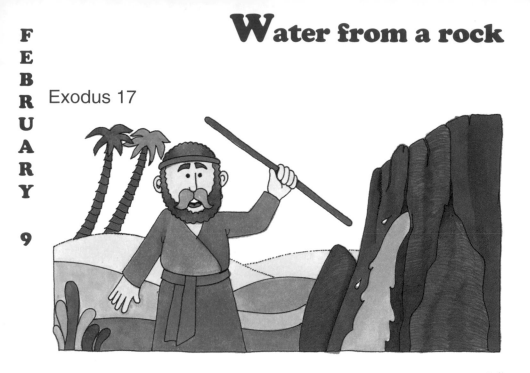

The Lord said to Moses, 'Take your shepherd's staff, the one you used when you struck the water of the Nile. I will meet you by the rock at Mount Horeb. Strike the rock, and water will come pouring out. Then the people will be able to drink.' (Ex 17:5-6)

The people moved on and eventually came to Rephidim. There was no water to be found there. Again they grumbled and complained to Moses. 'Give us water to drink!' they demanded.

'Quiet!' Moses said. 'Why are you arguing with me? And why are you testing the Lord?' They were really trying the Lord's patience. But the people were very thirsty. They kept on grumbling. Finally Moses asked the Lord what to do. The Lord told him to take a few leaders of Israel with him. They had to walk until they found a big rock at Mount Horeb. Then Moses had to strike the rock and water would come pouring out.

Moses did exactly as he was told. When he struck the rock, fresh water gushed out. Moses gave this place two names: Massah, which means the place of testing (the people tested the Lord); and Meribah which means the place of arguing, since this was where the people argued with Moses.

💡 **Remember:** We must do what the Lord tells us to do.

Israel beats the Amalekites

Exodus 17

As long as Moses held up the staff with his hands, the Israelites won. But as soon as he lowered his hands, the Amalekites were on the winning side. (Ex 17:11)

While the Israelites were at Rephidim, the Amalekite army decided to make war against them. Moses put Joshua in command of the Israelite soldiers. Moses watched the battle from the top of a hill. He held the staff which the Lord had given him up in the air. Aaron and a man called Hur were with Moses. As long as Moses held up the staff the Israelites were winning, but the minute he lowered his hands, the Amalekites started winning.

Eventually Moses' arms became tired so Aaron and Hur found him a stone to sit on. Then they stood one on each side of him, holding up his hands. In this way, Joshua and the Israelite army crushed the army of Amalek.

Moses built an altar there to thank the Lord for giving them the victory. The Lord took very good care of His people. He gave them food and water and He helped them when they had to fight for their lives. The Lord still cares for His children. He looks after us every day of our lives. If we look around us we will see what God does for us.

💡 **Remember:** Give thanks to God for everything He does.

The Israelites arrive in Sinai

Exodus 19

'Now if you will obey me and keep my covenant, you will be my own special people from among all the nations in the world. And you will be to me a kingdom that worships me every day. I will set you aside so you will be mine.' *(Ex 19:5-6)*

Three months after the Israelites left Egypt, they set up camp at the foot of Mount Sinai. Moses climbed the mountain and there the Lord told him that the Israelites would be His special people. God chose them from all the other nations on earth. They would belong to Him only. But from now on they had to do everything He told them.

Moses came down from the mountain and told the leaders of the Israelites what the Lord had said. When the Israelites heard this they immediately said, 'Of course we will do everything the Lord asks of us.'

So Moses went back up the mountain to bring the people's answer to the Lord. The Lord said Moses had to tell the people to start cleaning up that very day. They had two days to wash themselves and their clothes and clean up the whole camp. On the third day the Lord would come down to Mount Sinai. Then nobody would be allowed near the mountain.

💡 **Remember:** We are special in the eyes of the Lord.

Moses goes up the mountain

Exodus 19

Moses spoke and God answered him with thunder. (Ex 19:19)

The Israelites set up camp at the foot of Mount Sinai. At sunrise on the third day, there was a mighty thunderstorm. A thick, dark cloud came down on the mountain. A loud horn blast was heard. Moses went to the mountain to meet the Lord.

Mount Sinai was covered with smoke because the Lord had come down to it in the form of fire. The smoke billowed into the sky and the whole mountain shook with a mighty earthquake. As the horn blast grew louder and louder, Moses spoke, and God thundered his reply for all to hear.

As Moses climbed up the mountain, God came down from the sky to the top of the mountain. Giant flames leapt around the mountain and the whole mountain shook. The horn blasts grew louder and then the Lord's voice could be heard like thunder.

He told Moses to climb to the top. There God spoke to him. Moses had to warn the Israelites not to climb the mountain or they would die.

The Lord sent Moses to fetch Aaron. Then He gave them the Ten Commandments.

 Remember: The Lord is God. Bow before Him.

The ten commandments

Exodus 20

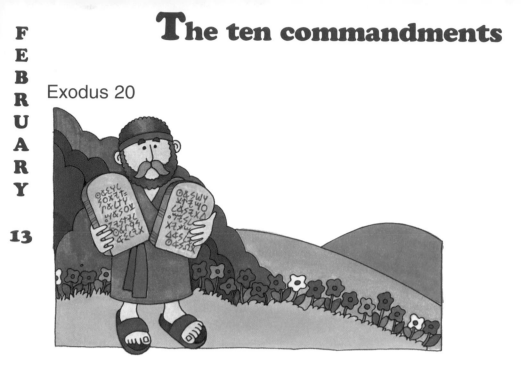

'I am the Lord your God, who rescued you from slavery in Egypt.' (Ex 20:2)

The Lord gave Moses ten laws which the people of Israel had to obey. We call these the Ten Commandments.

The first commandment says we are not allowed to worship any other god. We must serve only the Lord.

The second commandment says we are not allowed to make or worship any idol. We can make a god of sport, television and things like toys. If they become more important to us than the Lord, then they are like gods, and that is wrong.

The third commandment says we are not to use the Name of the Lord casually. Only when we speak to the Lord and mean every word we say, are we allowed to use His Name.

The fourth commandment says we must rest one day of the week. We Christians make Sunday our day of rest and go to church to praise the Lord together with other believers.

The fifth commandment tells us to obey our father and mother. The Lord gave them to us. They have to take care of us. That is why we must love and respect them.

💡 **Remember:** The Lord asks for obedience.

The ten commandments

Exodus 20

'Do not murder.' (Ex 20:13)

We also need to obey the Ten Commandments the Lord gave the Israelites as they are meant for all God's children.

The sixth commandment says we are not allowed to kill anybody. Every single person's life is important to the Lord.

The seventh commandment tells married grown-ups they are not allowed to fall in love with anybody except their own wife or husband. Our parents must love only each other.

The eighth commandment forbids us to steal. We should not take anything that does not belong to us. The ninth commandment says we may not lie. We must always tell the truth no matter how difficult it might be!

The tenth commandment tells us we mustn't be envious of what others have. We mustn't nag our parents for a new bicycle like our friend's or for clothes and toys just because 'everybody else' has them. The Lord tells us to be satisfied with what we have.

Remember: The things we do reflect our relationship with God.

The golden calf

FEBRUARY

15

Exodus 32

When the people thought Moses was taking too long to come back down the mountain, they went to Aaron, 'Look,' they said, 'make us some gods who can lead us. This man Moses, who brought us here from Egypt, has disappeared. We don't know what has happened to him.' (Ex 32:1)

Moses was on the mountain for some time while the Lord talked to him. God gave Moses many laws. These laws were necessary for the Israelites to know what the Lord wanted them to do.

The Israelites got tired of waiting and decided to make their own god. They brought Aaron all their gold. He melted it down and made a god that looked like a calf. The people were pleased with it and said, 'This is our god who brought us out of Egypt.'

Aaron told the people that the next day there would be a festival for the Lord. The feasting started early the next morning.

The Lord was very angry about this. He told Moses to go and check what was going on. The Lord decided to destroy the Israelites but Moses begged Him not to.

The Lord heard Moses' prayer and decided not to punish Israel with death.

Remember: The Lord hears our prayers.

Moses smashes the stone tablets

Exodus 32

When they came near the camp, Moses saw the calf and the dancing. He was so angry that he threw both stone tablets on the ground, smashing them. (Ex 32:19)

After Moses had pleaded with the Lord to spare the lives of the Israelites, he went back down the mountain carrying two flat stones. On both sides of these two stones, he had written God's laws.

As he came closer to the camp, he saw the calf and the dancing. He was furiously angry and threw down the stone tablets. He grabbed the calf and threw it into the fire. When the metal had cooled, he ground it into powder and mixed it with water. He made the people drink it.

Then Moses stood at the entrance of the camp and shouted, 'All of you who are on the Lord's side, come over here and join me.' Everybody who didn't go over to him was killed that day. The next day Moses asked the Lord to forgive his people for sinning.

God hates sin. We mustn't think we can get away with doing wrong just because nobody has seen us do it. The Lord knows everything we do.

Remember: We must pray to God to keep us from doing wrong.

Moses prays for Israel

Exodus 32

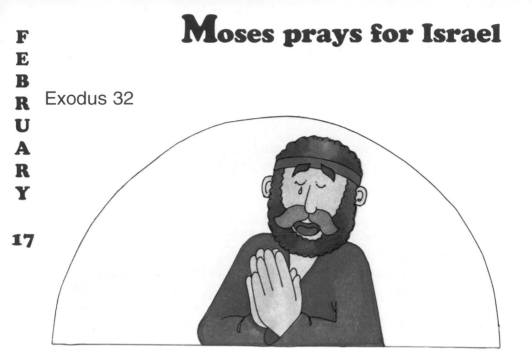

Moses went to the Lord and said, 'These people have done a terrible thing. They made themselves a god of gold. But now, please forgive their sin.' (Ex 32:31-32)

When Moses had taken action against those who were not willing to listen to the Lord, he went back up the mountain to talk to the Lord. Moses asked Him to forgive the people's sins. Moses was willing to be punished instead. The Lord could rub his name out of the books He kept in heaven if only He would forgive the Israelites.

But the Lord refused to punish Moses in their place. He told Moses everyone who had sinned would have to take their own punishment.

Moses loved the Israelites. Even though they did wicked things, he was prepared to give his life for them. He was willing to be punished in their place. Jesus expects us to love others. He gave his life for us, so God would forgive us. We must pray for others and help them and not think only of ourselves.

☼ **Remember:** We must be kind to other believers.

Moses and the Lord meet in a tent

Exodus 33

Moses set up a tent far outside the camp. This was where he and the Lord met. Everyone who wanted to know the Lord's will, would go there. (Ex 33:7)

It was time for the people to move on. The Lord was still angry with them over the golden calf. He told the Israelites He would not travel along with them again.

The Israelites were unhappy that the Lord would not be travelling with them. They cried a lot. Then the Lord let them know that He would decide what to do with them later on.

Moses put up a tent outside the camp. He said this was the tent where he spoke to the Lord. Anybody who wanted to know the will of the Lord could go there. They would tell Moses what to ask the Lord. Then Moses would go into the tent by himself. Every time he went inside, a big cloud came down and hung at the entrance while the Lord spoke to Moses.

Whenever the people saw the cloud they would bow low in respect for the Lord. Inside the Tent of Meeting the Lord spoke to Moses, face to face, as a man speaks to his friend.

Remember: God speaks to us through the Bible.

The Lord travels with Israel

Exodus 33

Then Moses said, 'Lord, if You don't go with us, don't let us move a step from this place. Then let us stay right here.' (Ex 33:15)

Moses remembered that the Lord had told him that He wasn't going to travel with Israel again. The people were much too sinful. So Moses asked the Lord, 'Who will travel with us now?' God said, 'Moses, do you want Me to come along so you can have peace?'

Then Moses answered that they weren't going anywhere without the Lord. He was not prepared to travel without Him. Not even an angel would be good enough to take care of them. The Lord Himself had to come along, otherwise it would be the end of the Israelites.

Moses reminded the Lord that He had called them His special people. Surely this made them different from all the other people on earth. This was the reason the Lord should go with them. The Lord answered Moses' prayer and promised to travel with them.

To this day, the Lord is with all His children. We don't have to pray that the angels will guard us. We must ask God Himself to look after us. He is the One who protects us. He is the One at our bedside when we sleep peacefully at night and He is the One who is there when we are afraid. All we have to do is hold His hand tightly.

🔆 **Remember:** The Lord keeps us safe.

The fiery cloud

The day they finished setting up the Tabernacle where the Lord's laws were kept, the cloud covered it. At night the cloud looked like a pillar of fire until morning. (Num 9:15)

A while later the Lord told Moses to make two stone tablets like the first ones. He had to climb Mount Sinai. On top of the mountain the Lord spoke to him. Once again the Lord gave Moses the Ten Commandments.

The Ten Commandments were kept in the Tabernacle. It was a tent especially made by the best craftsmen in Israel. Bezalel and Oholiab were in charge of everybody who decorated the Tabernacle. They also built an ark out of acacia wood. The cover was made of pure gold. The tablets with the Ten Commandments were placed inside the Ark. When the Tabernacle was finished they gave it over to God. A cloud covered the Tabernacle, which was the sign that the Lord was there. Whenever the cloud lifted from the Tabernacle, the Israelites knew it was the signal to move on. But if the cloud stayed, they would stay until it moved again. At night it looked like a column of fire.

 Remember: The Lord never leaves us by ourselves.

The Lord wants offerings

Leviticus 1-5

The Lord called Moses to the Tabernacle and said to him, 'Give the following instructions to the Israelites: Whenever you bring offerings to the Lord, you must bring animals from your flocks and herds.' (Lev 1:1)

The Lord told the Israelites to bring Him offerings. They had to take a sheep or a cow or a pigeon and put it on an altar. Then they had to burn it as a sacrifice to the Lord. The animal had to be healthy and slaughtered in front of a priest. The priest would sprinkle the blood of the animal around the altar. Then they offered it to the Lord on the altar.

If people had sinned they could bring a guilt offering to the Lord. This was a good way of asking the Lord to forgive them for their sins. But people could also bring an offering of thanks to show the Lord how thankful they were to Him for being so good to them. Farmers often brought the Lord an offering of their first ripe grain or fruit. This was a way of thanking the Lord for giving them enough to eat.

Today we don't bring offerings of animals or fruit to the Lord anymore, because Jesus was sacrificed in our place. He took all our sins on Him when He died on the cross. He was punished for all we have done that is wrong and God has forgiven us.

-ϙ́- **Remember:** Jesus paid for all our sins.

The Lord gets angry if we don't listen

Moses told Aaron, 'The Lord says, "Anyone who brings Me an offering must realize I am mighty and holy. They must respect Me. I must be glorified before all the people."' (Lev 10:3)

One day two of Aaron's sons, Nadab and Abihu, brought the Lord an offering. But they did it in the wrong way, disobeying the Lord's instructions. The Lord sent fire to burn them up and they died.

Someone who brought the Lord an offering had to know exactly what to do. He had to show the Lord great respect otherwise it was like mocking the Lord. Moses told Aaron this was what his sons had done. They thought they could play games with the Lord, but God will not allow that.

We may never make jokes about the Lord. Also, when we pray we must really mean what we say. The Lord wants us to respect Him. The Lord lives in heaven. He is God. We are just ordinary people. So we must bow down before the Lord. God makes time to listen to us. And He opens His hand full of love and gives us everything we need.

 Remember: The Lord's children love Him.

The people leave Sinai

Numbers 10-11

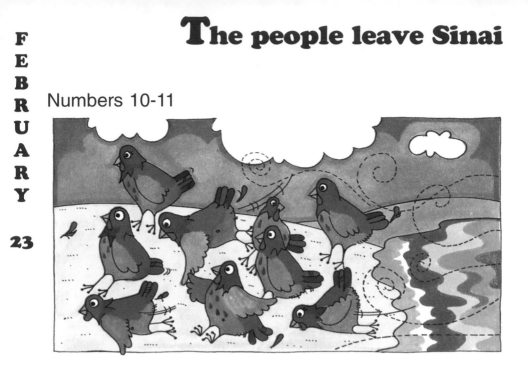

The Lord sent a strong wind. It brought quail from the sea and let them fall into the camp and all around it! (Num 11:31)

The people moved away from Sinai with the Ark of the Lord ahead of them. They soon began to complain again and blamed the Lord for the rough time they were having. So the Lord sent a fire in which a lot of people burnt to death. Moses prayed to the Lord and the fire stopped.

Later on the Israelites started complaining about the food. They were no longer satisfied with the manna the Lord sent them. They wanted meat. Moses was annoyed. He told the Lord he was not prepared to lead the people any longer. So the Lord sent His Spirit upon seventy Israelites. They would help Moses to keep the people under control.

God also sent the Israelites the meat they asked for. Quail fell from the sky into the camp and all around it. There was more food than they could eat. But God was angry because the people were never satisfied. Many of them died that day.

Some people are forever complaining and it is wrong. We should be satisfied with what the Lord gives us and thank Him every day for food and clothes and a place to stay.

💡 **Remember:** Christians should not moan and grumble.

Twelve scouts explore Canaan

The Lord said to Moses, 'Send twelve men to explore the land of Canaan, the land I am giving to Israel. Send one leader from each of the twelve tribes.' (Num 13:2)

While the Israelites were in the desert of Paran, God told Moses to choose twelve men to go and explore Canaan.

After exploring the land for forty days, the men came back. They said to Moses, 'It is a magnificent country – a land flowing with milk and honey.' As proof they showed him a branch with a bunch of grapes they had cut from a vine. Two men had to carry it. But ten of the explorers were worried about the people living there: 'We can't fight them. They are stronger than we are!' they said. But Caleb and Joshua did not agree.

The ten scouts who were afraid then started telling fibs about the Canaanites, saying some of them were giants. This scared the Israelites so much that they wanted to stay where they were. They had already forgotten the Lord's promise to help them. Sometimes people have so little faith. Every time something goes wrong, they give up. We must not do this!

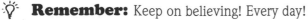

Remember: Keep on believing! Every day!

Forty years in the desert

Numbers 14

Then the Israelites plotted among themselves, 'Let's choose a new leader and go back to Egypt!' (Num 14:4)

The Israelites didn't want to go and live in Canaan anymore. They were too scared. So they decided to choose a new leader and go back to Egypt.

Moses was shocked. He and Aaron went down on their knees and begged the people not to do this. Joshua and Caleb, two of the scouts, also told them they were making a big mistake. The Lord was on their side.

Then the Israelites started talking about stoning Joshua and Caleb. But suddenly God's glorious presence appeared above the Tabernacle. Everybody saw this. The Lord told Moses He was going to destroy the Israelites. He had had enough of them!

Moses begged God to forgive them once again. The Lord answered Moses' prayer. He spared the lives of the Israelites. But God decided that not one of them would set foot in Canaan. For forty years they would wander around in the desert. Only after their death would their children be allowed into the promised land.

The Lord is patient with us. He keeps on giving us another chance. But we must say we're sorry if we have done something wrong, and we must not do it again.

🔅 **Remember:** The Lord never likes to punish us.

Korah's rebellion against Moses

Numbers 16

Then Moses said to Korah and his followers, 'Tomorrow morning the Lord will show us who belongs to Him and who is holy. Only those who are chosen will be allowed to come to His altar.' (Num 16:5)

One day a group of Israelites told Moses they didn't want him to be the leader of Israel any longer. The Lord had chosen them to be the new leaders.

Moses told them to come to the altar the next morning, where the people brought their offerings to the Lord. There the Lord would show who the true leaders of the people were.

The next morning all the Israelites came to see what would happen. Then the mighty power of the Lord was seen. He was furious with the people. He wanted to punish them with death but Moses and Aaron begged Him not to punish everybody for the sins of a few.

So the Lord decided to punish only those who were on the side of Korah, Dathan, and Abiram. The ground suddenly split open beneath them. The earth swallowed them up and they died.

The Lord hears us when we pray. Just think how many times He listened when Moses prayed for the Israelites.

 Remember: We should not repeat bad behaviour.

Buds on Aaron's staff

Numbers 17

Then the Lord said to Moses, 'Take twelve wooden staffs, one from each of the twelve tribes of Israel. Write each tribal leader's name on the staff. Then put these staffs in the Tabernacle in front of the Ark of the Covenant where I meet with you. Buds will grow on the staff belonging to the man I choose.' (Num 17:1-5)

The very morning after the death of Korah, Dathan and Abiram the people were complaining again. Once again the great power of the Lord was seen at the Tabernacle. He had had enough. He sent a plague, a terrible illness, which killed thousands of Israelites.

When Moses saw what was happening he said to Aaron, 'Quick, bring an offering to the Lord!' The plague ceased.

Then the Lord told Moses to take twelve staffs from the leaders of the twelve tribes. The staffs were put in the Tabernacle for the night. The tribe whose staff had blossoms on it the next morning, would be the one chosen by the Lord to put an end to the rebellion.

The next morning Aaron's staff had blossomed. This was the sign that from now on only Aaron and his sons could bring offerings to the altar of the Lord. They were to be the Lord's priests and work in the Tabernacle. The Levites had to help them.

💡 **Remember:** It really helps to pray for others.

The bronze snake

Numbers 21

Moses made a snake out of bronze and put it on top of a pole. When those who were bitten looked at the bronze snake, they didn't die! (Num 21:9)

One day Aaron died. All Israel mourned him for thirty days. Then they made war against Arad, king of the Canaanites. The Lord helped Israel to win the war. From there, the Israelites travelled towards the Red Sea. The people grew impatient again along the way and complained to Moses: 'Why have you brought us out of Egypt to die here? There is nothing to eat here and nothing to drink. And we hate this wretched manna!'

So the Lord sent poisonous snakes and many Israelites were bitten and died. Moses prayed again. The Lord told him to make a bronze snake and put it on top of a pole. Those who were bitten would live if they looked at it.

Just as the snake saved the lives of the Israelites in the desert, Jesus came to our rescue. He was also put on a wooden pole to free us. If we look up at Him and believe in Him, He gives us everlasting life.

 Remember: The cross of Jesus brings salvation.

Balaam blesses Israel

Numbers 22

The Lord opened Balaam's eyes. Then he saw the angel of the Lord standing in the roadway with a drawn sword in his hand. Balaam fell face down on the ground before him. (Num 22:31)

The Israelites won all the battles against their enemies. So when they set up camp in Moab, the people there were terrified. The Moabite king, Balak, quickly thought of something to stop them. He sent a prophet called Balaam to put a curse on Israel.

Balaam saddled his donkey and started off. But the Lord sent an angel to stand in the road and block his way. The donkey wouldn't go on. Balaam couldn't see the angel so he was angry with the donkey. Eventually the donkey lay down in the middle of the road, because it couldn't pass the angel. Balaam hit the donkey three times. Then the Lord opened his eyes and he saw the angel.

The angel told Balaam to do exactly what the Lord told him. When Balaam met with the king, he blessed the Israelites instead of cursing them. King Balak couldn't believe his own ears. But Balaam just did what the Lord told him.

🔅 **Remember:** God changes the life of sinners every day.

God's children must love Him

'Listen closely, Israel: The Lord is our God, the Lord alone! And you must love the Lord your God with all your heart, all your soul, and all your strength.' (Deut 6:4-5)

The Lord explained to the Israelites exactly how He wanted them to live. He promised them the land of Canaan if they obeyed Him.

The most important thing the Lord taught them was that He was the only God. They were not allowed to worship any other god. He alone was their God and they should love Him very much. They had to think about Him every day and obey Him.

The Israelites had to talk to their children about everything the Lord told them. Every child had to be taught from the very beginning that he or she must love the Lord more than anybody. They should also learn to do what the Lord said. It was as if the parents had to write the Lord's laws on the hands of their children and on their foreheads.

To this day, mothers and fathers are expected to love the Lord. Grown-ups may never be too busy for the Lord, nor must children. We must all learn to listen to the Lord.

 Remember: The Lord is the only God there is.

Care for those who suffer

Deuteronomy 15

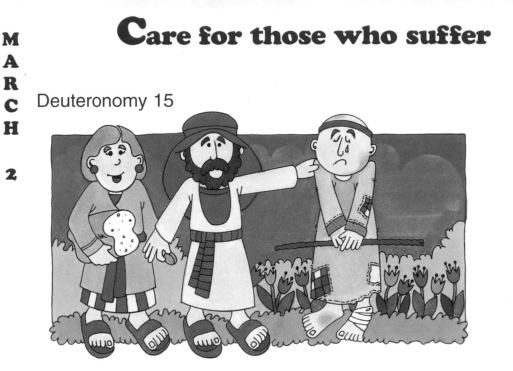

But if there are any poor people in your towns when you arrive in the land your God is giving you, do not be hard-hearted or tightfisted toward them. Remember they are Israelites, the same as you. Help them! (Deut 15:7-8)

The Lord likes people to care for one another. That's why He told the Israelites to open their hearts and hands to those who were poor. If one Israelite saw that another Israelite was going hungry or didn't have clothes to wear, he had to help and the Lord would bless him. God promised to look after every person who gave to others in need. Such a person would always have plenty to live on.

God doesn't want us to believe in Him just because we want to go to heaven, although that is important. He also wants us to do good deeds for Him. We must care for one another.

We must use some of our pocket money to help others, not spend it all on ourselves. We should try doing something good with it, and see what happens! The Lord will bless us once we start helping others.

Remember: We should care about our friends.

The Lord's covenant with Israel

Deuteronomy 29-30

'Today I am giving you a choice between the road of life and happiness, and the road of problems and death. Love the Lord your God and keep his laws. If you do this, you will live and become a great nation. God will bless you and the land you are about to live in.' (Deut 30:15-16)

The Lord called all the Israelites together in Moab. He said Moses must tell them about a new agreement He was going to make with them. First the Lord reminded them how good He had been to them. He had rescued them from Egypt and helped them win many battles against other nations.

The Lord wanted Israel to be his people once more. They must have nothing to do with the gods of other nations. They had to listen to Him only and then He would be their God forever.

Every Israelite had a choice: If he didn't want to listen to the Lord, he would die without Him. But if he obeyed Him, He would take care of him and treat him well.

The Lord doesn't force us to do what He says in the Bible. We have a choice. Naturally the Lord wants us to make the right choices. We must choose to love Him and do what is right.

 Remember: We must choose to serve the Lord every day.

The song of Moses

Deuteronomy 32

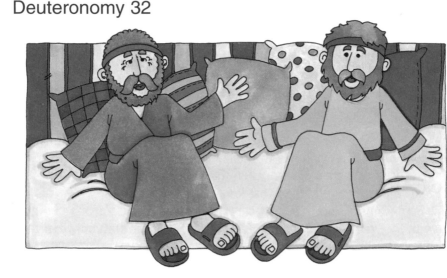

'Indeed, the Lord fights for his people. He takes care of them, because He sees their strength is gone.' (Deut 32:36)

When Moses spoke to the Israelites about God's new covenant with them, he was already a hundred and twenty years old. He told the Israelites that he would not go into Canaan with them. The Lord had chosen a new leader in Moses' place – Joshua. He led the Israelites in wars against the kings of the Amorites and Sihon and Og.

Moses took Joshua inside the Tabernacle with him. There the Lord told Moses that the Israelites would start doing terrible things again, once he was dead. Moses had to teach the Israelites a song so that when they sang it, they would remember everything the Lord had done for them. When they sinned, the song would be a witness against them.

The song told of how the Lord had taken Israel in his arms and protected them when He led them out of Egypt. He had shown them exactly what He wanted them to do and they were never alone. The Lord gave His people only the best. Yet they ran after other gods. That's why He decided to punish them. But, the song said, the Lord is a merciful God who would forgive and protect them.

☀ **Remember:** God cares for us and protects us.

Moses dies

Deuteronomy 33-34

Then the Lord said to Moses, 'This is the land I promised to Abraham, Isaac, and Jacob. I said, "I give this land to your descendants." I have now allowed you to see it, but you will not set foot in it.' (Deut 34:4)

Shortly before he died, Moses blessed all the Israelites. He had a blessing for each of the twelve tribes of Israel. Every tribe heard that the Lord would be with them in a special way.

When Moses had finished, he started climbing Mount Nebo. From one of the peaks, the Lord showed him the land where the Israelites were going to live. The Lord told Moses this was the land He had promised to Abraham, Isaac and Jacob a long time ago.

Moses died all alone on the mountain. The Lord buried him. The Israelites mourned Moses' death for thirty days.

The Lord used Moses in a wonderful way. He loved the Lord very much and he loved the Israelites, even though they were troublesome. He prayed for them often and asked God not to punish them.

If we love God, we will obey Him, care for others and pray to Him.

Remember: We should pray for our friends every day.

Joshua: God's new hero

Joshua 1

'Be strong and courageous! Do not be afraid or discouraged. I, the Lord your God am with you wherever you go.' (Josh 1:9)

Joshua took over after Moses' death. He had to lead the Israelites across the River Jordan into the promised land. The Lord spoke to him before he started on the journey. He told Joshua that He would be with him all the time. What a wonderful promise! But Joshua had to keep every word of the Lord locked away in his heart, and do what he was told. He had to walk in the ways of the Lord every minute of every day.

The Lord also told Joshua never to be afraid. He had a very difficult job. He had to lead a large nation into a new country, and the people could be very difficult at times. They didn't always listen to the Lord but Joshua knew that God would help him every step of the way.

The Lord wants us to be brave, like Joshua. We don't need to be afraid when the Lord is with us. The most powerful Person in the whole world is on our side and is there to look after us!

Remember: The Lord is with us always.

Two spies go to Jericho

Joshua 2

Then Joshua secretly sent out two spies from the Israelite camp. He told them, 'Spy out the land Canaan, especially the city of Jericho.' (Josh 2:1)

Joshua decided to send two spies to Canaan. He especially wanted to know how strong the city of Jericho was.

In Jericho the two men stayed at the house of a woman called Rahab. She had a very bad reputation. Someone saw the men there and told the king. He sent soldiers to Rahab's house to look for them but Rahab hid them and told the king's men they had already left the city.

When the soldiers had gone, Rahab begged the two men to ask the Israelites to spare her life and her family's when they attacked Jericho. They promised to do this. Rahab's house was built into the city wall, and the men were able to climb down the wall on a rope.

Before the two men left, they told Rahab she must leave the scarlet rope hanging from her window. Then they could guarantee her safety when they attacked the city.

The two men went back to Joshua and told him, 'The Lord will definitely give us the land. Everybody there is terrified of us.'

🔅 **Remember:** No problem is too big for God.

Twelve stones

Joshua 3-4

So the men did as Joshua told them. They took twelve stones from the middle of the River Jordan, one for each tribe, just as the Lord had told Joshua. They carried them to the place where they camped for the night. (Josh 4:8)

Joshua and the Israelites prepared to cross the Jordan. Joshua told the priests to lift up the Ark of the Covenant and lead the people across the river.

As the feet of the priests touched the water, the Lord cut the flow of the water. The priests carrying the Ark stood in the middle of the river on dry ground, while the Israelites crossed over.

When all the people were safely across the river, the Lord told Joshua to call the twelve leaders, one from each of the tribes of Israel. They each had to pick up one stone from the River Jordan and take it with them. Later they would use these stones to build a memorial at the place they camped for the night. This was to remind them and their children that the Lord had helped them cross the River Jordan without getting wet. As soon as the priests walked out on the other side of the Jordan, the water flowed again.

💡 **Remember:** The Lord still does miracles today.

Jericho is destroyed

When the Israelite soldiers heard the sound of the horns, they shouted as loud as they could. Suddenly the walls of Jericho collapsed. And the Israelites took the city. (Josh 6:20)

The people of Jericho knew the Israelites were going to attack, so they locked all the gates of the city. Joshua told the priests to march around the city once a day for six days, carrying the Ark of the Covenant. The army of Israel would march with them, some in front and others behind them. Joshua told them, 'Not a single word from any of you until I tell you to shout. Then shout!'

On the seventh day the Israelites marched around the city seven times. The seventh time around, as the priests sounded their horns, Joshua gave the command: 'Shout!' The walls of Jericho collapsed. The soldiers charged into the city and killed everybody but Rahab and her family. The soldiers took all the gold and silver for God.

The Lord gave the Israelites a great victory. He is so strong He can do anything.

-ॗ- **Remember:** Our God is a great God.

Achan's sin

Joshua 7

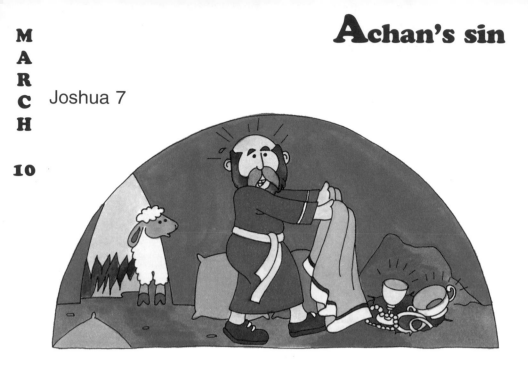

The Israelites had to give the Lord all the gold and silver they took from Jericho. But some of them kept it for themselves. A man named Achan stole some of these things, so the Lord was very angry with the Israelites. (Josh 7:1)

Joshua sent some of his warriors to attack Ai. But the army of Ai defeated the Israelites.

Joshua was upset and wanted to know why they lost when the Lord had promised to help them. God told Joshua it was because the Israelites were disobedient. They had taken some of the gold and silver for themselves instead of giving it to Him.

The following morning Joshua called all the Israelites together. The Lord identified Achan as the guilty one. He admitted that he had taken two kilograms of silver and half a kilogram of gold when they captured Jericho. He had also helped himself to some clothing and had buried everything under his tent.

Joshua told Achan it was his fault that a lot of soldiers had lost their lives in the battle against Ai. Achan had brought trouble upon the Israelites and he and his family were killed.

💡 **Remember:** The Lord sees everything we do.

Ai is defeated

Then the Lord said to Joshua, 'Do not be afraid or discouraged. Take your whole army and attack Ai. I will give you the king of Ai, his people, his city, and his land.' (Josh 8:1)

After the death of Achan and his family, the Lord told Joshua to attack Ai again. This time they would be victorious. Joshua made a clever plan. He hid thirty thousand men close behind the city and told them to be ready for action. Then he and the rest of the army attacked Ai from the other side. The king of Ai and his soldiers fought back. Joshua and his men pretended to be losing and they retreated. The army of Ai went after them leaving the city unprotected. The soldiers who had been hiding took the city and burnt it down. Joshua and his men then turned to face the king of Ai and his army and defeated them.

Joshua built an altar on Mount Ebal to thank the Lord for giving them the victory. He read the law of the Lord to all the Israelites, reminding them to obey God.

Remember: We should be glad that the Lord cares for us.

The sun and the moon stand still

Joshua 10

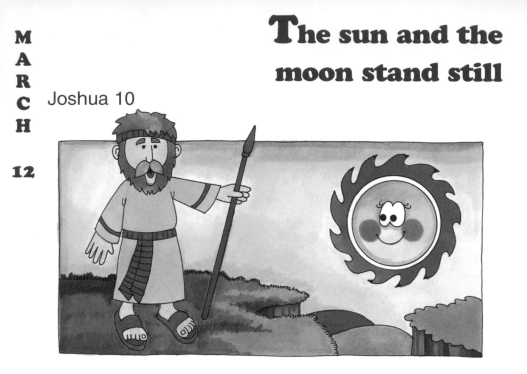

On the day the Lord helped Israel win the battle against the Amorites, Joshua prayed to the Lord in front of all the people of Israel. He said, 'Sun, stand still over Gibeon. Moon, stand still over the valley of Aijalon.' (Josh 10:12)

The five Amorite kings were very angry when they heard that the Gibeonites had made peace with Israel. They decided to attack the city of Gibeon. The Gibeonites immediately asked Joshua for help.

The Lord told Joshua He would give the Israelites victory over the Amorites and He did. At one stage Joshua asked the Lord to make the sun stand still so that they could finish the battle. The miracle happened – the sun stood still. Never before had anything like this happened.

The Lord is so mighty that even the sun listens to Him. If the Lord wants to, He can bring the whole world to a standstill. He has the sun and the moon and the stars in the palm of His hand. He will also do great things for us if we ask Him.

💡 **Remember:** The Lord does wonderful things for His children.

Joshua asks Israel to serve the Lord

Joshua 24

'If you are not willing to serve the Lord, then choose today whom you will serve. Would you prefer the gods your ancestors served? Or will it be the gods of the Amorites in whose land you now live? But as for me and my family, we will serve the Lord.' (Josh 24:15)

Joshua won one battle after the other against the Canaanite kings. In the end he defeated thirty-one kings. Later on he took the whole land of Canaan and divided it among the twelve tribes of Israel.

At the end of his life, Joshua called the Israelite leaders together. He told the people how good the Lord had been to them. Then he told them to choose who they wanted to serve. They could either serve the Lord or the gods of the land where they now lived. But regardless of their decision, he and his family would always remain faithful to the Lord.

The people answered, all together, 'We would never turn our backs on the Lord and worship other gods.' But Joshua was not satisfied: 'The Lord is a holy God. He won't allow people to serve Him just when it suits them.' But once more the Israelites promised to serve the Lord.

 Remember: We must love the Lord with all our heart!

The Israelites do not obey God

Judges 2

While Joshua was alive the Israelites served the Lord. After he and all the people of his time died, another generation grew up who did not know the Lord. They didn't know about the mighty things He had done for Israel. (Judg 2:7, 10)

While Joshua was alive, the Israelites obeyed the Lord, but after his death it was a different story. The next generation grew up knowing nothing about the Lord. The Israelites turned their backs on the Lord and started worshipping the gods of their new country.

The sins of Israel made the Lord very angry. They had forgotten all the promises the Lord had made to their fathers and grandfathers.

How can we make sure that we grow up knowing about the Lord? We must read the Bible and go to church every Sunday. If we don't love the Lord when we are little, we are going to grow up without Him and nothing can be worse than that.

🔆 **Remember:** We must read the Bible and go to church every Sunday.

The Lord sends judges

Judges 3

The Israelites cried out to the Lord for help. Then He sent a man to rescue them. His name was Othniel, the son of Caleb's younger brother, Kenaz. The Spirit of the Lord was with him. He ruled over Israel. (Judg 3:9-10)

The Israelites were very sinful, so the Lord allowed a Mesopotamian king to have control over them for eight years. Then the Israelites started praying. The Lord heard their prayers and He sent a judge to rule over them. He was called Othniel. He made war against the king of Mesopotamia and won. As long as Othniel lived, there was peace in Israel.

After Othniel's death Israel lost a war against King Eglon of Moab. The Israelites worked for him for eighteen years. Once again the Israelites started praying and the Lord sent Ehud to the rescue.

Ehud arranged to meet alone with King Eglon. As soon as the servants had been sent out of the room, Ehud pulled out his dagger and killed the king. He gathered the Israelites together and they attacked and defeated the Moabites.

The Lord notices when people suffer, even if they are sinners.

 Remember: The Lord never sleeps or rests.

Deborah and Barak

Judges 4

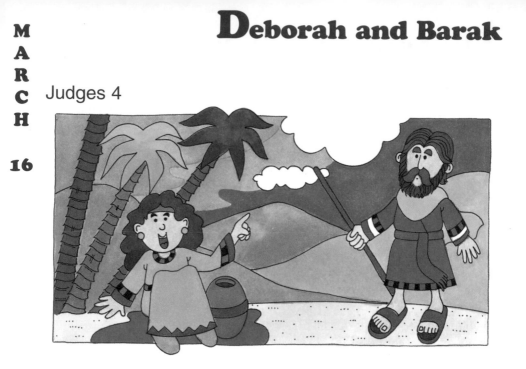

The Israelites cried out to the Lord for help. At that time Deborah, the wife of Lappidoth, was the leader of the Israelites. (Judg 4:3-4)

After Ehud's death the Israelites started doing evil things again. So the Lord handed them over to King Jabin, the Canaanite king who lived in Hazor. Sisera was in command of his army.

During that time a woman was the leader of Israel. Her name was Deborah. One day the Lord told her that Israel would win the battle against Sisera. She sent for Barak to be Israel's commander. Barak said, 'I will go, but only if you go with me!' 'Very well,' she replied, 'I will go with you, but the victory will be the Lord's, not yours.'

That day Israel's ten thousand soldiers defeated Sisera's army. Sisera tried to escape and hid in the tent of a woman called Jael. He was very tired. When he was fast asleep Jael took a tent peg and drove it through his head with a hammer. She called Barak to show him that Sisera was dead. That same day Barak captured King Jabin. The Canaanites were defeated.

After Israel's great victory, Deborah and Barak sang a song and praised the Lord. They were very happy that the Lord had helped them. We can do nothing without the Lord.

💡 **Remember:** The Lord helps His children in times of hardship.

God calls Gideon

Gideon said to God, 'I will put a piece of sheep wool on the ground tonight. If it is wet with dew in the morning but the ground around it is dry, then I will know that You are going to help me rescue Israel as You promised.' (Judg 6:36-37)

After a while the Lord gave the Israelites into the hands of the Midianites. Again the Israelites prayed for help. God sent an angel to a man called Gideon.

Gideon hurried home to fetch an offering for the Lord. The angel told him to put it down on a rock. Suddenly fire flamed up from the rock and burnt the offering. Gideon realized the Lord was there with him.

To make sure God really wanted him to rescue Israel, Gideon asked the Lord to give him a sign. He left a piece of sheep's wool outside that night. If the wool was wet the next morning and the ground around it was dry, then he would know that this was what he must do. It happened just that way but Gideon still wasn't sure. He said to God, 'Please don't be angry with me, but this time let the wool stay dry and the ground around it be wet.' The next morning it had happened just like that, so Gideon knew what he had to do.

Remember: Only ask God for good things.

Gideon defeats the Midianites

Judges 7

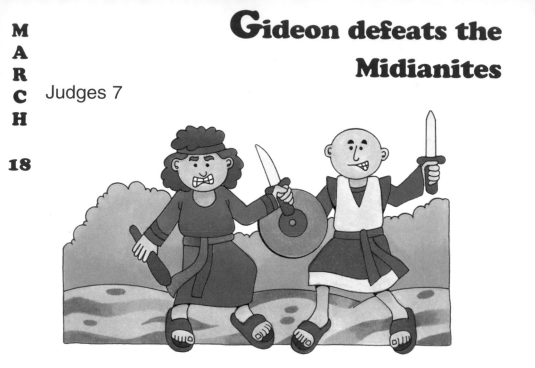

The Lord told Gideon, 'With these three hundred men I will rescue you and give you victory over the Midianites.' (Judg 7:7)

Gideon and his men prepared to make war against the Midianites. God told him he had too many warriors so Gideon sent home twenty-two thousand men who admitted they were scared. That left ten thousand soldiers – still too many. So the Lord sent them to the river to drink water. Three hundred men drank the water from their cupped hands. They, and they alone, were chosen to be Gideon's army.

Gideon divided his men into three groups. He gave each man a ram's horn and a clay jar with a torch in it. That night they went to the Midianite camp. Suddenly, they blew their horns and broke their jars. They held the blazing torches in the air and shouted, 'A sword for the Lord and for Gideon!'

The Midianites started rushing around in a panic. Some even fought each other in the confusion.

The Lord used three hundred warriors to defeat a powerful army. He is not interested in how strong or clever we are. He uses ordinary people. We don't even have to wait until we are grown up. God will use us just the way we are if we will give our lives to Him.

☀ **Remember:** One believer can make a difference.

Samson, the strong man

Judges 13

'One of these days you will have a son. His hair must never be cut, because he will belong to God from birth. He will rescue Israel from the Philistines.' (Judg 13:5)

The Israelites were oppressed by the Philistines for forty years. During that time, the Lord sent an angel to a woman in Israel. He told her she would have a son. He would be special because he would help Israel against the Philistines. He would not be allowed to drink any wine or beer or have his hair cut.

The woman told her husband, Manoah, about the angel's visit. Manoah then prayed that the angel would come to them again and tell them exactly what the Lord wanted them to do.

The angel came back later. After he had told them how to raise the boy, Manoah prepared an offering for the Lord. Then the Lord did something amazing. Flames from the altar shot up toward the sky, and the angel of the Lord went up to heaven in the flame.

Later on the baby boy was born. His parents called him Samson and the Spirit of the Lord was with him.

 Remember: The Lord always cares about children.

Samson's riddle

Judges 14

'What is sweeter than honey? What is stronger than a lion?' (Judg 14:18)

Samson decided to marry a Philistine girl who lived in Timnah. One day when he was on his way there, a lion attacked him but the Lord helped him to kill the lion. Later, when Samson went back to Timnah for the wedding he saw that a swarm of bees had made some honey in the carcass of the lion.

Samson threw a party at Timnah and invited thirty Philistine men. He said, 'Let me tell you a riddle: From the one who eats came something to eat; out of the strong came something sweet.' He promised to give each of the Philistines a set of clothes if they could solve the riddle within seven days. If they failed they each had to give him a set of clothes.

Three days later they were still trying to figure it out. Then they told his wife to get the answer from Samson. She nagged Samson until he told her: 'What is sweeter than honey? What is stronger than a lion?'

On the seventh day the Philistines brought Samson the answer. He went to Ashkelon, killed thirty men and gave their clothes to the others. Then he left his wife and went back home to his parents.

💡 **Remember:** We should choose our friends carefully.

Samson fights the Philistines

Then he picked up a donkey's jawbone that was lying on the ground and killed a thousand Philistines with it. (Judg 15:15)

Some time after this, Samson decided to visit his wife in Timnah again, only to discover that her father had given her to another man in the meantime. He told Samson to marry her sister. This made Samson so angry that he went out and caught three hundred foxes. He tied their tails together in pairs, and fastened a torch to each pair of tails. Then he chased the foxes through the fields of the Philistines. Everything was burnt down.

The Philistines wanted to kill Samson for what he'd done, but they couldn't find him. So they attacked the Israelites, thinking he was among them. The Israelites caught Samson, tied him up and took him to the Philistines. But Samson snapped the ropes on his arms. He picked up a donkey's jawbone that was lying on the ground and killed a thousand Philistines with it.

The Lord gave Samson this great strength. He used it to help the Israelites against their enemies.

 Remember: God is always there to help us.

Samson and Delilah

Judges 16

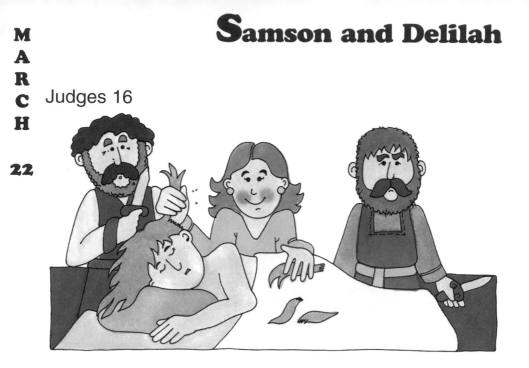

Then Samson prayed to the Lord, 'O God, please make me strong again, just this once, so that I may pay back the Philistines for poking out my eyes.' (Judg 16:28)

Samson fell in love with a Philistine woman named Delilah. The leaders of the Philistines went to her secretly. 'Find out from Samson what makes him so strong,' they said.

Delilah kept asking Samson what made him so strong. Every time he gave her a different reason. In the end, after Delilah went on nagging him, he told her the truth. If his hair was cut, his strength would go. When he fell asleep with his head in her lap, Delilah had his hair shaved off. Then the Philistines came, put him in chains and blinded him.

In the Philistine prison Samson's hair started growing again. One day the Philistines held a festival in the temple of the god Dagon. Samson was brought out to perform for them. As he stood between the two pillars which held up the roof of the temple, he prayed that the Lord give him back his strength once more. He put his arms around the two pillars and pushed against them with all his might. The temple crashed down on the people. Samson died with them that day.

🔅 **Remember:** The Lord can do anything.

Naomi and Ruth

Ruth 1-2

Ruth said to Naomi, 'Don't ask me to leave you and turn back. I will go wherever you go and live wherever you live. Your people will be my people, and your God will be my God.' (Ruth 1:16)

There was a famine in Israel, so a man called Elimelech and his wife Naomi decided to move to Moab with their two sons. The sons married Moabite girls called Ruth and Orpah, but as the years passed first Elimelech died and then his sons.

Naomi decided to go back to Bethlehem. Her two daughters-in-law wanted to go with her but she told them it would be better for them to stay in Moab. Orpah turned back, but Ruth refused to go. She went to Bethlehem with Naomi and said she wanted to serve God and be an Israelite.

In Bethlehem Ruth picked up leftover grain in the fields of a man called Boaz. When Boaz saw Ruth gathering the grain he told the harvesters to drop some heads of barley on purpose for her to take home. Naomi was very thankful. She said the Lord would bless Boaz.

Sometimes life is hard. But the Lord always has a plan for the lives of his children. Even if we suffer, we must never stop believing.

💡 **Remember:** Care about those who suffer.

Ruth and Boaz get married

Ruth 4

So Boaz married Ruth ... (Ruth 4:13)

Naomi told her daughter-in-law Ruth to go to Boaz and ask him to help her. So one evening she went to the threshing floor where Boaz was lying fast asleep. Ruth lay down at his feet. When he woke up, she asked him to help and protect her.

Later, after Ruth had gone home, Boaz asked the leaders of the town for advice. He wanted to buy Naomi's land in order to help Ruth and Naomi. Boaz first asked a relative of Naomi's if he wanted to buy the land, but he wasn't interested so Boaz went ahead.

Soon afterwards Boaz married Ruth. They had a son whom they named Obed. Everybody was happy that the Lord had been so good to Ruth and Naomi.

The Lord loves all His children. He will lead us along the right path if we ask Him. Sometimes it takes a long time for His plans for our lives to work out, but we should trust Him always.

🔅 **Remember:** The Lord is always good to us.

Hannah's promise to the Lord

'In that case,' Eli said to Hannah, 'Cheer up! May the God of Israel give you what you have asked of Him.' 'Oh, thank you, sir!' she exclaimed. (1 Sam 1:17-18)

A man named Elkanah had two wives, Peninnah and Hannah. Peninnah had children, while Hannah did not.

Every year Elkanah and his wives would travel to Shiloh to worship and sacrifice to the Lord. All the women there would make fun of Hannah because she was childless.

One day Hannah went to the temple in Shiloh to pray. She asked the Lord to give her a son. If He did she would give the boy back to Him.

While she was praying, Eli the priest watched her. He saw her lips move, but she made no sound. He thought she was drunk. 'Oh, no sir!' she said to him, 'I'm not drunk! But I am very sad and I was pouring out my heart to the Lord.' Eli told her that God would answer her prayer. She could go back home.

The next day Hannah went back home with her husband. She was not worried anymore. She believed that the Lord had heard her prayer.

 Remember: Every little child is a gift from God.

Samuel hears the Lord's voice

1 Samuel 3

Meanwhile, the boy Samuel worked for the Lord by helping Eli in the temple. In those days messages from the Lord were very rare. (1 Sam 3:1)

Hannah's prayer for a son was answered. She had a child and she named him Samuel. When Samuel was old enough, she took him to Eli the priest in Shiloh as she had promised the Lord. Samuel worked in the temple. Every year Hannah visited him. The Lord gave her five more children.

One night Samuel was asleep in the temple near the Ark of God. Suddenly the Lord called, 'Samuel! Samuel!' The boy thought it was Eli. But Eli said he hadn't called him and Samuel should go back to bed. It happened a second time. When it happened the third time, Eli realized it was the Lord calling Samuel so Eli told Samuel that if he heard the voice again he should say, 'Yes, Lord, your servant is listening.'

The Lord then told Samuel that He was going to punish Eli and his family. Eli's sons were bad and Eli didn't discipline them. When Eli wanted to know what the Lord had said, Samuel told him. Eli answered, 'It is the Lord's will. Let Him do what He thinks best.'

☀ **Remember:** The Lord also uses children in His service.

The Philistines steal the Ark of the Lord

As Samuel grew up, the Lord was with him, and everything Samuel said was wise and helpful. All the people of Israel knew that Samuel was truly a prophet of the Lord. (1 Sam 3:19-20)

Samuel grew up and the Lord was with him. Samuel brought all the messages the Lord gave him to the people.

At the time, Israel was at war with the Philistines. They defeated the Israelite army, so the soldiers of Israel decided to fetch the Lord's Ark in Shiloh. Eli's sons, Hophni and Phinehas, helped carry the Ark to where the battle was being fought. When the Ark arrived at their camp, the soldiers sharted shouting with joy.

When the Philistines heard all the shouting, they began to panic. 'Their God has come into their camp!' they cried. 'Fight as you never have before!' That day the Philistines killed thirty thousand Israelites and took the Ark. Eli's sons were also killed.

Others must see that we belong to the Lord. We must listen to what the Lord teaches us in the Bible. Then our friends will notice that we have a special Friend on our side. We shouldn't be embarrassed to talk about Him.

💡 **Remember:** People can see if we serve the Lord.

The Philistines send the Ark back

1 Samuel 5-6

The Philistines carried the Ark of God into the temple of Dagon and placed it beside the idol of Dagon. But when the citizens of Ashdod went to see it the next morning, Dagon had fallen with his face to the ground in front of the Ark of the Lord! (1 Sam 5:2-3)

The Philistines took the Ark of God to a city named Ashdod. There they put it in the temple of Dagon, one of their gods. The next morning when they went into the temple, they found the idol of Dagon, face down on the ground. The next day the same thing happened.

After this, the people of Ashdod started getting ill. So they sent the Ark to a place called Gath. Everybody there also fell ill. From there the Ark was sent to Ekron. The same thing happened there so the Philistines decided to send the Ark back to the Israelites.

The Philistines sent gifts of gold along with the Ark. When the Ark arrived at Beth-shemesh in Israel, some of the people were curious and sneaked a look into the Ark. Seventy of them died. So the people offered guilt offerings to the Lord. Then they sent the Ark to a place called Kiriat-jearim. There it was kept in the house of Abinadab for twenty years. Abinadab's son, Eleazar, was in charge of the Ark and there was peace in Israel again.

💡 **Remember:** The Lord does not allow people to mock Him.

The Israelites want a king

M
A
R
C
H

29

All the leaders of Israel met at Ramah to discuss the matter with Samuel. 'Look,' they told him, 'you are now old, and your sons are not like you. Give us a king like all the other nations have.' (1 Sam 8:4-5)

Samuel's two sons were not like him. They took bribes and they did not serve the Lord. The leaders of Israel were worried about this, because Samuel was already very old.

So the leaders asked Samuel to give them a king. Samuel didn't want to. He asked the Lord's advice. The Lord said, 'Do as they say, and give them a king.' He knew they wouldn't listen to Samuel's warnings anyway. The big mistake the people made was to think that the Lord was not good enough to be their king any longer.

So Samuel told the people they could have a king but he warned them about how a king would treat them. Many Israelites would have to work for the king. They would also have to pay taxes. By the time they started complaining, it would be too late and the Lord would not listen.

But the Israelites refused to change their minds. 'Even so, we still want a king,' they said.

 Remember: We must listen to what the Lord says in the Bible.

Saul, the first king of Israel

1 Samuel 9-10

When Samuel noticed Saul, the Lord said, 'That's the man I told you about! He will rule my people.' (1 Sam 9:17)

One day a man from the tribe of Benjamin went to look for his father's donkeys. His name was Saul. He couldn't find the donkeys anywhere. His servant told him about Samuel. Perhaps he could help them. So they went to the town where Samuel was.

Now the Lord had told Samuel the day before that He would send someone to him. Samuel had to anoint him as the new king of Israel. When Samuel saw Saul, the Lord said, 'This is the man!'

Later, after they had eaten, Saul started back. He and Samuel left the house together. Outside the town, Samuel anointed Saul as king. That day the Spirit of the Lord came upon Saul. Everybody could see the Lord was working through him.

Later Samuel called the people together at Mizpah. There he told them that God had chosen Saul to be their first king. All the people shouted, 'Long live the king!'

The Lord does great things! Even now He gives His Spirit to everyone who bows before Him. The Holy Spirit will live in us too if we love the Lord. He shows us the right way and helps us to love God.

💡 **Remember:** God wants us to live for Him every day.

Saul defeats the Ammonites

1 Samuel 11

But Saul replied, 'No-one will be killed today, for today the Lord has rescued Israel!' (1 Sam 11:13)

The Ammonite king attacked a city of Israel, called Jabesh. His soldiers surrounded the city. The citizens of Jabesh promised to be the king's servants if he would spare their lives. The king said, 'All right, but only on one condition. Only if I can take out the right eye of every one of you!'

Messengers went to Saul in Gibeah, and told him what the Ammonite king wanted to do. The Spirit of the Lord made Saul become very angry. He took two oxen and cut them into pieces. He sent the pieces throughout Israel with the message: 'This is what will happen to the oxen of anyone who refuses to follow Samuel and Saul into battle!' Then Saul attacked the Ammonites. Saul's army won the battle and saved the people of Jabesh. The soldiers were very happy about winning. They wanted to kill everyone who was against having Saul as king. But Saul stopped them. The Lord had helped them to win. No Israelite would be killed.

Then Saul went to Gilgal. There, before the Lord, the people crowned him king. Saul and all the Israelites were very happy.

Remember: Praise the Lord for His love.

Samuel talks to
the Israelites

1 Samuel 12

'Don't be afraid,' Samuel said. 'You have done wrong to ask for a king, but make sure now that you worship the Lord with all your heart.' (1 Sam 12:20)

One day Samuel spoke to the Israelites again. He said he had always told them what the Lord wanted. He also told them it was wrong to ask for a king. But the Lord would not hold this against them. If the Israelites and their king worshipped the Lord and listened to His voice, all would be well. But if they didn't, there would be hard times ahead for them.

Then Samuel prayed. Suddenly the Lord sent thunder and rain. All the people were terrified of the Lord and of Samuel.

'Pray to the Lord your God for us, or we will die!' they cried.

Samuel told them not to be afraid. They just had to hold on to the Lord's hand, and He would be with them.

The Lord is mighty and important. If He tells us to listen, then we must listen. It's the best thing we can ever do because it pleases the most powerful Person in the whole world. Just think, it is possible for us, for ordinary, puny little people to make the Lord happy!

💡 **Remember:** The most important Person in the world is with us.

Saul sins

1 Samuel 13

Samuel said to Saul, 'You have done a foolish thing. Why have you offered the burnt offering yourself? You have disobeyed the command of the Lord your God. If you had obeyed, you would have been king over Israel for the rest of your life. But now you will not be king much longer. The Lord has chosen a man after his own heart.' (1 Sam 13:13-14)

One day the Philistines declared war against the Israelites. The men of Israel lost their nerve and ran away. King Saul and his soldiers were still in Gilgal waiting for Samuel to bring an offering to the Lord before they went to fight the Philistines.

When Samuel took too long to come, Saul decided to offer the burnt offering himself. Just then Samuel arrived. He was very angry with Saul. He told Saul he had made a big mistake. He had offered the burnt offering himself knowing that only Samuel was allowed to do it. As a result the Lord would take his kingship away from him.

We must not think we're always right. We should listen to our parents and to what they tell us about God.

 Remember: We must obey our parents' teachings about God.

God chooses David as king

1 Samuel 16

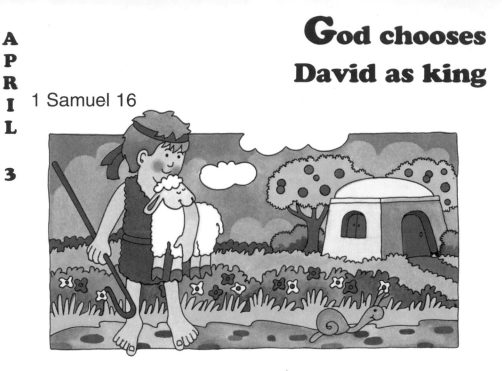

God's Spirit made David strong. (1 Sam 16:13)

King Saul didn't do what the Lord wanted. This upset the Lord and He decided to choose another king. He knew that one of Jesse's sons would make a good king.

The Lord sent Samuel to show everybody who the new king would be. Jesse called his sons and wondered which one the Lord would choose. As each son came before Samuel the old prophet shook his head and said, 'No, not this one.' When Samuel had seen all of Jesse's sons, he said, 'The Lord has not chosen any of these. Don't you have any other sons?' 'There's the youngest,' Jesse answered. 'But he's out in the fields watching the sheep.' Surely it couldn't be him! Then Samuel said to Jesse, 'It's not important to the Lord what a person is on the outside. It's the heart that counts.'

So Jesse sent for David. When he walked in, Samuel knew he was the king that the Lord had chosen, and he told the others that David was their new king. From then on, the Holy Spirit worked in David in a very special way. He made David strong so that he could be a good king one day.

🔅 **Remember:** God looks into our hearts to see if they are clean.

God watches over David

Psalm 23

The Lord is my shepherd. (Ps 23:1)

David was a shepherd and he watched over his sheep. He was often alone in the fields with them, but he was not afraid. He knew the Lord was with him always. In a lovely poem (Psalm 23) he tells us why he was never afraid.

This is what he says: The Lord is like a shepherd to me. I am like his sheep. He takes good care of me. He gives me everything I need. When I'm tired He lets me rest like a sheep rests on soft green grass. When I am thirsty He gives me cool water. So I needn't worry about a thing.

When He is with me, I feel safe. I can handle anything. When I don't know the right thing to do, He helps me. He leads me in the right ways. Even when I feel I'm all alone in the darkest night, I am not scared, because the Lord is with me. He comforts me. With Him, I am safe.

The Lord takes good care of His children. If we believe in Him, we need never be afraid. He will watch over us just like a good shepherd watches over his sheep.

Remember: God Himself looks after us.

David does his duty

1 Samuel 16

'I heard the boy, David, play the harp. The Lord is with him.' (1 Sam 16:18)

David was only a shepherd boy but the Lord, Who loved him very much, chose David to become king. God's plan was for David to be King Saul's helper in the palace at first so that he could learn how things were done before he became king.

David was a very talented harp player. When King Saul was tired or troubled, David would play the harp. It made the king feel better and calmed him down. All the other tasks he had to do for the king, David did well. He worked hard because he loved God very much and obeyed Him. David knew it would hurt God if he did something wrong and he knew that the Lord was helping him every day.

David wrote a poem about God Who always helps His children.

He says in Psalm 27: The Lord is the one who always helps me. So why should I be afraid? I can always go to Him. I know the Lord will help me. That's why I feel strong, because I put my trust in the Lord.

Remember: We can always go to the Lord.

A shepherd believes and wins

1 Samuel 17

'All right, go ahead. And may the Lord be with you.' (1 Sam 17:37)

David knew no fear. One day as he was watching his father's sheep, a vicious lion snatched one of David's lambs. David didn't run away. He went after the lion and killed it and took the lamb from the lion's mouth. He also killed a bear once.

David was very brave. One day David's father asked him to take his brothers something to eat. There was a war going on and they were soldiers. When David arrived with the food, he heard Goliath the giant making fun of the Israelites. Everybody was too scared to fight the giant.

David told the king he wasn't afraid of Goliath. He would fight him. At first the king was not happy about this. Goliath had been a soldier for many years. David was only a shepherd boy. But David said to him, 'Don't worry about a thing. The Lord helped me to kill the lion and the bear. He will also help me win the fight against Goliath.'

'All right, go ahead,' King Saul said. 'And may the Lord be with you.'

And the Lord did help David!

Remember: Trust the Lord!

Goliath

1 Samuel 17

'You come to me with sword, spear and javelin, but I come to you in the name of the Lord Almighty.' (1 Sam 17:45)

The Philistines were the enemies of God's people. They made war against them. The Philistines had a very strong man on their side whose name was Goliath. He was a giant and a very good fighter. Everybody was terrified of him. He mocked the Israelites. He made fun of them because their God couldn't even help them against him. He was too strong. But he was mistaken, as he soon found out.

David loved God and God loved him. He knew God would help him, so he wasn't afraid of Goliath. David put his catapult and five smooth stones in his pocket. When Goliath saw this young boy, not even armed for battle, he was furious. He thought they were joking. He started swearing and shouted, 'Come over here, and I'll give your flesh to the birds and the wild animals.'

David walked towards him and, with one stone, hit him between the eyes. Goliath the giant fell down dead. The Philistines were terrified. They turned and ran off in all directions. They realized that God is stronger than any human being.

-ঀৢ- **Remember:** God is stronger than any human being.

God saves David from Saul

1 Samuel 18-19

Saul was afraid of David, because the Lord helped him. (1 Sam 18:12)

King Saul soon noticed that David was very popular with the people. The Lord was very good to David. Saul became jealous of David. Saul didn't always listen to the Lord. He was disobedient. Sometimes he acted as if the devil was in him.

One day when David was playing the harp for Saul, Saul hurled a spear at him. David ducked, and the spear missed him. Then Saul chased David away from the palace. He decided to kill David.

Another time Saul sent soldiers to capture David. They knew he was with his wife Michal. But Michal warned David and she thought of a clever plan to save him. She put a rope out of the window and he climbed down it and ran away. Then Michal made up the bed so the soldiers would think that David was in it. She told them David was ill. It gave David a chance to get away. By the time the soldiers realized they had been fooled, it was already too late. Once again the Lord had protected David.

 Remember: The Lord protects His children.

David and Jonathan

1 Samuel 20

Go in peace. (1 Sam 20:42)

David and King Saul's son, Jonathan, were best friends, but Saul was jealous of David and wanted him dead. David had to go into hiding. He told Jonathan he needed his help. He wanted Jonathan to find out if Saul was really serious about killing him. Jonathan arranged a special signal with David which would give him the answer. He would shoot an arrow at a target. David had to hide nearby. If Jonathan said to his helper, 'The arrow is close, this side,' David would know he was safe. But if Jonathan said, 'The arrow is over there, on the far side,' David would know Saul was going to kill him.

Jonathan asked Saul if he was determined to kill David. 'Yes, of course,' Saul answered. Jonathan went off with his bow and shot an arrow. 'The arrow is over there, farther on,' he called out loudly to his helper. This was the sign for David to run for his life. Jonathan was sad that he would never see his friend again, but he knew he had to help save his life.

We must also do what's best for our friends, even if it sometimes hurts.

Remember: Always do the right thing, even if it sometimes hurts.

David spares
Saul's life

Saul said to David, 'You are a better man than I am.' (1 Sam 24:18)

The Lord took good care of David and He helped him. This made King Saul very jealous. He gave orders to his soldiers to find David and kill him. Saul went along to search for David. They travelled far in the hot sun and eventually they were very tired. At a cave, Saul decided to rest for a bit. He didn't know that David was hiding in the cave. Saul lay down and fell asleep. David went up to him quietly and cut off a piece of Saul's clothing. David's men wanted him to kill Saul. 'Now's your chance,' they whispered. But David refused. He didn't want to do anything that would not please the Lord.

When Saul woke up, David showed him the piece of cloth. 'I would never harm you, my king,' David said. Saul saw that David could have killed him, but he hadn't. This made him sad and he cried. He was so nasty to David, yet David did not try to pay him back.

Then Saul knew that the Lord does not want us to hurt others, no matter how jealous we are.

🔆 **Remember:** Never hurt other people.

Choose your friends carefully

Psalm 1

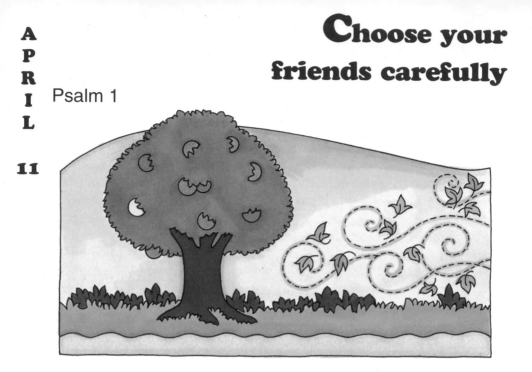

It is good not to listen to the wrong advice. (Ps 1:1)

The wrong friends can make us do wicked things. They often try to get us to do something that we know is wrong. Psalm 1 tells us about this.

We shouldn't listen to bad friends. We must ignore thèm when they tell us to be naughty because doing wrong makes the Lord unhappy.

We can think of it like this: A tree is planted beside a lovely stream. Its leaves are a shiny green and its fruit is good. Someone who listens to the Lord is like this tree. Someone who does not listen to the Lord, is like a handful of dried-up leaves blown away by the wind. One day the Lord will punish people who don't love Him. The Lord tells His children what they must do, but wicked people don't listen to Him. See what Psalm 1:6 says: Truly, the Lord walks alongside the person who listens to Him.

If we listen to Him, we are like a lovely green tree with delicious fruit. We please the Lord and make Him proud of us.

Remember: We must not listen to bad friends.

David becomes king

1 Chronicles 11

The Lord, Who is the most powerful of all, was with David. (1 Chr 11:9)

Remember the Philistines didn't like God and His people. They soon made war against the Lord's people again and killed King Saul and his son, Jonathan. The Philistines believed they were winning but they were mistaken! God had other plans. He had not said David would be king for nothing. He also had plans for His people and He was not going to allow the Philistines to win.

And that's the way it happened. The Lord helped David and his men to defeat the Philistines. God also gave David a very special city to live in – Jerusalem. David wanted God to be there with him and the people always. He knew that the Lord is actually everywhere but the Lord promised to be with them in Jerusalem in a very special way. That's why, later on, a temple for the Lord was built in Jerusalem.

If we believe in God, He will be with us in a special way.

 Remember: God loves us in a special way.

David helps others

2 Samuel 9

David said to Mephibosheth, 'I want to be kind to you. I promised Jonathan.'
(2 Sam 9:1)

David never forgot his friend Jonathan. He promised him that he would always help him and his children whenever he could.

The Philistines killed Jonathan but he had a son. The boy, Mephibosheth, fell when he was little and hurt both legs badly, making it difficult for him to walk.

David became king but he didn't forget his promise. When he heard that Mephibosheth was still alive he sent someone to fetch him straight away. David was very kind to Mephibosheth. He took care of him as he had promised Jonathan. Jonathan had been dead for a long time but David kept his promise. If we make a promise, we must keep it.

If we love the Lord, we must never promise to do something and then not do it. A promise is a promise!

🔆 **Remember:** Never, ever lie!

The Lord takes care of David

Please keep me safe, Lord. You are my shelter. (Ps 16:1)

David knew he couldn't do anything without the Lord. He wrote a beautiful poem, Psalm 16. In it he says how important the Lord is to him. The Lord is with him all the time, which makes him happy and makes him feel safe. He is no longer afraid. This is what David wrote:

Lord, let me be with you always. Keep me safe, God. I am yours. To me nothing is more important or better than You. I want to have nothing to do with people who don't love You.

Lord, You take care of me. Everything I have, You gave me. It is because of You that I am alive. I am so happy with everything You have given me – thank You very much. Thank You too for teaching me to do the right thing, because You are always with me. With You I am safe. You teach me the right way to live. You give me only good things. I'm glad that I can always be with You.

The Lord does all this for every one of his children. If we believe in Him, we are His children. He will take good care of us. We must remember to thank Him every day!

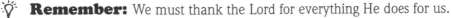

Remember: We must thank the Lord for everything He does for us.

Lord, You know me. You made me

Psalm 139

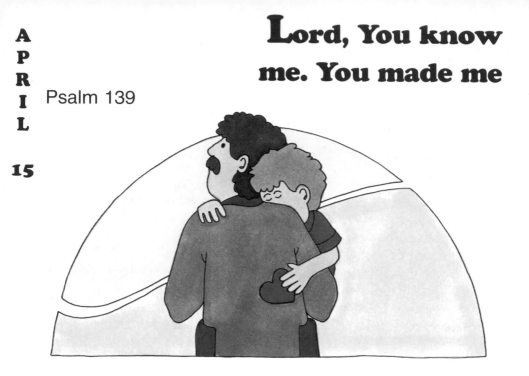

Lord, You know everything about me. (Ps 139:1)

There was once a man who wondered if he could hide away from the Lord. Would he be able to do something secretly, so that no-one knew – not even the Lord? That man was David. This is what he says in Psalm 139:7-12:

Is there a place I can go where God is not? I tried hiding in the graveyard but God was there. I tried to go as far east as I could, and to the west, but I couldn't hide from God, because He was everywhere.

Then I tried hiding from God in the pitch-darkness. But to God it's never really dark. He can see in the dark. Then I knew that the Lord knows what I think, almost before I have thought it. He knows what I am going to say and what I am not going to say. When I sit down or stand up, the Lord knows it, because He made me. Even before I was born, He already knew me. Even then He held me close, because He loved me.

The Lord loves us and knows each one of us just as much as He did David.

🔅 **Remember:** The Lord never stops loving us.

David says thank you to God

Your goodness and love will be with me all my life. (Ps 23:6)

Imagine there is a man who is so poor he doesn't even have food to eat. He has to live on the scraps he can pick up. Suddenly a rich man comes along and invites him to dinner. He gives him only the best food and most delicious cold drinks and the poor man is encouraged to eat and drink as much as he wants. How would the poor man feel? I think he would be very happy. This is how David feels about God because God treats him so well. In Psalm 23 David says God is like the rich man who invites someone to a scrumptious dinner. This is what David says:

Lord, you invite me to a feast. You make me feel so important. You are so kind and nice to me. Now those who made fun of me are silent. They have nothing to say.

David never gets tired of talking about the goodness of the Lord. God looks after all His children like this. We must remember to say thank you.

 Remember: God looks after all His children.

Trust the Lord

Psalm 146

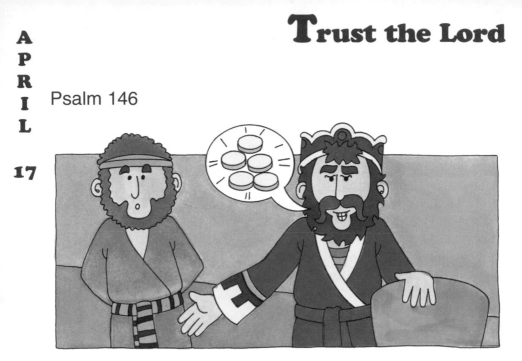

Don't put your trust in people. (Ps 146:3)

There was once a man called Peter who learnt a very important lesson. He trusted a rich and powerful king who promised to help him. Peter had to work for him and serve him. Peter thought, 'Now I'm going to be very important too and have everything I want.' That's what the king promised him. Peter forgot all about God and served only the king. Then the king died and Peter was left on his own ...

In the Bible there was a man like Peter and this is what he learnt:

Don't put your trust in powerful or important people. They are, after all, only human beings. They aren't always going to be there to help you. One day they will die and then they can't do what they promised anymore. It's much better to put your trust in the Lord and to serve Him. He never dies. He will always be there to help you. The happiest person is the one who trusts the Lord.

This should be a lesson to us too.

🔅 **Remember:** We can always trust the Lord.

David makes a mistake

Lord, I have made a mistake. Please forgive me. (2 Sam 24:10)

One day David decided to go and check how many soldiers he had. If he had plenty, he thought he wouldn't have to rely on the Lord so much. Then he realized this was a mistake. Having a big army was not enough. He should be putting his trust in the Lord alone. God sent a messenger to David. 'The Lord gives you three choices,' the messenger said. 'You must choose one:
- For seven years there will be no food.
- Your enemies will pursue you for three months and you will constantly be on the run.
- For three days the people will become very ill.'

David wondered which choice he should make. Finally he chose the three days of sickness. At the end of the first day, 70,000 people were dead. When David heard this he felt terrible. He begged the Lord to punish him instead. So the Lord gave him a second chance. If he would promise to obey Him always, God would forgive him. David promised and the Lord forgave him.

💡 **Remember:** If we sin, but confess, God will forgive us.

The Lord will watch over you

Psalm 91

With the Lord you are safe. You can trust Him. (Ps 91:2)

Life can be very difficult. One day someone is fine, and the next day he falls ill. We really want him to get better immediately but he doesn't. David desperately wanted to build the Lord a temple but the Lord wouldn't allow him to.

In Psalm 91 we learn not to lose heart when things go wrong. God will tell the angels to protect us. If we are scared, we should pray to the Lord. He will hear our prayers and because He loves us, He will keep us safe. Remember, the Lord is very powerful. Nobody is stronger than He is, so we can trust in Him.

The Lord is there to help us and when we are in trouble, we can rely on Him.

Remember: We must not lose faith when things go wrong.

Without the Lord, the work is useless

Psalm 127

20

The Lord takes care of His loved ones. (Ps 127:2)

David wanted so much to build a temple for the Lord, but the Lord didn't want him to do it. The Lord wanted Solomon, David's son, to build Him the temple. Sometimes things don't work out the way we want them to, because the Lord knows better. If the Lord isn't happy with something, we should just accept it.

This is what Solomon, the man who finally built the temple in Jerusalem, says in Psalm 127:

Unless the Lord helps build the house, the work of the builders is useless. If the Lord doesn't protect us, nobody can protect us. Our lives are in the hands of the Lord. People who do things with the help of the Lord, rather than trying to do it on their own, do it so much better.

We should always try our best. It doesn't matter if we lose, however hard we tried to win. It is much more important to use the talents the Lord has given us as best we can.

Remember: We should ask the Lord to do things with us.

David is disobedient

2 Samuel 11

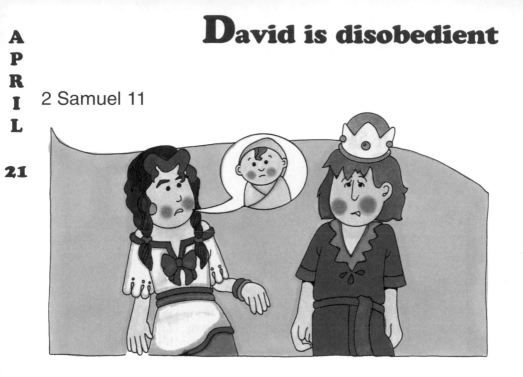

What David had done did not please the Lord. (2 Sam 11:27)

There was a war going on and David's soldiers had to go and fight. David stayed at home. One afternoon he saw a beautiful woman. She was Bathsheba, the wife of one of David's soldiers. David liked her and asked her to come and visit him. He knew it was wrong and meant disobeying the Lord.

A while later, the woman told David she was going to have his baby. David knew he could no longer hide the foolish thing he had done. He tried to think of a way to solve the problem. Eventually he sent Uriah, Bathsheba's husband, to fight on the front line. David hoped Uriah would be killed by the enemy and that's what happened. David was pleased because he could marry Bathsheba before the baby was born and he thought nobody would notice that he had been disobedient.

But God knew. We can hide nothing from Him. He knows every single thing that happens in our lives.

🔆 **Remember:** God knows everything.

David is punished

Why didn't you obey the Lord? (2 Sam 12:9)

One day Nathan, a prophet of God, visited David. He told David this story: There was a poor man whose only friend was a little lamb. He played with it and fed it with food from his own plate. At night they slept on the same bed. He loved this little lamb very much.

Nearby lived a rich man who owned many sheep. One day the rich man had a visitor. The rich man wondered what to serve for dinner that night. Then he saw the poor man's little lamb. 'Kill that lamb,' he told his servants. So they slaughtered the poor man's lamb.

When David heard this story he was furious with the rich man. 'Any man who does such a thing deserves to die,' he cried. 'Fetch me that man immediately!' Nathan answered, 'You are the man. You had another man killed and took his wife.' Then David knew the Lord had seen how disobedient he had been. He was so ashamed and he felt terrible. He asked the Lord to forgive him.

We can hide nothing from the Lord.

 Remember: We cannot hide anything from the Lord.

David is sad because he disappointed the Lord

Psalm 38

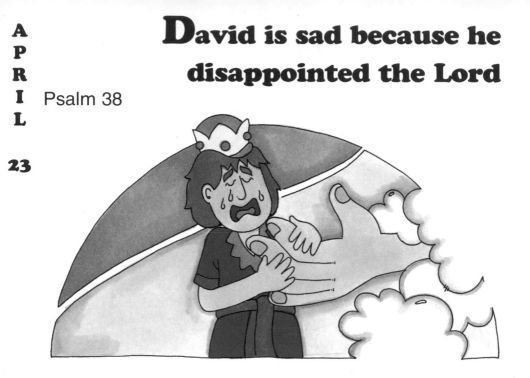

Please do not leave me, Lord. Do not go away. (Ps 38:21)

David was heartbroken because he had disappointed God. He had had a man killed so that he could have his wife. During this time he wrote Psalm 38. This is his prayer:

Lord, please don't leave me alone. Please stay with me. Don't let go of my hand. I know I have done a terrible thing, Lord. Help me, please Lord.

I feel like someone who has been shot with an arrow. I hurt so much it feels as if my whole body is covered with big sores. Lord, only You can make it better. Please forgive me. I want to, and will, obey You always. I want to do what You want me to.

God didn't abandon David and, if we make a mistake, He won't leave us either. We mustn't be ashamed to tell Him we're sorry. He knows all about it anyway. We just need to go to Him and ask Him to forgive us and He will!

💡 **Remember:** We need not be ashamed to ask the Lord's forgiveness.

Absalom turns against his father

2 Samuel 15

None of us will escape from Absalom. (2 Sam 15:14)

The Lord gives us mothers and fathers to take care of us. He wants us to respect them. King David had a son who did nothing of the kind, and it made David very sad.

Absalom, David's eldest son, was handsome and well built, but his heart was rotten. He didn't care if he hurt others or cheated them – and that included his own father. His father was the king so he had to punish wrongdoers. Absalom would go to the people and tell them that his father was no good. He said that if he became king he wouldn't punish them. Absalom stirred up the people against David even though David was his father.

One day Absalom told David he was going to Hebron to worship the Lord. In fact he was plotting rebellion against the king. David was taken by surprise. He had to flee from Absalom and his soldiers. Absalom took his father's place in the palace. His father had to go into hiding. But this was not the end of the story.

💡 **Remember:** We should love and respect our parents.

Absalom dies

2 Samuel 17-18

'O Absalom, my son, my son! If only I could have died instead of you!' (2 Sam 18:33)

David's soldiers were angry when Absalom took his father's place in the palace. They went to David and told him they would help him. David's troops didn't want him to be killed so they went into battle without him. David asked them not to harm his son, Absalom.

It was a bloody battle. David's soldiers fought hard and won. Absalom tried to escape on a mule but, as he rode under a tree, his long hair got caught in the thick branches. The mule ran on leaving Absalom dangling in the tree. That's where David's soldiers found him and killed him.

David went back to live in the palace again and he ruled the way God wanted. He was sad about the death of his son. Even though Absalom had treated him so badly, he still loved him.

🔅 **Remember:** Mums and dads love their children.

Our lives are in the Lord's hands

Psalm 31

I trust you, Lord. (Ps 31:14)

Things don't always work out the way we want them to. Even if we are Christians, bad things can still happen to us. The difference is, the Lord can help us when these things happen. Someone who doesn't love the Lord has no-one like Him to help him.

David writes in Psalm 31 that things went so terribly wrong for him at times that he thought he was going to die. He often said to himself, 'I've had it!' He even thought the Lord had forgotten about him. People were nasty and made fun of him. Even his own friends wanted nothing to do with him. David felt very lonely but he never lost hope because he knew how much the Lord loved him.

David trusted the Lord. He felt safe, because he could rely on the Lord helping him. The Lord looks after His children, so if we are children of the Lord we have nothing to worry about. The Lord will help us.

☆ **Remember:** The Lord keeps His children close to Him.

Solomon becomes a good king

1 Kings 3

'Lord, help me so that I can tell the difference between right and wrong.' (1 Kgs 3:9)

After David's death, his son Solomon became king. Solomon loved the Lord very much, just like his father did.

One day the Lord said to Solomon in a dream, 'What do you want, Solomon? Ask, and I will give it to you.'

'Lord,' said Solomon, 'I am still very young. I don't always know the right thing to do but I must rule over Your people. Help me so that I will always listen to You. Let me make the right choices. If You don't help me, I can't be a good king.'

The Lord was very pleased with Solomon's answer. Solomon could have asked for anything – to be rich or successful or to live for a long time. But he didn't think of himself. He asked God to give him wisdom so he would rule the people with justice and fairness. The Lord made Solomon wiser than anybody before or after him and he was a very good king.

It's always worth listening to the Lord and serving Him. Solomon knew that.

Remember: It is a pleasure to serve the Lord.

Solomon builds a temple

1 Kings 6 & 8

*'The Lord is wonderful. He has kept the promise He made to my father, David.'
(1 Kgs 8:15)*

Solomon was a good king who listened to the Lord and did what He said. Solomon wanted to build a temple for the Lord. God said to him, 'I want you to build Me a temple. Then I will be able to stay with you and My people in a special way. But it's not just the temple that's important. I also want My people to serve Me with all their heart.'

Solomon built a temple. It was beautiful inside. He brought the Ark to the temple and it was a sign that God was there.

The people were very happy and they celebrated because the Lord was there with them. The Ten Commandments that God gave Moses on Mount Sinai were in the Ark. From then on God was in the temple among His people, in a very special way.

But God is not only in a building. He also lives inside us. Whatever we are doing, He is with us.

☀ **Remember:** God is always with us.

Solomon is clever

1 Kings 3-4

God Himself gave Solomon wisdom. (1 Kgs 3:28)

The Lord made Solomon very wise.

One day two women came to Solomon. They lived in the same house. Their babies were born at about the same time. One baby died when its mother rolled over on it by accident one night. She got up and quietly swopped the two babies. She put the dead one down next to the other woman. The next morning when the woman woke up, she immediately saw that the dead baby was not hers. The two women started arguing. Both said the other one was lying. Solomon had to help them solve the problem.

Solomon listened carefully. Then he said, 'Bring the live baby here and bring a sword. Cut the child in two and give each woman half!'

The real mother was heartbroken. She couldn't bear her baby to be killed. She cried out, 'Oh no, give her the child. Please don't kill him.' Then Solomon knew she was the real mother. He said, 'You are the mother.' The news spread and the people who heard about it knew that God had made Solomon very wise.

🔆 **Remember:** God created us.

The Lord takes good care of His people

1 Kings 10

'It is because the Lord loves his people that He gave them such a good king.'

Solomon was a very wise man. People all over the world heard how clever he was. In a far-away land lived a beautiful queen, the Queen of Sheba. She too heard about Solomon. People said he was rich and that the Lord took care of him. She decided to go and visit King Solomon. She wanted to see for herself if he really was so clever and rich, so she packed many gifts of gold and diamonds and set off to visit Solomon.

She asked Solomon the most difficult questions she could think of. She listened open-mouthed as he answered every one. She realized why Solomon was so wise. The Lord loved him and was good to him. The Lord loved His people too and He wanted their king, Solomon, to be a good ruler. When the queen went back home she knew that the Lord takes good care of His people.

 Remember: God looks after His children.

Good advice for children

Proverbs 2-3

Discuss everything you do with the Lord. Then He will show you the right way. (Prov 3:6)

Solomon loved children. He wanted them to grow up the right way so he gave them some very good advice. He said:
• Always listen to good advice. Good advice is advice that tells us what the Lord wants us to do.
• We must be honest and must never lie or cheat.
• We mustn't even think about doing wrong.
• We must love others.
• People must be able to trust us. When they talk about us they must say, 'They never lie. So you can always believe them.'
• Pray often. We should ask the Lord every day to help us do the right thing.
• We must go to church and show we love the Lord.
• If we do something wrong, we must know the Lord can discipline us, like a father disciplines his child. This doesn't mean He doesn't love us. He does love us but He wants to teach us the difference between right and wrong.

💡 **Remember:** Do what pleases God.

More good advice for children

The person who understands what the Lord expects from him or her will be happy. (Prov 3:13)

If we live the way the Lord wants, we will enjoy life. Remember, the Lord made us. He knows what will make us happy and what will not:

• We must be kind and help people when we can.
• We mustn't hurt someone's feelings by being rude or by shouting at them.
• We mustn't worry too much or get scared. Remember, the Lord loves us. He will protect us.
• We mustn't gossip or say or think nasty things about people. Wicked people do this and they will get their punishment.
• If we are stronger than our friends we mustn't hurt or bully them. The Lord doesn't like that at all.
• We mustn't think we're better than others or ever make fun of anybody.
• We mustn't be so rude that we make others feel uncomfortable.

Remember: Be kind to other people.

Don't be lazy

Proverbs 6

Take a lesson from the ants, you lazybones. See how they work and learn from them! (Prov 6:6)

Solomon knew what the Lord expects from people. The Lord sees every step we take. If we do something wrong, the Lord sees it and will punish us. His advice was:

Don't be lazy. Watch the ants and see how hard they work. They don't have teachers or leaders. They have no-one to tell them what to do, but when winter comes and it's difficult to find food, they have stored up more than enough. They worked all summer to do this. Let this be a lesson to us. It's good to do our duty and to work hard. Lazy people get nothing done. They say, 'I want to sleep a little later. I just want to rest a little longer.' They lie around all day, doing nothing. Such a person mustn't think he or she is going to get something for nothing. They are going to struggle their whole life long.

The Lord likes hard-working children. He gives us many gifts – strength and good health and talents. He doesn't want us to waste these. That is why He is pleased when we use our strength and our talents.

:bulb: **Remember:** The Lord likes diligent children.

Don't cheat others

Proverbs 6

My child, listen to what your father and mother tell you. Keep it in your heart. (Prov 6:20-21)

Solomon had more good advice. Someone who lies to others is no good, he said. They make trouble wherever they go. The Lord doesn't like people who are forever lying and fighting.

A child must listen when his or her father and mother speak. They will try to give their children the best advice. We know they don't want their children to hurt others or do wrong things. Imagine someone's in a pitch-dark room. He can see nothing and doesn't know what to do. The good advice of a mum and dad is like a light shining into that dark room. Suddenly, he knows what to do and what not to do. If we listen to the good advice of our parents we will be happy.

The Lord gave our parents the responsibility to teach us what is right and what is wrong. We must listen to them. Read the Bible with them every day and pray with them.

🔆 **Remember:** We must obey our parents.

More good advice

Proverbs 7-10

A cheerful heart is good medicine. (Prov 17:22)

Solomon goes on to say in Proverbs:
• Having a good friend is better than being rich and having no friends.
• We must stay away from anyone who is out to hurt us. If we come too close to such a person, he or she will burn us like fire.
• A wise person thinks first and then speaks. It is stupid to speak without thinking.
• Someone with a friendly smile makes everyone around them happy.
• We can plan what we want to do, but it is God who decides if it will really happen.
• Don't tell stories about others, even if everybody likes listening.
• A child of the Lord doesn't get angry without good reason.
• It is better to be honest and to stay poor than to cheat people and get rich.
• We mustn't fight back when someone fights with us. Then he'll stop, because it's no fun anymore.

🔅 **Remember:** Be friendly and make others happy.

Enjoy life while you are young

Ecclesiastes 11-12

It's wonderful to be young. Enjoy every minute of it. Do everything you want to do, but remember: you will have to explain everything you do to the Lord. (Ecc 11:9)

Solomon had special advice for young people.

He said they should be happy to be alive, remembering that they won't live forever. Just as the night draws near so death comes closer. It should not frighten them. Instead, they should enjoy life every day.

Solomon goes on to say that young people must enjoy life while they can because, before they know it, they'll be old. Their chance to be young will be over. They should do everything they enjoy doing, but should also take care that it's not something that will displease the Lord. They shouldn't do anything which makes them feel bad or which is going to hurt them or others. Young people should do what is right and remember to keep on loving the Lord. Then if things go wrong, they will have Someone to help them.

Remember: Enjoy life.

Live every day
to the full

Ecclesiastes 5 & 9

It is good for people to enjoy the life the Lord has given them. (Ecc 5:18)

Solomon said that even if things go wrong, we must still enjoy life.

Often things happen to us that we don't like. We get upset and unhappy. But remember that it will pass.

If things are not going the way we would like them to, we should try thinking about all the good things the Lord gives us. We have food, clothes, a place to sleep. We can get up tomorrow morning and live for the Lord. These are all presents the Lord gives us and they should make us very happy. Solomon asks who can eat or be happy if the Lord doesn't make it all happen.

Where do all the good things we have come from? The Lord gives us everything. Surely He wants us to enjoy what He gives us.

Remember: The Lord wants us to enjoy what He has given us.

A time for everything

Ecclesiastes 2-3

Be happy and enjoy everything the Lord gives you. (Ecc 3:13)

Life is not always the same. It changes. Sometimes we are sad. Sometimes we are glad. Sometimes a person plants a tree and sometimes he chops it down. Sometimes we like someone and sometimes not. There is a time for everything.

The Lord wants us to enjoy life – when things go well and also the times when they don't. He wants to be proud of us. We mustn't be slapdash when we do something, because we are special to the Lord. He has put us in a very special place in life.

We don't always understand why some things happen, but we must believe that the Lord knows best. We mustn't give up hope. Even when we're having a hard time, we should thank the Lord for all the good things He gives us.

If things happen in our lives that make us unhappy, we shouldn't sit around and mope but think about all our blessings.

Remember: Each one of us is unique in the eyes of the Lord.

Don't listen to the advice of wicked friends

1 Kings 12

The people asked the king to treat them well. (1 Kgs 12:4)

After King Solomon's death his son Rehoboam became king. He was still young and didn't know how to rule the people. Should he be strict or should he be friendly? If he was strict with them, they might get angry with him. If he was friendly with them, they might not do what he told them. He decided to ask the older people what to do. They told him to be friendly. Rehoboam still wasn't sure that this was good advice so he asked his friends who were the same age as he was. They said he should be strict. If people didn't listen to him he should punish them. Rehoboam took the bad advice of his friends and the people became angry with him. They rebelled.

We must be careful whose advice we take, even if it is our friends' advice. We should think carefully whether it's good or bad advice and only take it if it's good advice.

💡 **Remember:** Don't listen to the wrong advice.

The king starts worshipping idols

1 Kings 12-13

Please ask the Lord to help me. (1 Kgs 13:6)

King Jeroboam reigned in the country, not in a city. He was worried that people would prefer the city of Jerusalem because there was a beautiful temple there, so he built his own temple. But he didn't build it to serve the Lord. He put two gold calves in the temple. Jeroboam told the people to worship these calf idols and even appointed priests for these gods.

One day Jeroboam was worshipping the gods. He brought a sacrifice to offer on the altar. A man of God, a prophet, came to him and said, 'All these evil priests are going to be killed. I will give you a sign to show you that I am telling the truth. This altar will split apart.' King Jeroboam pointed his finger at the prophet and told the guards, 'Grab that man!' As soon as he spoke, the king's hand became paralysed in that position.

Jeroboam begged the prophet to make his hand work again so the man prayed to God. The king regained the use of his hand. He learnt his lesson – never to worship idols but to serve the true God only.

🔆 **Remember:** We must serve only the Lord, nobody else.

We must obey the Lord

1 Kings 13

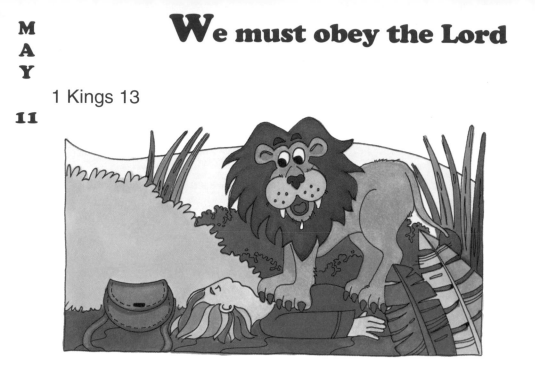

You have disobeyed the Lord! (1 Kgs 13:21-22)

If the Lord asks us to do something we must do what He says. There once was a prophet who took the king an important message. The king wanted to treat him to a nice meal but the prophet answered that the Lord had told him not to eat anything before he was back home.

On his way home he met someone. This man lied and said an angel had come to him and told him to give the prophet food to eat and water to drink. The two of them went to the man's house. While they were eating, God sent the prophet a message: 'You did not do what the Lord told you. So you won't be buried in your home town.' As the prophet made his way home after the meal, a lion attacked him and killed him. The man who had lied to him heard the news. He fetched the prophet's body and buried it. 'This is what happens if you don't do as you're told,' he said.

If our best friend says something that we know is not what the Lord wants, we mustn't listen to our friend.

🔆 **Remember:** God's children do what God wants them to do.

Elijah and the ravens

1 Kings 17   **12**

The Lord sent ravens to bring Elijah food. (1 Kgs 17:4)

King Ahab ruled over God's people. He was married to Jezebel. She was not one of God's people. She didn't like the Lord and she worshipped another god. His name was Baal. She wanted Israel to worship Baal too instead of God and she built many temples for this false god.

God was angry. He wanted to show the people He was the strongest and that Baal was useless. He did something that only God can do. He sent His prophet, Elijah, to Ahab. Elijah told the king, 'From now on there will not be a drop of rain. The Lord will decide when the rain will fall again.' From that day on, it stopped raining.

The king was angry with Elijah for bringing such bad news. Elijah had to go into hiding. He camped beside a brook in the fields. Nobody knew where he was but the Lord looked after him. He sent the ravens to take Elijah food to eat every day.

·ᛩ· **Remember:** Worship only God. He takes care of us.

A widow takes care of Elijah

1 Kings 17

'The Lord says there will always be plenty of flour in the jar.' (1 Kgs 17:14)

For a long time there was not a drop of rain. The plants died. The rivers dried up.

Elijah was very hungry and thirsty. Near where he was hiding lived a woman. Her husband had died and she was very poor. Elijah went to her and asked for some water. She didn't mind helping Elijah. He also asked her for a bite of bread. The woman wanted to give Elijah some bread, but she had only a handful of flour and a little cooking oil left. When that was gone there would be nothing left for her and her son to eat. But then a wonderful thing happened. Elijah told the woman to make the three of them some food. Even though there was not nearly enough flour, God would help her. The woman did what Elijah said. She trusted the Lord and started baking bread and to her surprise, no matter how much oil and flour she used, there was always enough left in the jars. It was a miracle. Only God can do something like this!

Even if we sometimes have a hard time, we mustn't lose heart. God knows best and He will help us.

💡 **Remember:** The Lord can do wonderful things.

The Lord can help us

1 Kings 17

'Now I know for sure you are a man of God. What you say is true. The Lord speaks through you!' (1 Kgs 17:24)

Elijah stayed with the widow and her little boy. It was better than staying in the field by the brook. The widow helped him and cooked for him. One day her son fell ill. He grew worse and worse and finally he died. The widow was very sad. She asked Elijah if God was angry with her. What had she done wrong? Why did her little boy die?

Elijah comforted her and told her she could trust the Lord. He said she should bring the boy to his room. He put the boy down on his bed and then knelt down and prayed. 'Lord, please don't let a terrible thing like this happen to this woman. She helped me. Please let this child come back to life.'

After Elijah had prayed, the Lord brought the child back to life. Elijah took him to his mother. She was so happy and she knew it was God Who had helped her.

When we feel down or sad we should pray and ask the Lord to help us – and He will, in His own way.

 Remember: We should pray when we are feeling down or sad.

Elijah proves there is only one true God

1 Kings 18

'O Lord, answer me so these people will know that You are God.' (1 Kgs 18:37)

Many people thought Baal, an idol, was stronger than the Lord. Queen Jezebel told them it was so. But Elijah knew that only the Lord was really God. One day the Lord told Elijah to show the people how powerful He is.

Elijah challenged all the priests of Baal: 'Let Baal come and light a fire for all of us to see.' The priests of Baal brought wood for the fire and put it on the altar. They prayed and prayed all day long, but nothing happened. They kept on praying even when they were exhausted, but still nothing happened. Elijah mocked them: 'Shout louder,' he said 'maybe your god is asleep!' Then Elijah took twelve stones and made an altar. He piled wood on the altar and put the offering on top. 'Now bring water and pour it on the wood,' Elijah said. This was to make sure Elijah couldn't trick them, and in some way light the fire. Then he asked the Lord to light the fire. Immediately, before their very eyes, the Lord flashed down fire from heaven. Then the people knew: God is the only God and He is much more powerful than Baal. Then and there they killed the priests of Baal.

Our Lord is real and He is very powerful.

‑ઌ̣- **Remember:** The Lord really exists!

God sends rain

1 Kings 18

The Lord gave special strength to Elijah. (1 Kgs 18:46)

The Lord was very angry when the people started believing in the god Baal and He told them He was the only true God. But there were people who didn't believe Him. So God showed again how powerful He is. He said it would not rain again until He gave the word. The drought was terrible and Elijah decided to ask the Lord if it could please rain again.

Elijah climbed to the top of a high mountain. There he prayed. At first nothing happened. But Elijah didn't stop praying.

When Elijah was praying for the seventh time, his friend told him he could see a little cloud on the horizon. It was only the size of a man's hand. Elijah knew immediately that the Lord had answered his prayer. He ran to tell the king but before he reached the palace, it started raining heavily.

We can really trust the Lord. If we pray and He doesn't answer us the first time, ask again. He will answer us, in His own time.

 Remember: Pray often. It's the only way to speak to God.

The queen wants to kill Elijah

1 Kings 19

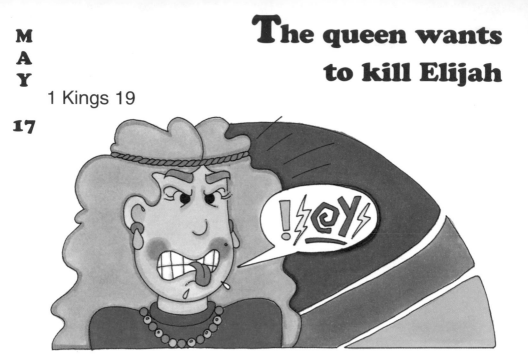

'Lord, I have served you heart and soul.' (1 Kgs 19:14)

Jezebel was a wicked queen. She wanted the Israelites to worship her gods. Elijah had proved that Baal was useless, which made Jezebel very angry. She decided to kill Elijah and he had to hide away in the desert. He was frightened and miserable. It seemed to him Jezebel had killed everyone who loved God and that he was the only one left. He worked so hard for God and yet he had to hide. He couldn't understand why. Suddenly an angel stood before him. The angel gave him food and water and told him to eat so that he could regain his strength. The Lord still had a lot of work for him to do.

Elijah walked to Mount Horeb and there he waited for the Lord. First a mighty windstorm hit the mountain and afterwards there was a terrible earthquake. After the earthquake there was a fire. But the Lord was not in any one of these. Then the Lord came past, very quietly. God comforted Elijah and reminded him that He always protects His children. We need to remember that too. The Lord will protect us so we have no need to worry.

Remember: The Lord will always be with us.

God gives His people another messenger

'Where is the Lord, the God of Elijah?' (2 Kgs 2:14)

Elijah served the Lord faithfully, but he was coming to the end of his life. He had a very good friend called Elisha. The two of them went to the River Jordan. Elijah took his cloak and struck the water with it. Suddenly the river opened up and there was a footpath that led to the other side. When they reached the other side Elijah asked Elisha, 'What can I do for you before I die?' Elisha answered, 'I want to be just like you.' Suddenly they saw a chariot of fire drawn by horses of fire. It stopped between Elisha and Elijah. Then Elijah was carried into heaven by a whirlwind.

When Elijah disappeared, his cloak was left behind. Elisha picked it up and struck the water with it. Then he asked God to help him. Suddenly a footpath opened up across the river and everybody realized that Elisha was like Elijah – a man of God. The people of Jericho asked him to help them. The water in their town was so foul that they couldn't drink it. He asked for a bowl of salt and put the salt in the water. Immediately the water became pure and drinkable.

Remember: The Lord gives us leaders to help us.

The Lord helps in wonderful ways

'You know my husband served the Lord.' (2 Kgs 4:1)

One day a woman who was very poor came to Elisha the prophet. Her husband, who had served the Lord faithfully, had died. She had no-one to provide for her anymore and she had no money to buy food. She'd borrowed money from other people but couldn't pay them back. They wanted their money and threatened her with jail.

The woman begged Elisha to help her. Elisha asked her what she had. 'Nothing at all, except a little bit of cooking oil,' she said. Elisha told her to borrow as many empty bottles as she could from her friends and to fill them with cooking oil from her bottle. She did as he said.

Amazingly, she poured and poured but the oil didn't run out until all the bottles were full. The woman was able to sell the oil and pay her debts. She even had enough money left over to live on.

The Lord takes care of people who need Him in amazing ways.

Remember: God helps those who need Him.

An axe floats on the water

And the axe floated on the water. (2 Kgs 6:6)

Elisha did many wonderful things because the Lord helped him. One day he went with some men who wanted to build a place to live. As one of the men was chopping down a tree his axe fell into the river. The man was worried. The axe didn't belong to him. He had borrowed it. He didn't know what to do. Elisha asked, 'Where did it fall in?' The man showed him and Elisha cut a stick and threw it into the water where the axe had fallen. The axe floated up to the surface of the water. The man stretched out his hand and grabbed it. Sometimes the Lord makes things happen that we do not expect.

Another day Elisha was on his way to worship. Some boys made fun of him because he was bald. 'Go away, you baldy!' they teased him. Elisha turned around. He warned them to stop. He was God's servant. In making fun of him, they were mocking God. The boys wouldn't listen. The next moment two bears came out of the woods and attacked the boys. Forty-two of them died.

We must show respect for the Lord. If we do we will make Him happy.

 Remember: We must always show respect for the Lord.

Will the Lord help?

2 Kings 6

If the Lord doesn't help you, what can I do? (2 Kgs 6:27)

The king of Aram and his whole army went to Samaria. The king wanted to take the city and ordered his soldiers to surround it. Nobody could enter or leave the city. The people couldn't fetch food or water. Eventually they ate all the available food. They started getting very hungry, but there was nothing to eat. Even a donkey's head cost a lot of money. They were so hungry they ate dove droppings, and paid a lot of money for it!

A woman asked the king to help her. She told him how hungry they were. She and her friend had decided to eat their children – one day her son and the next day her friend's son. First they ate her son but when it was the other woman's turn she hid her son.

When the king heard this he was very shocked. He said to the woman, 'I can't help you, only the Lord can. Only He can save us from the terrible situation we are in.'

Then he went to Elisha, the prophet. He said, 'I don't think the Lord can help us anymore.'

🔅 **Remember:** We know the Lord can help us.

Nothing is impossible for the Lord

2 Kings 7

This is what the Lord says, 'By this time tomorrow you will have more than enough food.' (2 Kgs 7:1)

The Lord helps His people and Elisha was able to tell the king, 'The Lord has good news for you. Food is very scarce now. But by this time tomorrow you will be able to buy a big bag of flour for next to nothing.'

'Impossible!' many people said.

Then four men in the city decided to join the enemy. If they stayed in the city they would die of hunger and if they left and the enemy killed them, so what? But there was a chance that they might not be killed and be given something to eat. But when they reached the enemy camp there was no-one there! The Lord had sent a noise that sounded like a great army approaching and when the enemy soldiers heard it, they panicked and ran off, leaving all their food and money behind. The four men went back to the city and told the guards. The gates were flung open and the people ran out of the city and helped themselves to food.

Elisha's words came true. Nothing is impossible for the Lord.

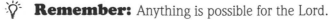

💡 **Remember:** Anything is possible for the Lord.

Our Lord is everywhere and always there for us

1 Kings 20

'Then you will know that I am the Lord.' (1 Kgs 20:28)

The people who didn't like the Lord wanted to take Israel's country. They thought the Israelites worshipped mountain gods so they would be able to defeat them easily if they fought them on the plains, since their gods wouldn't be there. They assembled a great army to fight against Israel. The Israelite army looked like a little flock of goats in comparison, but the Israelites were not afraid.

The battle started. Even though there were very few Israelites, they had the Lord to help them. A hundred thousand of the enemy died. The rest ran away to hide behind the walls of a nearby city. But the city wall fell in on them, killing twenty-seven thousand men.

The enemies of Israel learnt their lesson that day. They discovered that the God of the Israelites was everywhere and always ready to help His people.

Remember: The Lord is always with us.

Don't be disobedient

1 Kings 20

'Well, it's your own fault. You have decided on your own punishment.' (1 Kgs 20:40)

The king of Aram who thought the Lord lived on mountains only, soon found out how wrong he was. So he told Ahab, the king of the Israelites, how sorry he was about everything. He wanted to be King Ahab's friend and Ahab was flattered. He believed what the king of Aram said. But the Lord was not happy. He told one of His prophets, 'Get someone to beat you black and blue.' The prophet obeyed and afterwards bandaged up his face. He stood by the roadside and King Ahab didn't even recognize him when he passed by.

Then the prophet said, 'Sir, I had to guard a prisoner. I was told, "If he gets away you will either die or pay a fine." While I was busy doing something else the prisoner escaped.'

'Well,' King Ahab said, 'you have brought your punishment on yourself.'

Then the prophet took the bandage off. 'Sir, you have just brought punishment on yourself. The Lord told you to kill that king. Now you will have to die in his place.'

We must do what the Lord tells us to do.

💡 **Remember:** We must obey the Lord.

The Lord shows His power

2 Kings 5

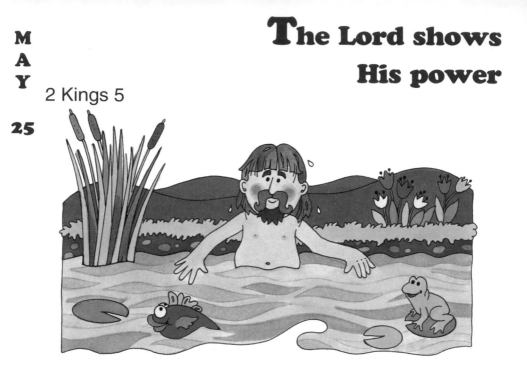

'I know at last there is no God in all the world except the God of Israel.' (2 Kgs 5:15)

A certain man called Naaman became very ill. Nobody could make him well again. Naaman didn't know God. There was a young girl though, who knew God, and she knew He could help people. She worked for Naaman's wife and she told Naaman to go and see a prophet who would help him. Naaman went first to the king of Israel and asked for his help. The king was sad. He couldn't heal people.

When Elisha the prophet heard about it he suggested that Naaman came to see him. Naaman stopped at Elisha's house. Elisha didn't even come to the door. He sent Naaman a message: 'Go and wash yourself seven times in the River Jordan.'

Naaman was furious. He thought Elisha would do something special, or at least see him. He decided to go home. But his friends said he might as well follow Elisha's advice. After all, it wasn't difficult. Naaman did what Elisha had told him and the Lord healed him. He went back to Elisha and said, 'Now I know there is no God in all the world except the God of Israel.'

💡 **Remember:** Our God is the only true God.

Honesty is the best policy

2 Kings 5

'I work for the Lord. I won't take gifts for it.' (2 Kgs 5:16)

Namaan wanted to give Elisha lots of presents and money but Elisha wouldn't take anything. The Lord healed Naaman, Elisha said, he didn't do it.

Naaman said he wasn't going to worship idols anymore. He now knew who the real God was. He wanted to serve only Him. Then he set off for home.

Elisha's servant, Gehazi, overheard their conversation. He thought this was his chance to get his hands on some money, so he ran after Naaman and told him Elisha had sent him because he had changed his mind. He wanted a lot of money and clothes to give to two of his friends.

Naaman gave Gehazi much more than he asked for. Gehazi hid it away in his room. But you can't cheat the Lord. When Gehazi went to Elisha, he asked, 'Where have you been, Gehazi?'

'I haven't been anywhere,' he answered. But Elisha knew the truth and because Gehazi had lied he fell ill with the same disease that Naaman had suffered from. It doesn't pay to lie.

☀ **Remember:** Dishonesty does not pay.

Disobedience is punished

1 Kings 21

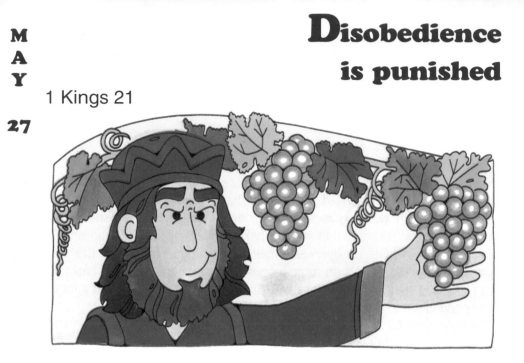

'Ahab, you did not do what the Lord said. You are going to be punished.' (1 Kgs 21:22)

A man called Naboth had a lovely vineyard. King Ahab wanted this vineyard with its delicious grapes but Naboth refused to sell it.

Ahab was upset. When he told his wife Jezebel about it she said, 'You are the king. You can do what you like.'

Jezebel was an evil queen. She came up with a wicked plan. She arranged a special festival and invited many people. She gave Naboth a seat right at the front and put two crooks next to him. The festival had barely started when these two bad men leapt to their feet. 'Naboth has cursed God and the king,' they shouted. Naboth was taken outside the city walls and stoned to death. Then Ahab took his vineyard.

But the Lord saw it all. He sent Elijah, the prophet, to Ahab to tell him that dogs would would lick his blood from the street just as they had licked up Naboth's blood and that they'd eat the body of Jezebel at the city wall. Elijah's words came true. It's useless to plan evil deeds and think God won't know. He knows everything.

🔆 **Remember:** The Lord sees everything.

Hezekiah was a good king

'O, Lord, I have always tried to be faithful to you and to please you.' (2 Kgs 20:3)

Hezekiah was a good king. He did what the Lord wanted. One day he became very ill. One of God's prophets visited him and told him that he was going to die. Hezekiah was very sad. He wanted to live a little while longer. He prayed earnestly to the Lord Whom he had obeyed all his life.

The prophet was still making his way out of the palace when God sent him back. He had to tell Hezekiah that the Lord had heard his prayer. He would get well and would live for another fifteen years. Then the prophet told Hezekiah's servants to make an ointment from figs and put it on Hezekiah's sore. They did as he instructed and Hezekiah started feeling better straight away! Just to make sure that the prophet wasn't lying to him Hezekiah asked God to give him a sign to prove that he was healed. The Lord said he would make the sun move backwards. It happened and Hezekiah knew that the Lord had answered his prayer.

 Remember: The Lord hears our prayers.

Never forget about the Lord

2 Kings 20

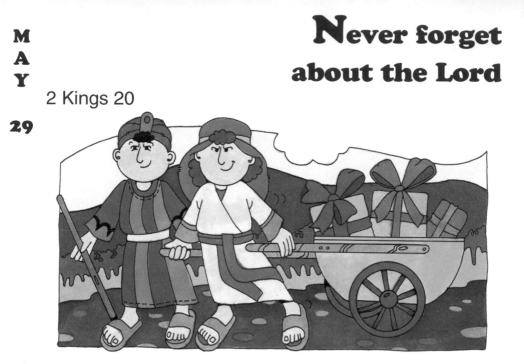

'This message you have given me from the Lord is good.' (2 Kgs 20:19)

The news that the Lord had healed Hezekiah spread quickly and as far afield as Babylon.

The Babylonians were planning to take Hezekiah's country from him. They sent people to find out how strong Hezekiah's God was. They had heard about Him, but wanted to see for themselves.

The spies from Babylon brought many gifts. They made Hezekiah feel so important that he forgot all about the Lord. He showed them everything he owned, even his money and weapons. The spies knew exactly how strong Hezekiah was, but Hezekiah didn't tell them how strong the Lord really was because he had forgotten about Him.

The spies went back to their king and told him he could defeat Hezekiah. Hezekiah was not so very strong and they hadn't seen anything of his God. Then God's prophet went to Hezekiah. He'd heard what had happened and that the Babylonians were going to attack. But the Lord waited until Hezekiah had died before Israel was taken so his final years were years of peace.

⚙️ **Remember:** Never forget the Lord.

If we don't serve the Lord it hurts Him

'Come back to the Lord.' (Hos 14:2)

The Lord's people, Israel, did not serve Him anymore. They ran after all kinds of gods. The Lord warned them about their behaviour. He wanted them to see that what they were doing was wrong.

He sent his prophet, Hosea, to get married to a very bad woman. Hosea was kind to her but she treated him cruelly. Although she was married to Hosea she had other boyfriends. Hosea was very upset and the people saw how sad he was. They knew he treated his wife well even though she treated him like dirt.

Hosea started preaching to the people. He told them they made the Lord just as sad as he was.

The Lord treated them well, but they disobeyed Him and ran after heathen gods. They were just like his wife.

They must come back to the Lord, Hosea said. They must stop sinning and promise to serve the Lord again. Then the Lord would take care of them.

-�czᷢ- **Remember:** We should not sin but serve the Lord.

Like clay in the potter's hands

Jeremiah 18

As the clay is in the potter's hand, so are you in My hand. (Jer 18:6)

God sent Jeremiah, His prophet, to a man who made clay pots and jars. There he found the potter working at his wheel. The jar he was making didn't turn out as he had hoped so the potter squashed the jar into a lump of clay again.

Patiently he started all over again and this time he made a beautiful pot, just as he had planned.

Then the Lord said to Jeremiah, 'I am like the potter and the people are like clay. I can do with them what I like. If they obey Me, I can shape them into lovely jars. If they don't do what I say I can squash them like clay.

Tell the people to obey Me. If they live as if I am not here, I will punish them. Then they will be like useless lumps of clay.'

But the people wouldn't listen to Jeremiah. They wanted to get rid of him so he wouldn't keep on at them.

What will God do to such people? They should remember that if they turn against God, He might turn against them.

 Remember: The Lord will punish those who do not serve Him.

The people refuse to listen

Jeremiah 36 & 38

The Lord said, 'I will hand over the disobedient people to the king of Babylon.' (Jer 38:3)

The people of Israel were very disobedient. Although the Lord was good to them they refused to obey Him. Straight after worshipping the Lord they would go and worship other gods. Jeremiah preached and preached. He told them the Lord did not like them worshipping other gods but they wouldn't listen.

Finally Jeremiah wrote everything down in a book. The king read the book then threw it into the fire. The people grabbed hold of Jeremiah and threw him into a water tank which had a thick layer of mud at the bottom. When the king heard about this he told them to pull Jeremiah out. He talked to Jeremiah secretly and asked him what was wrong. Jeremiah told him God didn't want His people to worship idols but the king wasn't really listening to Jeremiah. He wanted to have his own way, but the Lord would make him pay for his disobedience.

Remember: The Lord will make sinners pay.

The fall of Jerusalem

Jeremiah 39

The Babylonians burned Jerusalem and the palace and tore down the walls of the city. (Jer 39:8)

The people of Jerusalem did not do what the Lord told them. Jeremiah did his best to warn them. He preached all the time but no-one listened to him. They kept on disobeying God and worshipping idols.

The Lord allowed Nebuchadnezzar, the king of Babylon, to attack Jerusalem. Nebuchadnezzar's army was very strong. His soldiers surrounded the city and built a high wall around Jerusalem so that nobody could enter or leave. After four months the people in the city were famished. In their desperation they made a big hole in the wall around the city. The king and his soldiers tried to escape through the hole but the Babylonians caught them. Then Nebuchadnezzar's soldiers went into the city and tore everything down. Nothing was left standing, not even the beautiful temple. The houses were burnt down and all the important people taken to Babylon to work there as slaves. Their farms were given to strangers. The people had thought they could manage without the Lord. They had made a big mistake!

💡 **Remember:** We cannot manage without the Lord.

The exile begins

So the people of Judah were taken from their land. (2 Kgs 25:21)

When Zedekiah, the king of Jerusalem, tried to escape through a hole in the city's wall Nebuchadnezzar's soldiers chased after him and caught him. They took him to Nebuchadnezzar. He was very cruel. First he made Zedekiah watch as his sons were killed in front of him. They then blinded Zedekiah, put him in chains and locked him away in a Babylonian prison.

There in the foreign land of Babylon, the people began longing for the Lord again. They started feeling sorry that they had not obeyed the Lord. They wished they could worship the Lord again in their own country and in the temple, but they feared it was too late.

We should not make the same mistake. We must serve the Lord while we have the chance.

Remember: We must serve the Lord the best we can.

The Lord helps where no-one else can

Daniel 2

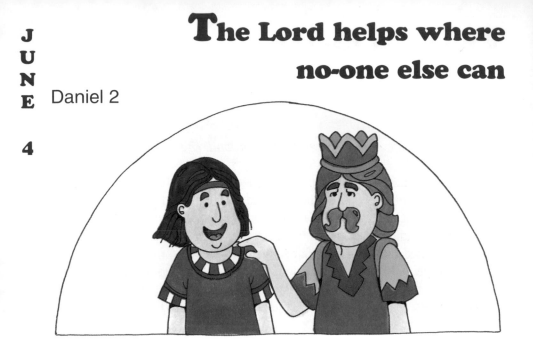

Truly your God is the most powerful of all gods. He is more important than kings. He knows everything. (Dan 2:47)

Daniel was one of the Jews who was captured and taken to Babylon. He was clever so the king let him work in the palace.

One night the king had a dream which scared him. He wanted to know its meaning so he called all his cleverest people together. In case they tried to lie to him he set them a test. They had to describe his dream. Of course no-one could. How were they supposed to know what he had dreamt?

The king was furious, but then Daniel said he would help him. Daniel prayed to God and asked Him to explain the dream to him. God answered Daniel's prayer and he went back to the king and was able to tell him exactly what his dream meant. In his dream the king had seen a huge and powerful statue of a man. The head was made of gold, but the feet were of clay. The whole statue collapsed and was smashed to bits. Daniel said it meant that Nebuchadnezzar's kingdom would break up like the statue.

King Nebuchadnezzar realized that the Lord had helped Daniel. He said, 'Your God is the God of all gods.'

Just think, this God is also our God.

🔆 **Remember:** Our God is the God of all gods.

The Lord rescues His children from a fire

Daniel 3

'Our God Whom we serve will save us.' (Dan 3:17)

The king of Babylon soon forgot how powerful the Lord is. He made a gold statue and said everybody must worship it. Anyone who didn't, would be thrown into a blazing fire. Daniel's three friends, Shadrach, Meshach and Abednego refused. They said they worshipped only the Lord. Even if they were thrown into the fire it was all right, because they trusted the Lord and He would help them. The king was very angry. He had the fire made seven times hotter and ordered his men to throw Shadrach, Meshach and Abednego into the flames. The fire was so hot that the men who threw the three friends into the furnace were burnt to death. Then an amazing thing happened. In the flames, King Nebuchadnezzar saw not three, but four men. An angel was there with the three friends.

The king called to them to come out and Daniel's three friends walked out of the fire. Not a hair on their heads was scorched nor were their clothes burnt. They didn't even smell of smoke! Nebuchadnezzar said, 'These men really trusted God. They didn't mind dying. It was more important to them to serve the Lord.'

Remember: Trust only the Lord.

Daniel thrown to the lions

Daniel 6

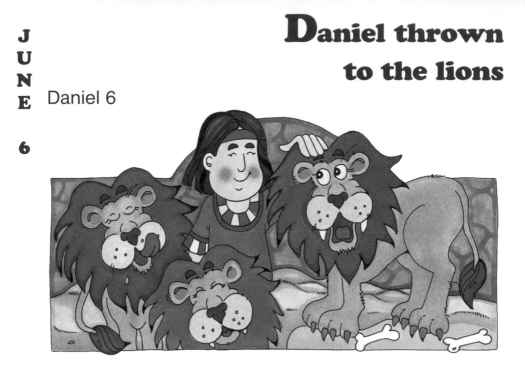

May your God Whom you worship so faithfully, rescue you. (Dan 6:16)

The king was very fond of Daniel, which made his other officials jealous. They thought of a scheme which would get Daniel into trouble. They knew how much Daniel loved God and that he would worship no-one else, so they said to the king, 'Your Majesty, you are so important and so powerful. Why not make a law that the people must pray only to you for a month?' The king thought this was a good idea so he made the law. 'Anyone who doesn't obey this law will be thrown to the lions,' he said. Daniel took no notice of the new law and continued to pray only to the Lord. That was just what his enemies were waiting for. They told the king Daniel was breaking the law. The king was very sad, but he was forced to throw Daniel to the lions. 'I hope your God can help you,' he told Daniel.

That night the king couldn't sleep. Early the next morning he hurried to the lions' den. He called out to Daniel and was overjoyed when he heard Daniel's voice: 'My God sent an angel to shut the lions' mouths.'

Daniel was taken out of the lions' den and his enemies were thrown to the lions and were killed.

·Ò· **Remember:** The Lord will deal with bad people.

Don't ever forget about the Lord

Daniel 4

'Everything the Lord does is right.' (Dan 4:37)

Nebuchadnezzar had another dream. He saw a big tree in the middle of the world. It was very tall and strong and reached up to heaven. It had fresh green leaves and was loaded with fruit – enough for all the people in the world. Wild animals rested in its shade and birds built their nests in its branches. Suddenly an angel came down from heaven and chopped the tree down. The fruit was thrown away and the leaves shaken from the branches.

Once again Nebuchadnezzar called on Daniel to explain this dream. At first Daniel was too afraid to tell him, but the king insisted. Daniel said, 'This tree is actually like you, Your Majesty. You have become very great and powerful. Everybody has seen how mighty you are. You think you can do everything, but you have forgotten about the Lord. Just remember the Lord has not forgotten about you. He will show you who is the mightiest. He will deal with you like the angel dealt with the tree.' A year later Nebuchadnezzar was no longer king. He was like the tree that had been axed.

🔆 **Remember:** We always need God.

Pride comes before a fall

Daniel 5

The king started thinking he was better than God. (Dan 5:20)

Nebuchadnezzar knew exactly how strong the Lord was, but he forgot about Him. He stopped noticing that the Lord took care of him. Nebuchadnezzar thought only of himself and, because he treated others badly, everybody was afraid of him. If he didn't like someone he would have him killed. Nebuchadnezzar thought he was more important than the Lord, but he was wrong. Before he knew it, he wasn't king any more and nobody took any notice of him. He had to go and live outside in the fields among the wild donkeys, eating grass like a cow. His hair grew wild and his nails were like the claws of an eagle.

Nebuchadnezzar learned the hard way that no human being is more important than the Lord. God is the most powerful of all. We are in His hands and we cannot carry on as if He were not there. We should thank the Lord every day for all He does for us.

💡 **Remember:** We should not carry on as if God were not there.

No-one messes with God

'Although you knew all about the Lord, you didn't want to serve Him.' (Dan 5:22)

Belshazzar became king after King Nebuchadnezzar. He also took no notice of the Lord.

One day he held a great feast. He took all the beautiful gold and silver cups from the temple. He and his guests drank from them, just to show they were not afraid of the Lord. Then suddenly they saw a finger. Like a pen, the finger wrote on the wall: 'Mene, Mene, Tekel, Parsin.' The king's face turned pale with fear. He didn't understand the words this finger wrote so he called for Daniel. Daniel told him the words meant: 'The Lord has watched everything you do. He "weighed" it. You have not listened to the Lord. You thought you could do what you wanted, and the Lord wouldn't mind. You laughed in His face and drank from the cups from His temple. Now you are going to find out, like Nebudchadnezzar before you, that there is only one God. And He is great and mighty.'

That night Belshazzar died.

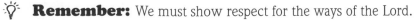

 Remember: We must show respect for the ways of the Lord.

God brings His people back to life

Ezekiel 37

Then you will know that I am the Lord. (Ezek 37:14)

The Lord promised to help His people again. He would not let them stay in a foreign country forever. The Lord explained it to Ezekiel by taking him to a large valley. The valley was filled with human bones. 'Do you think these bones can become living people again?' the Lord asked Ezekiel. 'I don't know, but You know Lord,' Ezekiel answered. Then the Lord said, 'Speak to these bones and say, "Listen dry bones, I am going to make you live again. Then you will know that I am the Lord."'

As Ezekiel spoke, there was a rattling noise across the valley. The bones of each body came together, and every one settled in its right place. Then muscles and flesh formed over the bones and skin covered the bodies. They looked like human beings again, but they were not alive. Then the Lord sent His Spirit to breathe life into the bodies. They came to life and stood up. This story tells us what the Lord will do for His people. People who don't know Him are like dry bones. When the Lord becomes our God, He makes us come alive inside, like He did with those bones. If we believe in Jesus we will live with God forever.

⋅ဴ⋅ **Remember:** A child of God lives with Him forever.

Water gives life to trees and fish

Ezekiel 47

'If you believe in Me, I will give you rivers of living water.' (John 7:38)

A desert is a lifeless place. Ezekiel says people who don't serve the Lord are like a desert. They are lifeless inside. The Lord showed Ezekiel in a dream that it won't stay that way forever. He dreamt that he was standing at God's temple in Jerusalem. All around the temple it was as dry as a desert. Suddenly water started flowing from underneath the temple. Ezekiel walked alongside this stream of water. It became deeper and deeper. Eventually it was like a deep river. It flowed into the Dead Sea, which is in the middle of a desert.

Then the most amazing thing happened. As the water flowed into the Dead Sea, it was suddenly swarming with fish. Fruit trees started growing. Their leaves never turned brown and there was always fruit on their branches. Ezekiel wondered what his dream meant. It meant that the Lord would bring His people out of exile. But it has another meaning as well. Jesus says that when the Holy Spirit enters the Lord's children, they will come alive and live for God.

☀ **Remember:** A child of God should live for Him.

God's people go back to Jerusalem

Ezra 1 & 8

Then the exiles who came back, worshipped the Lord. (Ezra 8:35)

Good news for the Jews! King Cyrus said they could go back home. They had been slaves in a foreign land long enough.

Ezra was a good man. He had to take his people back to Jerusalem and rebuild the city. They also had to build a temple for the Lord.

But what would happen when they reached Jerusalem? Strangers were living there. Surely these people wouldn't just let them take the land and build houses and a temple there? But the Lord helped them. The king gave Ezra a letter which said the people in Jerusalem must help Ezra and his men. No-one would ignore that order.

Everybody who wanted to go along had to meet at a river. There they asked the Lord to help them and He took very good care of them. They had a safe journey and now they were interested in one thing only – they wanted to obey the Lord and do His will.

🔆 **Remember:** We are very privileged to learn about God.

The temple is used for the first time

Nehemiah 1-9

'Praise the Lord!' (Neh 9:5)

13

Ezra and his helpers struggled. It was not easy to build a temple if you didn't have the know-how and thieves kept stealing your bricks and tools.

At that stage Nehemiah worked for the king of Persia. He heard how his people in Jerusalem were struggling so he asked the king if he could go and help them. He knew a lot about building. The king gave him building materials and soldiers to protect them.

As soon as Nehemiah arrived in Jerusalem he started building. The guards the king sent along protected him and his workmen. Now nobody could stop them from building their temple and a wall around the city. Once again the Lord was taking care of His people.

It was not long before, once again, the people had a place where they could worship the Lord. They held a festival to celebrate the opening of their new temple. They were back in the land the Lord had given them and they were overjoyed. Each one of us is privileged to have a church where we can worship the Lord without anybody trying to stop us.

🔆 **Remember:** We are privileged to serve in a church of our own.

Sing a song for the Lord

Psalm 134, 135 & 137

Praise the Lord, for He is good. (Ps 135:3)

'**I**t is much better to worship the Lord in a proper temple,' the Jews said. With the Lord's help they had a beautiful temple on Mount Zion where they could serve the Lord. They were very happy and sang praises to God. First they sang: 'By the rivers of Babylon, we sat and wept. We thought about our temple on Mount Zion that had been destroyed. The people who held us prisoner made fun of us. They demanded, "Sing us one of those songs of Jerusalem! Sing a joyful hymn for your temple." But they knew it had been knocked down. How can we sing hymns for the Lord in a foreign land? But we will never forget you, Jerusalem. Every time we think of you, we will be joyful.'

Now that they had their own temple again they sang: 'Praise Him, you who serve in the house of the Lord. Praise the Lord, for the Lord is good; glorify His wonderful name with music. Lift your hands in holiness, and bless the Lord. The Lord be praised, for He lives here in Jerusalem. Praise the Lord.'

💡 **Remember:** Never forget to tell others that the Lord is important.

Also help your enemies

Esther 1-2

Mordecai heard about the plot to kill the king. So he told Esther. (Esth 2:22) **15**

Esther was beautiful. She was so lovely that King Xerxes asked her to marry him and so Esther was crowned queen. She was very happy in the beautiful palace but the king was not the same nationality as Esther. He was from Persia. Esther was a Jew, though the king didn't know it.

One day two men decided to murder the king. Their job was to guard the door of the king's palace, so it would be easy for them to kill him when he walked in the door. Mordecai, Esther's uncle, overheard the two guards talking about what they were planning to do. He went to Esther and told her. She informed the king and so saved his life. The king never forgot it.

Even though the Persian people didn't like the Jews much, Mordecai did the right thing. He helped someone even though that person didn't like him.

The Lord wants us to be kind to others, even if we don't always like them very much.

:bulb: **Remember:** We must help people even if we dislike them.

Serving the Lord is worthwhile

Esther 3-6

Mordecai worked for the good of his people. (Esth 10:3)

Life did not always go well for Esther and the people of the Lord. The king made a bad man, called Haman, prime minister. He said everybody must bow before Haman to show him respect and serve him. Mordecai, Esther's uncle, refused. He served only the Lord.

Haman was very angry about this. He decided to kill Mordecai. He had a gallows made on which he was going to hang Mordecai. Mordecai went to Esther for help. They had a problem. The king didn't know that Esther was a Jew so how could she explain to him why she wanted to help the Jews?

Esther was not only pretty, she was clever too. She prepared a delicious dinner for the king. He enjoyed it very much. Afterwards he told Esther he would give her anything she asked for. Esther told him that Haman planned to kill Mordecai and reminded him that Mordecai was the one who had saved his life when he found out about the plot to murder him. The king was furious with Haman. He hanged Haman from the very gallows he had had built for Mordecai. Then the king gave Mordecai Haman's job. It always pays to obey the Lord and do the right thing.

🔆 **Remember:** The Lord rejoices in our good deeds.

The devil tests Job

'When I was born, I came into the world with nothing. When I die I can take nothing with me.' (Job 1:21)

There was a good man named Job. He served the Lord with all his heart and God was good to him. One day the devil came to the Lord. The Lord asked him whether he had seen how religious Job was. 'Yes,' said the devil, 'but not without reason. It's because You have always looked after him well. But take away everything he has, and then You will see.' So the Lord answered the devil: 'All right, you may test him. Take whatever you want from Job, but don't harm him.' So the devil sent evil people to steal or break all of Job's belongings. Many terrible things happened to Job. He was left with nothing.

'Will Job be cross with the Lord, or not?' the devil wondered. But Job was not angry with the Lord. He said, 'I had nothing when I was born. I can take nothing with me when I die. The Lord gave me everything. Now He has taken everything back. Praise the Lord!'

Job didn't get angry with the Lord because he really loved Him.

 Remember: Sometimes the devil will also test us.

How can one be angry with God?

Job 2

'Should we accept only good things from the hand of God, and never anything bad?' (Job 2:10)

The devil thought Job would get angry with the Lord if he lost everything, but he was wrong. The Lord asked him again if he saw what a good man Job was. 'Yes,' said the devil, 'but a farm and other belongings are not so important. If You took away Job's health, that would be a different story. Job would be angry and forget all about You.' The Lord said the devil could give it a try. He made Job very ill. Big sores came out all over his body.

Job's wife said to him, 'It doesn't look as if the Lord is your friend anymore. Tell Him you are angry with Him and then you might as well die.' Job answered, 'Now you are really being stupid. You don't know what you are saying. I was happy with all the good things the Lord gave me. So shouldn't I also be satisfied if things are going wrong now?'

The devil was wrong. No matter how much Job suffered, he did nothing that would hurt the Lord. Job felt it was much better to be God's friend than to be rich or important.

Remember: Having a lot of money is not important.

Sometimes we don't understand the Lord

Job 4-5

You should be happy if the Lord shows you what to do, even if unpleasant things happen. (Job 5:17) **19**

Does the Lord only love us when all goes well? What happens if things go wrong? Does this mean He has forgotten us? Job's friends thought so. They said to Job, 'The Lord punishes those people He does not like. Look how you are suffering. He's not going to help you, that's for sure.'

But Job's friends were wrong. When things are going well for us, or when we are rich, it doesn't necessarily prove that the Lord loves us. The Lord always loves us whatever our circumstances.

Eliphaz, one of Job's friends, did give Job some good advice: 'If I were you, I would try talking to the Lord. I would ask Him why I am having such a hard time. Remember the Lord is great. We cannot always understand Him. So when the Lord lets something happen to you, it might be that He is trying to tell you something.'

Job thought about it. He decided to speak to the Lord.

 Remember: We cannot always understand the Lord.

God is not a human being.
He is far greater

Job 38

'Did you perhaps make the world, Job?' (Job 38:4-5)

Job decided to talk to the Lord. He knew the Lord and how great and powerful He is. Although it would not be like speaking to an ordinary person Job decided that he would speak to God and ask Him why everything was going wrong for him. He obeyed the Lord, so why was he suffering? Job wanted God to answer him and give him an explanation.

The Lord did answer him. A loud voice came to him in a strong wind: 'Job, do you think I don't know what I'm doing? Asking all these questions shows how little you understand. Now I want to ask you a few questions: Who made the world? Who made the waves of the sea and the clouds? Who makes the sun rise in the morning and the moon at night?' Job had no answer. So the Lord went on: 'Can you make the lightning strike? Or make the stars shine?' Job kept quiet.

As Job looked at creation he knew our Lord is greater and mightier than any human being.

Remember: The Lord is the creator of everything.

The Lord made it all

Job 39-41

'Job, you criticize the Almighty, but do you have the answers?' (Job 40:1)

21

The Lord went on talking to Job: 'Job, see for yourself how wonderful the world is. The baby deer are born without any help. They run around in the open fields and don't need anyone to look after them. Who do you think cares for them? Look at the hawk soar in the sky and spread its wings. Are you the one who makes it fly, Job?' Then the Lord showed Job a crocodile. 'Job,' the Lord asked again, 'can you catch a big crocodile with a light fishing rod? Will you try to keep his mouth closed with your bare hands? Do you think the crocodile will tremble with fear when you come near him? Will you give a crocodile to little children to play with? You can try to fight a crocodile, Job, but you won't try it twice. Who do you think made this fearless animal? Yes, I, the Lord, I made it. You are afraid of a crocodile that I made, but now you want to challenge Me?'

When we see the beautiful fields, the magnificent birds, the mighty mountains and the red sun setting, we realize, like Job did, how wonderful God's creation is and why He is the Lord we want to serve.

 Remember: The Lord created a beautiful world.

The Lord gives everything back to Job

Job 42

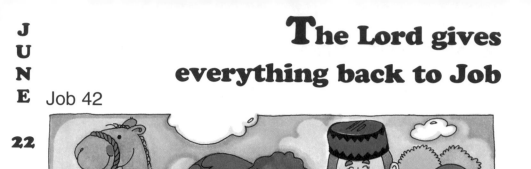

'Now I know that the Lord can do anything.' (Job 42:2)

The God we worship is great and mighty. Job learnt this when God spoke to him. In the end Job said: 'Lord, what can I say? You are so wonderful and great. I am nothing. I know You can do anything. When You decide something must happen, it does. I must admit, I wondered why things were going wrong for me but now I know how wonderful You really are.

'I have heard how You made the earth. You told me how You make the hawk fly, how You keep the huge hippo alive and well although it eats only grass. You also made the lion that roars and the cruel crocodile. And there are so many other things, O Lord, that prove how wonderful You are.

'I am ashamed, Lord that I doubted You. Now I know better. Before I just knew what people told me about You. Now I have seen You with my own eyes.'

Then the Lord knew that Job loved Him very much. He gave Job back everything the devil had taken away and Job was happy for the rest of his life.

 Remember: Things happen in the Lord's time.

You can't run away from the Lord

Jonah 1-2

'You have Your own good reasons for what You do.' (Jon 1:14)

The Lord had a special job for Jonah. He had to go and tell the people of the big city, Nineveh, that God was not happy with them.

Jonah was afraid so he boarded a ship that was going in the opposite direction to Nineveh. He thought he could get away from the Lord. How stupid could he be! The Lord sent a violent storm. The ship creaked and everyone on board thought it was going to sink. The sailors were terrified and started praying to their gods. All this time Jonah was fast asleep in the hold. When the ship's captain found him there he shouted at him: 'How can you sleep at a time like this? Get up and pray to your God! Maybe He will help us.'

Meanwhile the sailors had a toss-up to see who was the cause of the storm. They discovered it was Jonah. 'Who are you? What work do you do?' they asked him. Jonah answered, 'I worship the Lord who made the sea and the land.' 'So what did you do wrong?' 'I was disobedient. I didn't listen to the Lord,' Jonah owned up. 'Throw me into the sea, and it will become calm again.' They did and the storm died down, but it wasn't the end of the story.

💡 **Remember:** We cannot hide from the Lord.

The Lord forgives our greatest sin

Jonah 3

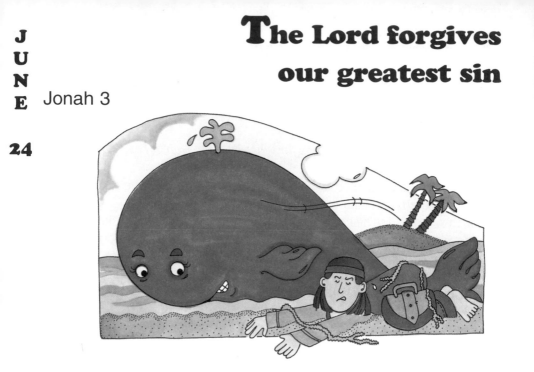

God saw they were sorry about their sins. He forgave them. (Jon 3:10)

The sailors threw Jonah into the sea but he didn't drown. God still had work for him to do so He sent a fish to swallow Jonah. He was inside the fish for three days and during this time he realized how disobedient he had been. Jonah asked the Lord to forgive him and because he was truly sorry the Lord did. Three days later the fish spat Jonah out onto the beach.

Jonah went to the evil city of Nineveh and talked to the wicked people there. He told them God was angry with them and was going to punish them. When the people of Nineveh heard this they felt very bad. They begged the Lord to forgive them. They pleaded with Him not to let them die. The Lord saw they were really sorry and wanted to do His will again so He forgave them and spared their lives.

The Lord forgives us too, if we are truly sorry.

💡 **Remember:** The Lord forgives us our sins if we are really sorry.

The Lord loves us

Jonah 4

J U N E

25

'Lord, You do things for us we don't deserve. You love us.' (Jon 4:2)

When Jonah saw the Lord wasn't going to punish the people of Nineveh, he was upset because he'd told them they would be punished. He didn't think they'd pay attention to his warnings but they did. They changed their evil ways which was why the Lord forgave them.

Jonah took a walk. He sat down just outside the city on a hill. While he sat there, a plant suddenly started growing next to him. Jonah was pleased. The sun was hot and the plant would give him some shade. Early the next morning a worm ate through the stem of the plant and the plant died. Jonah was furious. He'd have no protection from the burning sun.

The Lord asked Jonah, 'Why are you so angry? You didn't make the plant grow. It's not really your plant. Now remember, I made the people of Nineveh just as I made the plant. They are like my own plant. I must worry about them and help them.'

The Lord made us too. He loves us and wants only the best for us, and we must give Him our best.

 Remember: We must do our best for the Lord.

The Lord will help

Psalm 130

Wait and watch for the Lord. (Ps 130:7)

God's people knew the Lord would not forget them. He would come to them in a special way. In Psalm 130 the poet asks the Lord to come soon:

'Lord, I'm all alone,
I call out to You.
Please hear my cry for help.
Don't think of all my wrongdoings;
Please forgive me when I am bad.
Then I can keep on being Your child.
I trust You, Lord.
I know You never lie.
Like someone waiting for the sunrise,
I wait for You.
The Lord will not let us down.
He can really help us.
Look how He helped us when He sent Jesus to the earth.'

Remember: It hurts the Lord when we do wrong.

He died in our place

He carried all our sins. (Is 53:4)

Lionel kept lots of chickens in a chicken coop. One day the chickens scratched a hole under the fence and ran away. Lionel could have left it like that, but he didn't want to. They were his chickens. He started looking for them, and one by one, he brought them back.

The Lord also looks for us when we have strayed. We are often like naughty chickens who run away. We do things God doesn't like but He doesn't just let us go. He comes looking for us.

Isaiah, the Lord's messenger, tells us how the Lord looks for us until He finds us. We do wrong then we run away from God, but God has put our sins onto one Person – Jesus. We should have taken the punishment for our sins ourselves, but Jesus was punished in our place. He died so that we might become God's friends. God keeps on looking for us, because He loves us.

We must love Jesus. He came to make us children of God again. We can go and tell everyone this. We can tell them how wonderful God is.

 Remember: Jesus came to help us to become God's children.

The Lord is not an idol

Jeremiah 10

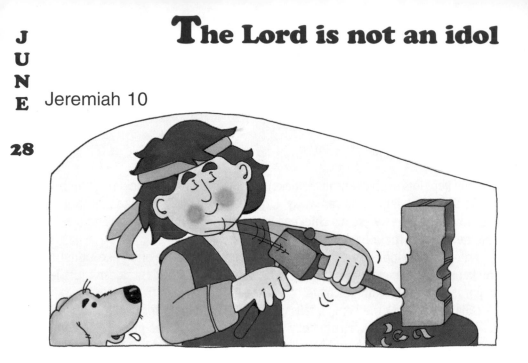

Lord, there is no one like You! You are great, and Your name is full of power.
(Jer 10:6)

Jeremiah tells us how people made idols. They cut down a tree and carved an idol out of it with their hammers and chisels. They decorated it with gold and silver. Then they nailed it to the ground so it wouldn't fall over. They called the wooden statue 'god' and they bowed before this 'god' and worshipped it. But their god stood there like a helpless scarecrow. It couldn't talk to them. It couldn't even walk. It was just a piece of dead wood.

The God we worship is much greater and stronger than this. He made the earth. He is alive and He takes care of us. He knows what we need and helps us with it. He is nothing like a dead idol.

Sometimes we think other things are more important than the Lord and we spend all our time and energy on these things. That is wrong, because we are making idols of them and nothing must be more important to us than the Lord.

Remember: Nothing should be more important than the Lord.

Come to me

Isaiah 1 & 55

Speak to the Lord while He is still near. (Is 55:6)

We know that the Lord never forgets His children. This is how He invites us to come to Him:

'Come to Me, so that we can sort things out.
No matter how bad your sins are, I can take them away.
Even if you are red with sin, I will make you as white as snow.
If you will only obey Me and let Me help you,
I will take good care of you.
But if you keep turning away from Me, you will pay for it!
If you need something, come to Me.
Even if you have nothing to give Me, come anyway.
I will give you what you need and it's all free.
Don't waste your time on things that are not really important.
Come to Me and I will give you everlasting life.
Ask while the Lord is still with you.
Talk to Him while He is still near.'

💡 **Remember:** We shouldn't waste our time on unimportant things.

A messenger of the Lord

Jeremiah 1

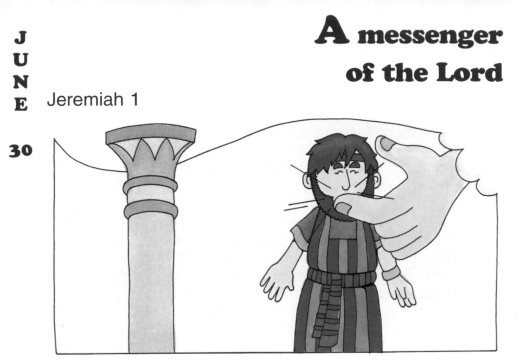

'O Lord, I'm too young.' (Jer 1:6)

Jeremiah was a priest in the temple. One day the Lord spoke to him: 'Even before you were born, I knew you. I decided then that you would be my special messenger.'

Jeremiah answered, 'O Lord, I am too young. I don't even speak well.'

The Lord said, 'Don't say you're too young. Go where I send you. Talk to the people. I will tell you what to say. Don't worry, I will be with you and take care of you.' Then the Lord touched Jeremiah's mouth and said, 'See, I have put My words in your mouth!'

From then on the Lord was with Jeremiah wherever he went. He told Jeremiah what to say to the people. For many years Jeremiah preached the message of God.

We mustn't say we're too young to work for the Lord. We can tell our friends and other people that the Lord is good. We can talk to our parents about Jesus. It makes the Lord very happy when we talk to others about Him.

☼ **Remember:** We should talk to our parents about Jesus.

People are excited because Jesus is coming

Malachi 3-4

'People who listen to Me are like a special treasure to Me.' (Mal 3:17)

The people in the last book of the Old Testament were excited. They knew God was going to send Jesus to us because He loves us so much. This is what Malachi says about it:

'The day will come when the Lord will punish wicked people and reward the good ones. He will come to those who serve Him. They will love being with Him. It will be like a flower enjoying the morning sun. He will heal the places where sin hurts them.

The Lord will take good care of them, because they are His. He will treat them like a father who looks after his children. He will make His children feel safe, and they will be happy.'

This is written in the last book of the Old Testament. The people were excited and happy. They were waiting for Jesus! When Jesus came He was like the sun shining down warmly on people.

Jesus healed us from our sins. That's why we are happy too. The devil is no longer our master. We are free, cheerful and happy because Jesus loves us and takes care of us.

Remember: Jesus makes us children of God.

God talks to His people again

Luke 1

'God has come to help His people! He has not forgotten His promise to them.'
(Lk 1:54)

God did not forget His people. There were times in the Old Testament when people forgot about Him. They turned their backs on God, but God loves His people and never gave up on them.

In the Old Testament God spoke to the people through His prophets. They promised that God would send Jesus to help all believers. The devil would not stand a chance against Him.

What God had promised, happened when Jesus came to us. Mary, Jesus' mother, sang a song:

'God has come to help His children. He promised to be very good to us and He has kept His promises. God is very powerful. He helps all who need help and we are happy.'

Mary sang this song because she knew that Jesus would bring people to God. We need never feel alone. God is always with us and Jesus can be our best Friend.

💡 **Remember:** Jesus can be our best Friend.

John the Baptist is born

Luke 1

'John will bring you great joy and happiness.' (Lk 1:14)

Zechariah and his wife Elizabeth were faithful believers who loved the Lord. They were sad though, because they didn't have a baby and were very old. One day Zechariah was in the temple. Suddenly an angel stood before him. Zechariah got the fright of his life. But the angel said, 'Don't be afraid! You will have a son. You must call him John. The Lord will use him to prepare the way for Jesus.' Zechariah said, 'How can this happen? I am an old man now.' The angel, Gabriel, answered, 'Since you don't believe me you won't be able to speak until the child is born.'

Elizabeth had a baby boy. The family came to congratulate her. 'What are you going to call him?' they wanted to know. 'John,' answered Elizabeth. 'But nobody in the family has that name,' they said. 'Let's go and ask Zechariah instead.' Zechariah couldn't speak, so he wrote down, 'His name is John.' From that moment he could speak again.

Zechariah had learnt that with God, nothing is impossible.

 Remember: Nothing is impossible for the Lord.

Luke 1

An angel tells what God is going to do

'Mary, God has decided to bless you.' (Lk 1:30)

Mary lived in Nazareth, a village in Galilee. She was engaged to Joseph. They were going to get married soon. Suddenly Gabriel appeared to her. He said, 'The Lord is with you!' Mary was very surprised. The angel went on, 'Mary, you are going to have a son. You must call Him Jesus. He will be very important because He is the Son of God.'

Mary was confused and asked, 'But how can I have a baby? I am not married.' The angel told her the Holy Spirit would give her the baby. That is why Jesus would be called the Son of God. 'Nothing is impossible with God,' he reminded her. So Mary said, 'I am willing to do what God wants.'

But Joseph was worried when he heard that Mary was pregnant. He didn't understand how it had happened. He knew he was not the father so he didn't want to marry her anymore. But the angel of the Lord came to talk to him as well. He told Joseph that the Holy Spirit had given Mary the baby and so they waited for the birth of Jesus together.

🔆 **Remember:** We must be prepared to do what God asks.

Jesus is born

Jesus was born and they wrapped Him snugly in strips of cloth. (Lk 2:7)

The Roman emperor, Augustus, said all the people had to be counted. They had to go to the towns where their fathers were born and register. Joseph went to Bethlehem and he took Mary with him. It was very close to the time when Jesus would be born.

When they finally arrived in Bethlehem all the inns were full. They had to stay in a stable because it was time for the baby to be born.

Mary wrapped Him warmly in cloths. There wasn't even a cot for Him, so she laid Him in a manger.

Mary and Joseph were very happy. Jesus wasn't born in a palace, but in a humble place where ordinary people could come and see Him.

God loved us human beings so much that He sent His Son for all of us, regardless of who we are. It doesn't matter whether we are rich or poor, good-looking or plain. Jesus came for us.

💡 **Remember:** Jesus wants us to be His friends.

They called Him Jesus and Immanuel

Matthew 1

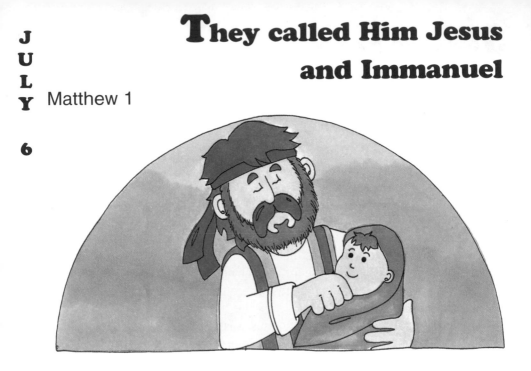

'Mary will give birth to a son, and He will be called Immanuel.' (Mt 1:23)

Everything happened exactly the way the angel said it would. The baby was born and Joseph named Him Jesus just as the angel had told him.

But Jesus had another name – Immanuel, which means 'God is with us'. Joseph couldn't help thinking back to a time long ago when God's people needed Him very much. Strangers wanted to harm them and take their country, but the Lord promised that they would not get what they wanted. The Lord would look after His people Himself. As proof of His love for them, and to show that He was with them, a baby boy would be born. He would be called Immanuel.

Every time the Israelites were afraid of their enemies, all they had to do was remember the boy, Immanuel. He would remind them that they were not alone. God was with them and so was Jesus. He reminds us that God is with us, always. We are never alone, because the Lord loves us.

-ợ- **Remember:** God is with us always.

Mary thanks the Lord

'Oh, how I praise the Lord.' (Lk 1:46)

Mary, Jesus' mother, wrote a poem to thank God for Jesus. This is what she said:

'In my song, I want to say how great the Lord is.
I am excited and happy.
God is going to take my sins away.
He took notice of me, Mary,
although I am not important.
He is so powerful;
That is why He can do such awesome things for us.
He takes such good care of people who serve Him.
There is nothing He cannot do.
If people don't like Him, He scatters them all over.
But if people love Him, He takes good care of them.
He keeps His promises.
He is good to His people.'

-ᑀ- **Remember:** Jesus does what He promises.

The angels were happy

Luke 2

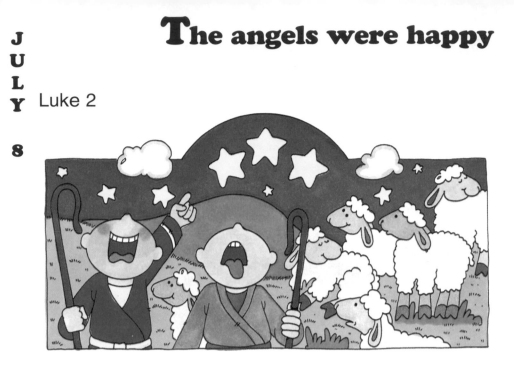

'Glory to God in heaven. And peace to everybody God likes,' the angels sang. (Lk 2:14)

There were some shepherds near the place where Jesus was born. They were in the fields outside the village watching over their sheep. Suddenly an angel stood among them. It was like a bright light shining on them. They were frightened. 'Don't be afraid,' the angel said to them. 'I have come to tell you something that will make you very happy. Jesus was born today. He is going to forgive all your sins. You will be God's special children. Go to the village. There you will find a baby lying in a manger.'

Suddenly the angel was joined by a whole choir of angels. They sang a lovely song: 'Glory to God in heaven. Peace to everybody God loves.'

Then the angels left. The shepherds said to each other, 'Let's go to Bethlehem. Let's go and find the baby.' They found Jesus and told everyone what the angels had told them. The people stood listening open-mouthed. Later that night the shepherds went back to their sheep. They sang and praised the Lord all the way there. This was their way of saying how great God is. They also thanked God for everything that happened that night.

🔅 **Remember:** Jesus helps us to become God's special children.

Not everybody is happy about Jesus

Matthew 2

Some wise men from the East asked, 'Where is the newborn king of the Jews?'
(Mt 2:2)

One day some wise men arrived in Jerusalem. They had seen a star that showed them a new king had been born. They didn't know exactly where, so they asked around if anybody knew where this new king was.

When King Herod heard that these men were looking for a new king he was very upset. He had a meeting with the leaders and asked them about this special king. They said, 'He will be born in Bethlehem.'

Herod invited the wise men to his palace. 'Go to Bethlehem and look for the child until you find him. Then come back and tell me so I can go and worship him too,' Herod told them. But Herod didn't want to take Jesus gifts. He wanted to kill Him.

The wise men found Jesus and gave Him the most beautiful gifts of gold, frankincense and myrrh.

God told the wise men in a dream not to return to Herod, so they secretly took a different route home.

💡 **Remember:** Jesus is the most important King of all.

Simeon and Anna are pleased to see Jesus

Luke 2

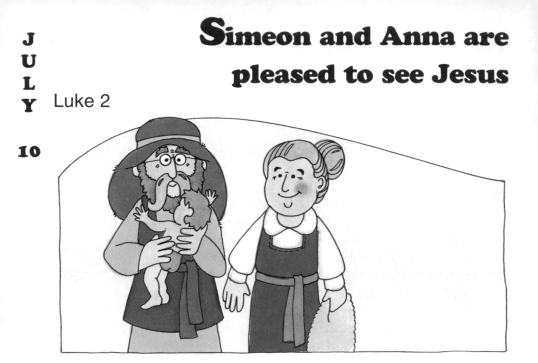

'Lord, I have seen how You will save Your people.' (Lk 2:30)

Simeon lived in Jerusalem. He loved the Lord very much and was looking forward to the day when Jesus would come. God told him he would not die before he had seen Jesus.

One day the Lord's Holy Spirit told Simeon to go to the temple. The baby Jesus was there.

When Simeon saw the child he picked Him up and took Him in his arms. He thanked the Lord: 'Lord, now I can die in peace. I have seen Jesus. He is the One who will take away our sins. He will shine for us like a light in the dark.'

Joseph and Mary were surprised by the things Simeon said so he told them, 'Jesus will save many people. But many will also be punished, because they will refuse to listen to Him.'

Anna, a woman who was also in the temple, came up to them. The Lord loved her. She served Him with all her heart. When she saw Jesus, she also thanked God. She couldn't stop talking about what Jesus would do for everybody.

☀ **Remember:** Jesus takes our sins away if we believe in Him.

Jesus also goes to the temple

Luke 2

Jesus grew stronger and cleverer by the day. God and all who knew Him, liked Him very much. (Lk 2:52).

Every year there was an important religious festival in Jerusalem. Jesus' parents always travelled there to celebrate it and took Jesus with them. When Jesus was twelve years old they were at the festival as usual.

After the celebrations were over, Jesus' father and mother and many other people started back home in a group. Nazareth was quite a distance from Jerusalem. Jesus' parents didn't realize that their son had stayed behind in Jerusalem. Towards evening they noticed that He wasn't around. They went back to Jerusalem to look for Him. They found Him in the temple talking with the priests. They were amazed that He was so clever.

Jesus' mother asked Him, 'Why did You stay behind? We were worried about You.' Jesus answered, 'Why did you look for Me? You should have known I would be here. My Father is here.' His parents didn't really understand what He meant. Jesus is the Son of God and the temple was God's house. Jesus grew up to be strong and clever.

Remember: Jesus is the Son of God.

God teaches Jesus everything

John 5

The Son does nothing by Himself. He does only what He sees His Father doing. (Jn 5:19)

How was it possible for Jesus to know everything? The Bible tells us that Jesus is God's Son. God taught Him everything, just like our parents teach us to do things.

This is the way God taught Jesus. He loved Jesus very much and Jesus loved Him. That's why Jesus did everything exactly the way His Father showed Him. One of the most important things that His Father showed Him was how we can become God's children again.

God sent Jesus to tell us how we can become the children of God so we need to know what Jesus says in the Bible. If we read our Bibles we will know what God wants us to do.

Remember: Jesus came to show us how to be children of God.

John tells the people about Jesus

Matthew 3

'Prepare a pathway for the Lord. Make a straight road for Him!' (Mt 3:3)

13

Jesus grew up. It was time for Him to start preaching to the people. God sent John the Baptist to prepare them for Jesus' coming.

John did not preach in a synagogue or in the temple but in the fields alongside the River Jordan. His food was locusts and wild honey.

John was a good preacher. His message was, 'Turn from your sins and turn to God. It is time for Jesus, our King, our Messiah to come. Prepare everything for Him.' People came from all over to hear him. They were glad that Jesus was coming and they wanted to be ready for Him. They didn't want to sin anymore. John baptized them in the River Jordan.

Then John saw many of the Jewish leaders, the Pharisees, coming to be baptized but they only pretended to serve the Lord. John spoke to them angrily: 'It's no use making out that you are good. You must live like people who love the Lord. God will treat a person well who lives the right way but those who make the Lord sad will be punished.'

🔅 **Remember:** Do only the things that will please God.

John baptizes Jesus

John 1

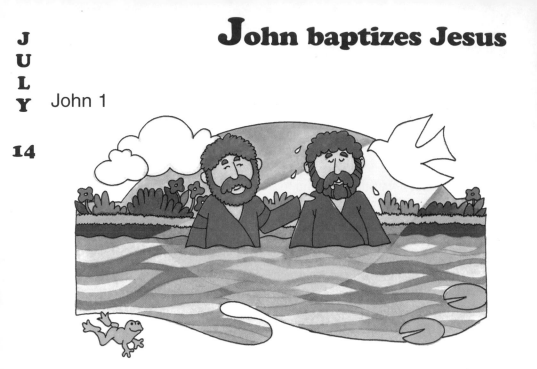

'Look! There is the Lamb of God who takes away the sin of the world!' (Jn 1:29)

One day John was standing at the river baptizing people. Many people came to hear him preach. Then he saw Jesus coming towards him. Jesus asked John to baptize Him too. At first John didn't want to baptize Jesus, but Jesus told him to do it. God wanted him to. Jesus wanted to show that He doesn't like sin at all. This was why John baptized people. Water washes us clean, and we are baptized because sin makes us dirty. We want to be washed clean from sin.

When John baptized Jesus, Something suddenly came down from heaven. It looked like a dove, but it was the Holy Spirit. The Holy Spirit gave Jesus strength.

Then God spoke from heaven, 'This is my Son. I love Him very much. He makes Me very happy.'

When this happened John knew that Jesus was the Son of God. He told everybody. He also said, 'Jesus will take our sins away.'

Now Jesus was ready to tell people about God.

Remember: Jesus came to tell us about God.

The devil wants to stop Jesus

Matthew 4

'Worship the Lord your God; serve only Him.' (Mt 4:10)

After Jesus was baptized, He went into the desert with the Holy Spirit. There the devil tried to make Jesus sin.

For a very long time Jesus had nothing to eat. He was very hungry. The devil said to Him, 'If You are God's Son, change these stones into loaves of bread.' But Jesus said, 'No, food is not that important. It is more important to listen to every word of God.'

Then the devil took Jesus to the temple. They went up on the roof. He said, 'If You are the Son of God, jump off! Surely the angels will help you so you won't get hurt.' Jesus said to the devil, 'The Bible says we are not to test God.'

The devil tried a third time. He took Jesus to a very high mountain. The devil showed Jesus the whole world from there. He said, 'I will give it all to You, if You will only kneel down and worship me.' Jesus said crossly, 'Get out of here, Satan!' The Bible says we must pray to God and no-one else. Then the devil went away defeated.

 Remember: The devil could do nothing against Jesus.

The devil wants to stop you too

Matthew 7, Luke 13

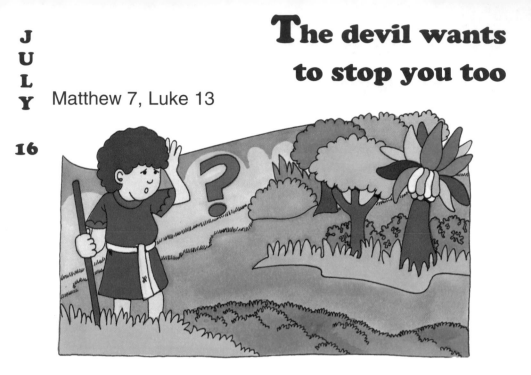

'Follow the narrow road that leads to the right door.' (Mt 7:13-14)

Someone once asked Jesus what sort of people would go to heaven. Jesus said, 'Try your best to serve the Lord. Some people try just for a short while. Then they give up and start listening to the devil. They won't go to heaven.'

We can choose which way we want to go – to keep trying even though it's hard or to give up because that's easier.

It's not always easy to listen to the Lord and to do the right thing. This is like walking along the difficult road. It might be hard, but this road takes us to heaven. If we don't listen, and choose the easy road, we won't find the door to heaven. That will please the devil! He wants to stop us from taking the road to heaven – but we're not going to let him!

Remember: Don't listen to the devil.

Whose side are you on?

Jesus said, 'Anyone who isn't working with Me is actually working against Me.' (Mt 12:30)

Once some people brought a man to Jesus. He had a devil inside him so he couldn't talk or see. Jesus chased the devil out of the man and he was healed.

The Jewish leaders, the Pharisees, didn't like Jesus. When they heard how Jesus had ordered the devil out of the man they said Jesus must be a friend of the devil's, and that's why the devil listened to Him. Jesus told them they were making a big mistake. 'I threw out the devil,' Jesus said. 'This means that I am not on his side.'

'I beat the devil,' Jesus went on. 'God's Spirit gives Me the power over demons and that's why the devil runs away when I speak. Say a strong man lives in a house. If you want to break into his house you must tie him up first. I overpowered the devil. I'm in charge, not the devil. If you're not on My side, you're against Me.'

 Remember: Jesus has defeated the devil.

We needn't be afraid of the devil

Matthew 8

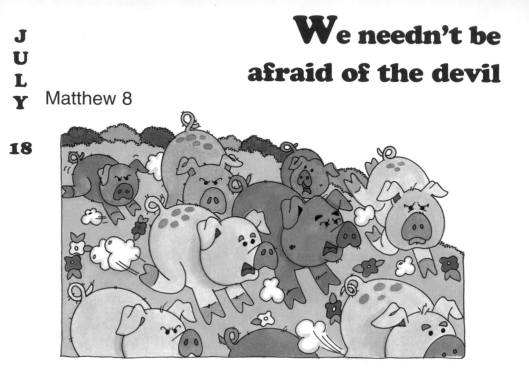

The devils started screaming at Him, 'Why are You bothering us, Son of God?'
(Mt 8:29)

One day Jesus walked past a graveyard. Two men who lived in the graveyard charged up to Jesus. They had devils inside them and everybody was afraid of them because they were very dangerous. When they saw Jesus, they stopped in their tracks and shouted, 'What do you want, Son of God? Have you come to hurt us?'

A large herd of pigs was feeding nearby. 'Please, don't send us to hell. Rather let us go into those pigs and live inside them,' the devils begged. 'All right, go!' Jesus told them. So the devils went into the pigs. The pigs started running wildly down the hillside and into the sea. They all drowned.

The herdsmen who looked after the pigs, ran to town. They told everybody what had happened and that Jesus had healed the two dangerous men. But the townspeople were bad. The two men weren't their problem. They didn't care about them, they were just worried about their pigs. They chased Jesus away. They wanted to get rid of Him!

💡 **Remember:** Always choose Jesus.

Jesus chooses His special friends

Luke 5

'From now on you'll be fishing for people!' (Lk 5:10)

One day Jesus was walking beside the lake. Many people crowded around to hear Him preach. Jesus asked some fishermen if He could sit in their boat. He used it as a kind of pulpit or platform. Jesus sat in the boat and told the crowds about God. When He had finished, He said to a fisherman called Simon, 'Thank you for letting Me use your boat. Now take it out to the middle of the lake and let your nets down.' Simon said, 'We've been fishing all night and we haven't caught a thing, but I'll try again.' He did as Jesus said and he and his friends caught so many fish that they had to load some onto a second boat.

Everyone realized how wonderful the Lord was. Simon went down on his knees before Jesus. 'Lord, I have so many faults. I am sinful. It is better if You go away from me.' But Jesus answered, 'Don't be afraid. I want you to help Me. You must go and tell people about Me. Just like you caught those fish, you must catch people for Me.' When they got back to shore Simon left his boat and followed Jesus. They became good friends.

Remember: Jesus loves us even if we sometimes make mistakes.

Jesus invites everybody

Matthew 22

'Tell everybody who has been invited the meal is ready.' (Mt 22:4)

Jesus said heaven is like a feast. A king once invited people to a feast but when everything was ready, the people who had been invited didn't turn up. They were too busy doing their own thing: one had gone to his farm and another said he had too much work. The king sent messengers to tell them, 'The meal has been cooked, everything is ready. Hurry!' But they were rude to the king's messengers and chased them away. The king was very angry. He sent his army to punish these people.

Then the king said, 'Go out and invite everyone you see to the feast.' Many people came. The hall was filled with guests.

Do you know who the first group of people are – those who were invited but didn't come? They are people who think they are so important that they don't need the Lord. They don't really love Him and the Lord will punish them.

The others who came to the feast are the people who listen to the Lord. They want to do what He says. That's why they come when He calls. They are not disobedient and one day they will be at God's feast in heaven.

💡 **Remember:** Jesus invites everybody to be His children.

Jesus also invites children

'Let the children come to Me. Don't stop them!' (Mk 10:14)

One day when Jesus was talking to the people, some parents brought their children to Him. They wanted Jesus to speak to the children, to touch them and bless them. But Jesus' friends told them not to bother Jesus. He was busy with the grown-ups. When Jesus heard this He was not pleased with His friends. He loves children so He said, 'Don't keep the children away from Me. They must come to Me. God loves children.'

Jesus looked at the grown-ups and said, 'If you want to serve the Lord, you must be like children. A child listens to what his father or mother says.

You must also listen to what the Lord says,' Jesus told them. 'When someone helps one of God's children, God is very happy and He will help that person. But if someone should harm one of God's children God will punish that person. It would be better for that person to tie a heavy stone around his neck and jump into the sea.'

It is true. God loves children.

-ᗢ- **Remember:** Jesus loves little children in a special way.

Even if you hide, Jesus still invites you

Luke 19

Jesus came to look for people. He wants to make them children of God. (Lk 19:10)

A rich man called Zacchaeus lived in Jericho. The people didn't like him because he was a tax collector and they said he took more money from them than he was supposed to. One day Jesus came past and Zacchaeus tried to get a look at Him, but Zacchaeus was short and couldn't see over the people's heads. Zacchaeus decided to run ahead and climb a tree beside the road. When Jesus came to the tree, He suddenly stopped and looked up: 'Zacchaeus, come down at once! I must visit your house today.' Zacchaeus quickly climbed down. He was very happy.

The people were angry with Jesus. Why did He choose to go to the home of a bad man? But Jesus changed Zacchaeus' whole life. Zacchaeus said, 'I will give back everybody the money I took from them. I will even give them extra.' Jesus said to Zacchaeus, 'Now you are My friend.' Jesus also spoke to the people who wondered why He had visited a man like Zacchaeus: 'I came to find sinners. Surely you know they also need God. I must help them to become children of God.'

Jesus invites us all to be His friends.

·Ọ· **Remember:** Jesus wants to help bad people become God's friends.

Jesus also invites people others don't like

'If you drink the water I give you, you will never be thirsty again.' (Jn 4:14)

One day Jesus and His friends had walked a long way. They were tired. When they came to a well, they sat down beside it to rest. Then Jesus' friends went into the village to buy some food.

A woman came to the well. She was not a Jew like Jesus, but a Samaritan. The Jews didn't like the Samaritans. They didn't even talk to one another. But Jesus was never rude. He asked the woman for some water. She was very surprised: 'I am a Samaritan. Why are you asking me for a drink of water?' Jesus said, 'I can also give you water. If you drink it, you will never be thirsty again.' Jesus was not talking about real water, but about spiritual water.

Say there is someone who wants to know God. One can say that person is 'thirsty' for God. Jesus can take that 'thirst' away. He can teach that person about God.

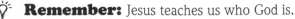

Remember: Jesus teaches us who God is.

Don't make the wrong choice, like the rich young man

Mark 10

'Then come back and follow Me.' (Mk 10:21)

We must choose if we want to be Jesus' friends or not. If we choose to be His friends we must do what He asks of us.

There was a rich young man who came to Jesus and asked, 'What must I do to be Your friend?' Jesus answered, 'You know what God wants. He told us that in the Ten Commandments.' The young man said, 'I've obeyed these commandments since I was a child.'

Jesus liked him very much and he said to the young man, 'Go and sell all you have. Give the money to people who need it. Then come, follow Me.' The man's face fell. He loved everything he owned more than he loved Jesus. He would rather stay and keep his riches than go with Jesus.

We have a choice too. We can choose to be Jesus' friends and do whatever makes Him happy.

Jesus loves us. He asks us to be His friends.

-ϙ́- **Remember:** Jesus wants to be our special Friend.

Jesus makes us happy

John said, 'Jesus must become greater and I must become less.' (Jn 3:30) **25**

It is great being Jesus' friend. The Bible tells us it's almost like going to a wedding. We go to a hall where all the delicious cake is as well as the other nice things to eat and drink. But we must wait there until the bride and groom arrive. It may feel like a long boring wait but when the bride and bridegroom finally arrive, everyone is very glad. Then the feasting can start and we don't have to wait anymore.

Jesus makes our lives as enjoyable as a wedding. If He is not there, it is boring. But when we become His friends, then we enjoy life. It's as if the bridegroom is there. At a wedding we like to do things for the groom. We feel special if he asks us to help him. When we are Jesus' friends, we really feel special. We want to do what He asks us. We want to make Him happy.

 Remember: We are special to the Lord.

The Lord makes everything new for His friends

John 3

'Unless you are born again, you cannot be the Lord's child.' (Jn 3:3)

When a new-born baby is born he is very tiny. His parents feed him and take care of him. He learns to walk and play. Later on he goes to school. But everything starts when the baby is born.

Jesus says we must also be born if we want to be God's children. We must be born again or reborn. Everything starts there.

The Holy Spirit helps us so that we can be born a child of God. This means that God becomes our Father in spirit. We then have an earthly father and a heavenly Father.

Just as a baby learns to eat and walk, we can learn from God how to be His children. He will teach us to do what pleases Him. Just as the parents of a little baby teach him everything, God teaches us, His children, everything. That is why Jesus said to Nicodemus, 'Unless you are born again, you cannot be the Lord's child.' The Holy Spirit helps us to be God's children in spirit. We must thank the Lord that we can be His children.

:bulb: **Remember:** We must thank God for the privilege of being His children.

Jesus invites us through the Bible

A farmer went out to plant some seed ... (Mt 13:3)

One day a farmer went out to plant some seed. As he scattered it across his field some seeds fell on a footpath. The birds came and ate them. Other seeds fell among stones. The ground was very shallow. The plants came up quickly. But they soon wilted in the hot sun because their roots were too small. Other seeds fell among thorns. The seeds tried their best to grow, but the thorns grew all over them. Other seeds fell on good soil. They grew well. They gave the farmer a bumper crop.

Jesus says the same thing happens with people who hear about Him. Like the seeds that fell on the footpath some people hear Jesus' words, but don't listen. The devil takes the words away. Others hear what Jesus says. For a while they are excited, but they soon forget all about it, like the seeds that fell among the stones. Then there are the people who are like the seeds that fell among the thorns. They listen to what Jesus says, but the minute something goes wrong in their lives they forget all about Him.

But the people who listen to Jesus and do what He tells them, are like the seeds that fell upon good soil. The words of Jesus grow well in them.

💡 **Remember:** Listen to and do what the Bible says.

Matthew 5

Jesus uses us like a light to invite others

'Let your good deeds shine like a light for all to see.' (Mt 5:16)

We must not be ashamed to be God's children. We must never try to hide it.

A child of the Lord is like a light in the world. When we switch on a light, everyone can see. If it's dark we need a torch. And what's the use of taking a torch along and keeping it in our pocket? The sensible thing to do would be to take it out, switch it on and let its light shine out. The Lord says a Christian is like a light. A Christian should tell other people about Jesus. We must shine like a light for all to see. If we are Christians, we shouldn't hide the fact.

A Christian is also like a mountain. A mountain cannot hide. And a Christian cannot hide. People should be able to tell by a person's life that he or she loves Jesus. So we must be friendly, good and helpful and love our friends and other people. We must copy Jesus' example. Then we will be like a light that shows other people how great God is.

 Remember: We must be the light of God for other people.

You must show others it's great to serve Jesus

Matthew 5

'You are the salt of the earth.' (Mt 5:13)

If food is without salt it has no flavour. In the old days salt was even more important than it is today. In those days people didn't have fridges. They put salt on the food and then the food didn't go bad and it could be stored for a long time.

But sometimes the salt became lumpy or it tasted bad. Then it couldn't be used with food.

The Bible says we are the salt of the world. We must work for the Lord in this world. We must tell people about Him and how wonderful it is to belong to Him. In this way we can make their lives better because they will get to know the Lord. Just as salt stops food from going bad, we will help them not to become bad.

We must live like children of Jesus. Then we are like salt. But if we do things the Lord doesn't like, then we become like that salt which is useless, and that hurts the Lord.

🔆 **Remember:** Our work must be like salt for the earth.

It's nice to be Jesus' friend

Matthew 13

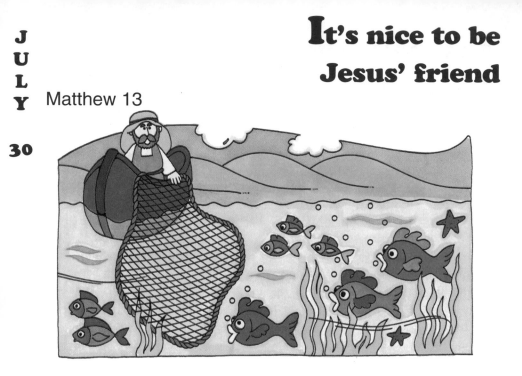

'If you want something of value, you will take all your money and buy it.'(Mt 13:46)

To know Jesus is more important than anything else.

Jesus told a story of a treasure that was buried in a field. A man heard about it. He was very excited and wanted this treasure so badly that he sold all his things and with the money bought the land to get the treasure.

This treasure is like being Jesus' friend. Nothing is more important than that. That is why we must give everything to be His friend.

To be a friend of Jesus is great. Not to be is terrible. Jesus said it's like a fisherman who catches many fish in a big net. He keeps the good fish and throws away the rest. The Lord does the same. If we serve the Lord we are the good fish whom He keeps with Him. But if we lead bad lives and don't love the Lord, He will cast us from Him.

There is nothing more important than being Jesus' friend.

Remember: Knowing Jesus is more important than anything else.

Jesus wants to be our best Friend

It is good to be the Lord's child and to live the way He wants you to. (Mt 11:29)

People often think it is difficult to be God's child. But Jesus came to show us that it's easy. It's fun to be Jesus' friend.

Let's hear what Jesus told the people: 'You don't need to go to school to know that the Lord loves you. Your parents can tell you Jesus loves you very much.' That's easy to understand.

Jesus also says, 'When you are afraid, come to Me and tell Me all about it. If you are sad, tell Me. If you don't know what to do, ask Me. I will help you.' The Lord wants to be like a good friend to us. He wants to be with us and He wants to help us.

It is great to have the Lord with us all the time. He is like the best friend ever.

🔅 **Remember:** Jesus is with us and wants to help us.

Children are very important to God

Mark 9

Anyone who wants to be important to God, must be prepared to help other people with everything. (Mk 9:35)

One day Jesus and His friends were together at home. He asked them what they had been doing all day. They were ashamed to tell Him because they had been arguing about which of them was the most important. Jesus knew this, so He said, 'Do you know who is the most important to God? It is someone who wants to help others. Someone who doesn't think only of himself. Someone who thinks of others too. These people like doing what the Lord wants them to. And God wants them to be kind to one another.'

Jesus called a small child over to Him: 'Someone who loves a child also loves Me. Christians should care for little children. This is what God wants. If you hurt even one of these little ones, God will punish you.'

When we are Jesus' children, we needn't worry. Even if something happens that scares us, we just need to remind ourselves that Jesus loves us and will watch over us. We don't need to be afraid because we are very important to the Lord.

🔆 **Remember:** As Jesus' children, we need not be afraid.

Jesus helps a little girl who believed

Mark 5

Jesus said, 'Get up, little girl!' And the girl immediately stood up and walked around. (Mk 5:41-42)

An important man, called Jairus, came hurrying to Jesus one day. 'My daughter is very sick. I think she is going to die,' he said. 'Please help her. Please come and make her well again. Don't let her die.' While Jesus was on His way there, Jairus' friends brought this message: 'Your little girl is dead. There's no use troubling Jesus now.'

Jesus heard them. He comforted Jairus: 'Don't be sad. Just trust Me.' Then Jesus went to Jairus' house. There were many people there crying bitterly. Jesus went into the house and asked, 'Why all this crying? The little girl isn't dead, she is only sleeping.' The people thought, 'How stupid of Him!' And they laughed. Couldn't He see she was dead?

Jesus told everybody to leave the house. Only the little girl's parents and Jesus' friends stayed behind. He walked over to the little girl and took her hand. Then He said, 'Little girl, get up!' And the girl immediately got up and walked around. Her parents gave her something to eat. The people couldn't believe it. Jesus is our Friend too if we believe in Him.

💡 **Remember:** Jesus helps His friends.

Jesus also helps grown-ups who believe

John 9

'One thing I know: I was blind, and now I can see!' (Jn 9:25)

One day a man who was born blind sat begging for money to buy food. Jesus was walking past but He saw him and stopped. He put a litle mud on the man's eyes. 'Go and wash your eyes in the Pool of Siloam,' He told the man.

The man did so and suddenly he could see! The people asked, 'But isn't this the blind man who always sits here begging?' 'Yes, I am that man!' he kept saying. 'But how is it that you can see now? What happened?' they wanted to know. So the man told them how Jesus made him see again.

There were people who didn't like Jesus – the Pharisees. They were angry when they found out that Jesus had healed the blind man. They were jealous. But the blind man kept telling everyone that Jesus was a good man – the Pharisees were wrong.

Some time later the man saw Jesus again. He knelt down before Him and said, 'You really are the Son of God.' And so he became Jesus' friend.

💡 **Remember:** Jesus is our Lord. We should worship Him.

Trust the Lord

Luke 5

Jesus said, 'Your sins are forgiven.' (Lk 5:20)

Jesus healed many people. They came from all over and crowded round Jesus wherever He was. One day people came to the house where Jesus was, carrying a paralysed man on a stretcher. They tried their best to get him to Jesus, but they couldn't push through the crowd so they went up onto the roof. They took off some tiles and lowered the sick man into the room below. They put him down right in front of Jesus. When Jesus saw the faith they had in Him, He said to the man, 'I forgive you all your sins.'

Before Jesus could say another word, the Pharisees said, 'Who does this man think He is? Everyone knows only God can forgive sins.' Jesus said, 'Anybody can say he forgives someone. But not everybody is powerful enough to do it. Come let me show you how powerful I really am.' Then Jesus turned to the paralyzed man and said, 'Stand up, take your stretcher and go home.' And right there, as everyone watched, the man did just that. He was overjoyed. He could not stop thanking the Lord. Once again Jesus had proved how powerful He really is.

Trust the Lord. He can do whatever He promises us.

💡 **Remember:** Nobody can be as strong as Jesus.

Our strength is from the Lord

John 15

'Those who stay near Me and I near them, they will do as I ask.' (Jn 15:5)

One day the Lord told a story to explain about being His friends.

He said He is like a fruit tree. His Father, God, is like the farmer who has to care for the tree. We are like the branches of the fruit tree. The farmer also cares for the branches. He cuts them back so that they can bear good fruit. Every branch that doesn't yield any fruit, He cuts off.

A branch that is not part of the tree cannot bear fruit, can it? A person who is not part of Jesus cannot do what He says either. When a branch is fixed to a tree, it gets its strength from the tree. Then lots of fruit can grow on it. Without the tree the branch can do nothing. It's the same with us. We must be good friends of Jesus. We must not let go of Him. We must be like a branch on a tree. Then He will make us strong. He will help us to do things which make God happy. We can pray and ask Him to help us, and He will.

We should be Jesus' branches. Branches want to be part of the tree always, otherwise they're useless. We too must stay close to Jesus.

💡 **Remember:** Always stay close to Jesus.

Jesus takes care of us

Matthew 6

'First live for God. Then He will give you all you need.' (Mt 6:33)

The Lord doesn't want us to worry too much. We must remember He will take care of us. Jesus explained it by saying: 'Look at the birds. They don't plant. They don't build barns to store food. So how do they stay alive? The Lord feeds them.'

We are more important to the Lord than a bird, so He will take even greater care of us. The Lord doesn't want us to worry too much. It is not good for us.

Let's also look at the wild flowers that grow in the fields. They don't make themselves clothes. Yet they are beautiful. They are sometimes prettier than the most expensive clothes one can buy in a shop. Do you know who dresses the flowers? The Lord Himself. He takes care of them.

We are more important than flowers and therefore God will take even better care of us.

Our Father in heaven knows what we need. He will look after us. We mustn't worry. All the Lord wants us to do is to listen to Him. We must be good because we are His children and He will give us all we need.

Remember: We need not worry. The Lord provides.

Jesus takes care of us – just trust Him

Matthew 8

Jesus said, 'Go on home. What you have believed has happened.' (Mt 8:13)

Once a soldier came to Jesus for help. This soldier was in charge of many other soldiers.

He said to Jesus, 'Please help. One of my men is in so much pain, he can hardly walk.'

Jesus said, 'All right, I will come.'

The soldier answered, 'Lord, You are too important to come to my house. Just say the word and the man will be healed. I know how it works. Among my men, I'm the important one. They do what I tell them. I give the orders and they listen when I speak. You also just say the word and it will happen.'

What the man said surprised Jesus. He said, 'This man really trusts Me. People like him are friends of God.' Then Jesus said to the soldier, 'You can go home. What you believed has happened.' The sick man was healed as Jesus spoke. We too can trust the Lord.

Remember: We can trust the Lord.

Jesus feeds many people

John 6

'I am the bread of life. Those who eat this bread will never be hungry again.' (Jn 6:35)

Jesus and His friends were at the Sea of Galilee. Crowds gathered on the shore. Many people were there hoping to be healed by Jesus. After a while the people started getting hungry. Jesus asked one of His friends, 'Philip, where can we buy bread for all these people?' Philip replied, 'I don't know. We'd need loads of money to buy all these people food.' Meanwhile one of Jesus' other friends came up to Him and said, 'There's a young boy here with a little food. He has five bread rolls and two dried fish. But it's not nearly enough for all these people.'

Then Jesus said, 'Tell everyone to sit down on the grass.' Thousands of people sat down. Then Jesus took the bread. He prayed, giving thanks to God for the food. Then He started passing around the bread and the fish. The people ate and there was more than enough food for every single one of them. There were even leftovers!

This is how Jesus takes care of us. He not only gives us food to eat. He also helps us to be children of God forever.

Remember: Jesus also provides our food.

You can't do without the Lord

Luke 12

The most important thing in a peson's life is not how much money he has. (Lk 12:15)

One day two brothers came to Jesus. They were arguing bitterly. Their father had died and they had to divide his money between them. They asked Jesus to help them. But Jesus saw they weren't really interested in Him, only in the money.

So Jesus told them a story. There was once a rich man with a big farm. He always had very good crops. In fact his barns were overflowing. 'What shall I do now?' he wondered. 'I know. I'm going to pull my barns down and build bigger ones. Then I'll have enough room to store up everything I own. And I won't need anybody anymore. I can sit back and enjoy life, because I am a rich man.' The Lord said, 'You fool! Tonight you are going to die in your bed. And what will you have then? What will the things you hoarded mean to you? You can't take them with you.'

Jesus told this story to teach us that it's no good having lots of things if we forget about the Lord. It's much better to work hard and make the Lord happy. Then we will be able to enjoy all the wondeful things He gives us.

🔆 **Remember:** Jesus is much more important than money.

We must always thank Jesus for taking care of us

He went to Jesus and thanked Him very much. (Lk 17:16)

One day Jesus came across ten men. They were all very sick. They had leprosy. The townspeople chased them out of their town because they were scared of catching the disease. The men didn't come close to Jesus but cried out to Him from a distance, 'Jesus, please help us.' 'All right,' Jesus said. 'Go into town and show the people you are not sick anymore.' On the way to the village their illness vanished.

Only one man turned back when he saw he was healed. He came back to Jesus to thank Him. He shouted, 'Praise God, I am healed!' Then he lay face down on the ground at Jesus' feet because he was so grateful. Jesus asked him, 'Where are the other men who were healed? Doesn't even one of them want to thank God?' Then Jesus told this man, 'You can go home now. Today you were not only healed. You saw how good God is. From now on you are God's friend.'

We must always remember to thank God for all He does for us.

Remember: Thank the Lord for everything He does for us.

We must do what Jesus asks

Luke 14

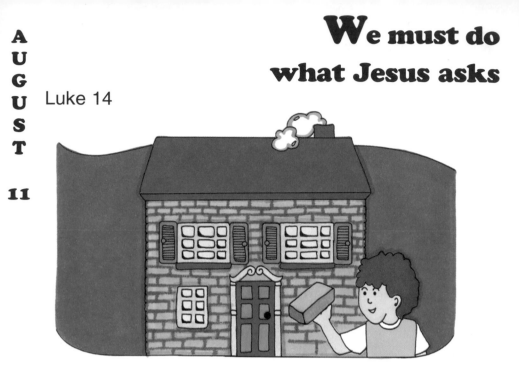

Jesus said, 'No one can become My friend without giving up everything for Me.' (Lk 14:33)

The Lord is our Friend and He is good to us so we must take care not to make Him sad.

When a house is being built the builders need many bricks, cement and a roof. Without bricks and cement, a builder can't build a house. People would laugh at him if he tried. They might say, 'He wants to build a house, but he doesn't have any bricks.' Jesus doesn't want us to be like that – saying we want to be His friends, and then doing nothing about it. It's like wanting to build a house without bothering to get any bricks.

What must we do to be Jesus' friends?
• First of all we must want to be His friend and to trust Him.
• Then we must ask what He wants us to do. We will find that answer in the Bible.
• Sometimes the Lord will ask us to do something we don't really feel like doing, but we must be obedient and do it.

These things are like 'bricks' that build our friendship with Jesus.

🔆 **Remember:** The Bible teaches us God's will.

Talk is cheap

'Son, go out and work on the farm today.' (Mt 21:28)

Going to church is important, but what we do there is even more important. We can sit in church and listen to what the minister is saying but still ignore it. We can sing a lovely hymn to the Lord, but not mean it. Then going to church isn't worthwhile. Going to church only works if we want to listen to the Lord and do what He asks.

Jesus told a story about this. Once there was a man who had two sons. He said to one of them, 'Son, please go and work on my farm today.' 'No,' the boy said, 'I don't feel like it.' Later he felt bad about it. So he went out and worked on the farm.

Then the father called his other son. He asked him the same. 'Yes father, I will go,' he said. But he didn't.

Which son did what the father wanted? The first one, of course.

It's no use us saying we want to serve the Lord. We must do it. If the Lord asks us to do something we must be willing to do it.

-`Ö`- **Remember:** Listen to the Lord.

Helping others is important to the Lord

Matthew 25

'If someone does what the Lord wants, he will be with God in heaven forever.'
(Mt 25:46)

One day the Lord will decide who goes to heaven and who doesn't. We call this the Final Judgment. Jesus will divide all the people into two groups. To one group He will say, 'God wants you to be in heaven with Him.' Do you know why? The Lord gives the answer: 'I was hungry and you fed Me. I was thirsty and you gave Me a drink of water. I was ill and you gave Me medicine.' When they ask, 'Lord, when did we do this for You?' Jesus will answer, 'When you help anyone who is My child you also help Me. If you give someone who is not important a glass of water, it's like giving it to Me.'

To the other group He will say, 'Go away from Me. You are the devil's children. I was thirsty and you wouldn't give Me anything to drink. I was hungry and you didn't even give Me a bite to eat.' They will be surprised and ask, 'When did we see You and not help You?' Jesus will then say, 'You were not willing to help the most unimportant of My children, so you don't want to help Me either.'

We must always help others.

💡 **Remember:** We must always help others.

What you do shows what you are

Matthew 7

'A healthy tree produces good fruit, and an unhealthy tree produces bad fruit.'
(Mt 7:17)

There are people who say they are the Lord's children but they do wicked things. They don't love the Lord. Jesus says we must watch out for these people.

Jesus gave the following example. Only peaches grow on a peach tree. So how will you know if the tree in your garden is a peach tree? By its fruit. If you have a tree that doesn't give you peaches you'll know it's not a peach tree. You'll be able to tell by its fruit what kind of tree it is.

It's the same with people. Watch what they do. Do they love one another? Watch what they say. Are they friendly and are they kind to children? If so, we can tell they are good people. But if a person does and says wicked things all the time, then we know that person is like a tree that is no use to anybody. We must not do wrong things but try to please the Lord. We must always try to grow good fruit in our lives.

 Remember: God's children should be friendly.

We must help one another

Luke 10

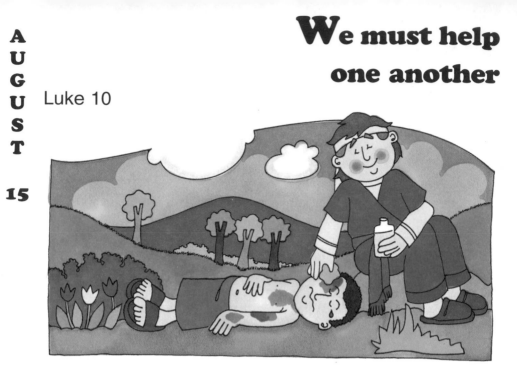

'Go and do the same.' (Lk 10:37)

The Bible says we must help our 'neighbour'. Who is our 'neighbour'? Jesus told a good story to explain it. One day a man was travelling from one town to another. He was attacked by robbers. They beat him up and took all his clothes and money. They left him lying in the road half dead. Two religious people passed by at different times. They saw the man but neither of them helped him. One of them even crossed to the other side of the road.

Then a Samaritan came along. The Jews didn't like Samaritans one bit. They wouldn't even talk to a Samaritan. He saw the man lying there by the roadside and felt very sorry for him. He knelt down beside him and helped him. He put ointment on his wounds and bandaged them. Then he took the man to the nearest inn where he could be looked after. He asked the innkeeper to care for the man and he paid the bill. 'If this is not enough I'll pay the rest when I come back,' the Samaritan said.

Who did the right thing? The Samaritan, of course. We must help others too whether we like them or not. If people need our help we must give it.

🔆 **Remember:** Even if we dislike someone, we should help them.

We must serve one another

'You ought to wash each other's feet.' (Jn 13:14)

In Jesus' time, people didn't have cars. They had to walk. They also didn't sit on chairs and eat at a table. They lay sideways on benches around a table. They always washed their feet before a meal. It was the servants' job to wash people's feet.

Jesus and His friends were getting ready for supper. Suddenly Jesus got up and fetched a basin and a towel. He started washing His friends' feet. His friends were surprised. It just wasn't done – an important person washing the feet of others! When Jesus came to Peter, Peter protested, 'Lord, you are not going to wash my feet.' Jesus answered, 'Well, if you don't want Me to wash your feet, then you are not My friend.' Peter quickly said, 'Then wash my hands and face as well, Lord.' 'No, only your feet,' Jesus answered. Jesus wanted this to be a lesson to His friends. We must never think about our own importance. In church we must be willing to do the unimportant little jobs for the Lord. If He needs us, no matter what for, we must do it.

 Remember: We must be ready to do anything for Jesus.

We must not hurt one another

Matthew 5

'Leave everything and go and make your peace with your brother.' (Mt 5:24)

The Lord doesn't like us to fight. He says fighting is almost like killing a person. It's not good to say things to our friends like, 'You idiot!' or to swear at them or spread rumours about them. It's almost like stabbing them with a knife, in the heart.

This is what Jesus says, 'God is angry with people who talk about others. If we are cross and feel like hurting someone, God gets upset with us.'

If we are in church and remember that a friend is cross with us then we must get up and go and make peace with that person. Afterwards we'll enjoy being in church much more.

We shouldn't look for trouble. Sometimes people hassle us but we must ignore it and not think, 'I'll pay you back, just wait!'

The Lord wants us to keep the peace. He doesn't want us to fight. We should try being friendly with people who are looking for trouble and in the end they won't have any excuse to start a fight.

Remember: Don't look for trouble, find peace.

Forgive one another

Matthew 18

'You must forgive one another.' (Mt 18:35)

One day there was a king who had many farms. He had a foreman on one of these farms. The king decided to bring his accounts up to date. He asked the foreman to help him. Then the king noticed that this man owed him millions of pounds. He couldn't pay it back. In those days a man who owed that kind of money was sold, together with his belongings, to pay off his debts. The king said this man must be sold. He begged the king, 'Oh sir, please be patient with me. I will pay it all.' The king felt sorry for him. He said he could go. He didn't have to pay back anything.

Outside in the street this same foreman came across a man who owed him a few pounds. He called out to him: 'Pay me – now!' 'Please be patient. I will pay you back,' the man answered. But the foreman wouldn't listen. He called the police. They arrested the man and jailed him.

When the king heard about this he couldn't believe it. He sent for the foreman and had him put in prison.

The Lord forgives our sins and He expects us to forgive others. If we don't, He might just decide not to forgive us either.

 Remember: We must forgive other people.

We must love our enemies

Matthew 5

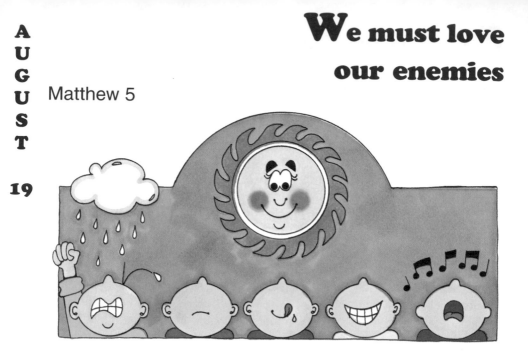

'Love your enemies. Pray for them!' (Mt 5:44)

There are people who say we don't need to love and help everybody. If we don't like someone, we don't have to help him or her. We can treat him or her any way we like – it doesn't matter. Jesus says 'no'.

Jesus wants us to be kind to people we don't like. Even if they hurt us, we must still pray for them and ask the Lord to help them.

The Lord gave us a good example. When He sends rain, does it rain only on the people He likes? No, it rains on all of us. It's the same with the sun. The sun doesn't shine only on some of us. The sun shines on both good and bad people.

So we can't pick and choose who we help because it's wrong not to help others. God's children must follow His example. We must not treat any person badly.

If someone really makes us very angry, do we still need to stay calm and friendly? Jesus says 'yes'. This is how His children should behave.

🔆 **Remember:** God's children should not treat others badly.

Jesus tells his friends what makes Him happy

'Never talk others into doing something wrong.' (Lk 17:1)

One day Jesus and His friends were talking together. Jesus told them how they should behave and answered their questions. What He said can help us:

• Sometimes we do things we shouldn't. It happens to us all but we should never talk others into doing something wrong. Take care.

• If our brother or our friend does something wrong, tell them not to do it. If they say they're sorry, don't sulk and stay angry with them. It doesn't matter how often this happens. Every time he says he's sorry, we must forgive him.

• Jesus' friends asked Him to give them more faith. 'Well,' Jesus said, 'with even a little bit of faith you can do great things. Just trust Me, I will help you.'

• If we have someone who does our housework would we go and clean her house all the time? No, because she works for us, not us for her. We work for the Lord – it's not the other way round. When He gives us something, all we can do is say thank you. We don't deserve it. And it's for free!

☀ **Remember:** We should work for Jesus.

We can talk to the Lord

Matthew 6

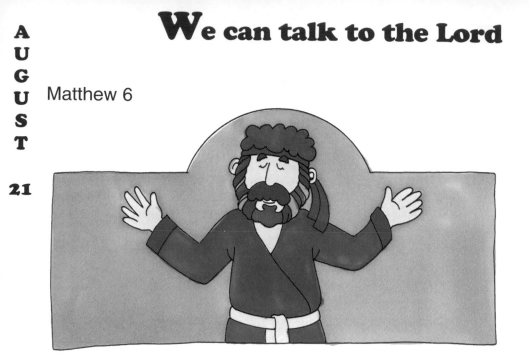

'Pray like this.' (Mt 6:9)

Jesus taught us how to pray:

'Our Father in heaven,
May people see how important You are. There is no-one like You.
May You rule over all like a great king.
Let the people on earth do Your will,
Just like all do in heaven.
Please give us our food for today.
Please forgive us for what we have done wrong,
Just as we forgive others who hurt us.
Please help us against the devil who wants us to sin.
Help us not to listen to him and do wicked things.
Amen.'

When we pray, we need to remember three things:
• We must worship and praise God and ask that everyone will serve Him.
• We can ask God to take care of us.
• We need to ask God to forgive our sins.

🔅 **Remember:** We should pray regularly.

Don't pray if you don't mean what you say

Matthew 6

'Your Father knows exactly what you need even before you ask Him!' (Mt 6:8)

Often people just pray without thinking about what they are saying. The Lord says praying is like talking to Him. We can talk to Him about anything and everything, but we must pray in the right way.

• It is wrong if we don't really care about talking to God but want other people to be impressed by seeing us pray. In Jesus' time people prayed at certain times of the day. Some people wanted others to hear how well they prayed. When prayer time came, they would go where many people were gathered. Then they prayed so that everybody could admire them. These people wanted to appear important and they forgot that they were talking to God.

• It is wrong if people think the longer they pray the more the Lord will listen. If we want to have a long talk with the Lord, that's fine. He will be pleased. But we mustn't think we're going to force the Lord into doing something just because of a long prayer. The Lord listens to us when we pray because He loves us, not because of the length of our prayers.

-�- **Remember:** The Lord listens to us when we pray.

God listens when we pray

Matthew 7

'Keep on asking and you will be given what you ask for.' (Mt 7:7)

'**A**sk and I will give you what you ask for,' the Lord said, 'Keep on looking and you will find. Knock and I will open the door to you. Those who ask will receive.' The Lord always listens to our prayers.

We need to remember that the Lord wants to give us only the best. To demonstrate it He said: 'A boy asks his dad for a slice of bread. Will his father give him a stone? Or if he asks for a fish, does he give him a snake? Of course not!' The Lord in heaven is much better than our fathers on earth. Our earthly fathers give us good things, but our heavenly Father gives us the best.

The Lord knows what is best for us.

Sometimes we ask for something and when He doesn't give us what we asked for, we think the Lord has not heard us. He has, but maybe what we asked for was not the right thing for us.

The Lord wants to give us something better. We must trust Him.

Remember, the Lord hears all our prayers. He answers them. He gives us what is best for us.

Remember: God knows best.

Live flat out for the Lord

Matthew 25

'Good work! Well done!' (Mt 25:21)

One day a man had to go on a long journey, so he gave each of his workers some money to do business for him while he was away. He gave one 5000 pounds, a second 2000 pounds and the third one 1000 pounds. Then he left on his trip.

The one who was given 5000 pounds began doing business straight away and soon doubled the money. The worker who had 2000 pounds did the same, but the man who received 1000 pounds dug a hole in the ground and hid the money in it for safekeeping. After a long time the owner came back home. The workers with the 5000 pounds and 2000 pounds each gave him double his money back. He said, 'Well done! You have done good work!' Next was the man with the 1000 pounds. He gave the 1000 pounds back to the owner. He said, 'Sir, I know you are a hard man so I hid the money. I was afraid I would lose it all.' The owner was angry. 'You lazy man,' he said. 'You could at least have put the money in a bank where it would have earned interest.' The owner took the money from him and gave it to the other two men.

The Lord has also given us talents. We must use them, not hide them.

Remember: We mustn't hide the talents God has given us.

A U G U S T

25

We need to give the Lord only the best

Luke 21

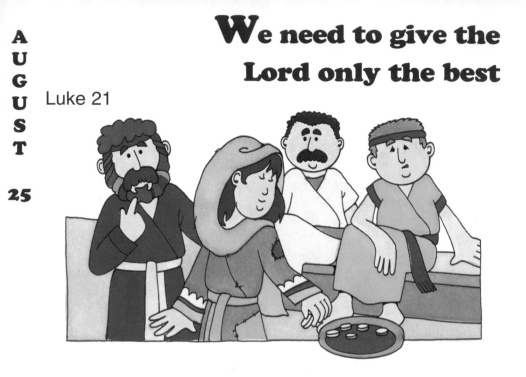

Jesus told them, 'This poor woman has given more than all the rest.' (Lk 21:3)

One day Jesus and His friends were at the temple. They watched as the people put their money into the collection box. There were many rich people. They put a lot of money in the box. Then a poor widow came by. She dropped a few coins into the collection box.

It wasn't much, but Jesus said, 'Do you know, this woman gave more than all the others? The other people put in a lot of money, but they could afford it, because they are rich. Even after giving a large sum, they have plenty of money left.

'This poor woman had only a few coins. She put all of them in the box. She has nothing left for food but she wanted to give the Lord the best she could, so she gave Him all she had.'

The Lord sees into our hearts. He wants us to give Him our best. It doesn't matter if it isn't as much as other people give as long as it comes from our hearts.

When we give to the Lord, it must be because we love Him – and that will make Him very happy.

💡 **Remember:** We must give to the Lord because we love Him.

Store up treasures in heaven

Matthew 6

'Store your treasures in heaven.' (Mt 6:20)

Some people want money so much that they work hard for it, but when they die their money means nothing to them. Their cars rust away. The moths eat their clothes and the food they stored up goes bad. They can take nothing with them.

Jesus says we shouldn't spend our time storing up money and possessions. We should spend our time on making the Lord happy. 'Store up treasures in heaven,' He said, 'There moths won't eat them and they will be safe from thieves.'

An old priest, Augustine, asked how we can get treasures in heaven. We cannot take them there by car or send them by train, so he said if you give something to everyone on their way to heaven, they can take it there for you. This is a way of getting treasures in heaven. If we give people smiles, we will get smiles back in heaven. If we help people, we will be helped in heaven. We could say that what we do for the Lord here on earth, He will do for us in heaven.

💡 **Remember:** Spend time making the Lord happy.

Jesus will take care of you

John 10

'I am the good Shepherd.' (Jn 10:11)

Jesus told a story to show how much He loved His friends. The story is about a shepherd and his sheep. He is a very good shepherd. He knows every one of his sheep. His sheep love him too. They want to be near him. In the morning when he comes into the sheep-pen, they are happy. They want to go into the fields with him to graze. They know the shepherd will take them to the best places. We should be happy when we wake up knowing we can spend the day with Jesus. We should try to please Him.

Jesus went on with the story. One day a wolf tried to catch the sheep. An ordinary shepherd would have left the sheep and run away in case the wolf attacked him. The good shepherd doesn't do that. He fights the wolf, even though he knows the wolf can kill him. He will give his own life for his sheep – that's how much he loves them. And that's how much Jesus loves us. He gave His life on the cross for us. One day our bodies will die but God will bring us back to life again to live with Him in heaven forever.

·¤· **Remember:** God will one day take His children to heaven.

When you are afraid, He is there

Matthew 8

'Why are you afraid? Don't you have faith in Me?' (Mt 8:26)

One day Jesus and His disciples started across the lake in a boat. Suddenly a terrible storm came up. A strong wind started blowing. The waves were so big they broke into the boat.

Jesus was so tired that He stayed fast asleep. Jesus' friends were afraid. They thought the boat was going to sink. They woke Him up, shouting, 'Lord, save us! We are going to drown.'

Jesus said, 'Why are you afraid? Don't you trust Me?'

Then He stood up. He told the waves and the wind to die down. Suddenly all was calm. Jesus' friends were amazed. The wind and the sea don't obey just anyone.

Jesus is with us now just as He was when He was in that boat with His friends. We may sometimes think Jesus has forgotten about us – that's what His friends in the boat thought – but it's not true!

We needn't be afraid. Jesus is with us always. We can be sure of that.

:'ᗉ': **Remember:** We need not be afraid because Jesus is with us.

You are never alone – Jesus is with you

John 5

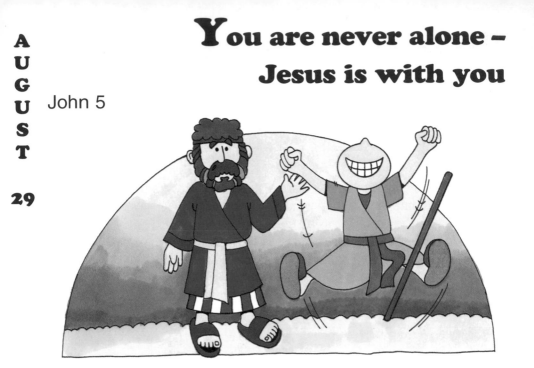

"Stand up, pick up your mat and walk!" (Jn 5:8)

One day Jesus walked past the Pool of Bethesda. Many sick people crowded around the pool. Some couldn't see and others couldn't walk. They believed the first one to jump in the pool when the water stirred, would be healed.

One of the men lying there had been sick for thirty-eight years. Jesus asked the man, 'Would you like to get well?' 'I can't, Sir,' the sick man said. 'I have no one to help me into the pool when the water is stirred up. While I am trying to get there, someone else always gets there before me.'

Jesus said to him, 'Stand up, pick up your mat, and walk!' Instantly the man was healed. He took his mat and walked away.

This happened on the Sabbath. The Pharisees saw what Jesus had done and were very angry. They said Jesus had broken the Jewish laws. They weren't even glad that Jesus had healed the man.

Jesus will be our Friend even if we have no other friends. So we are never alone, because Jesus is with us.

💡 **Remember:** Jesus' friends need not feel alone.

Jesus can do things for us that no-one else can

John 11

"I will give you everlasting life." (Jn 11:25)

Lazarus, one of Jesus' friends, was sick. His sisters sent Jesus a message to come and help His friend. Jesus didn't go at once. He waited for a few days. People didn't understand why but Jesus had His reasons.

Four days later Jesus arrived at Lazarus' house. His sister, Martha, came running to Jesus: 'Lord, if You had been here, my brother would not have died.' Jesus answered, 'Don't worry. I will bring him back to life again.' Martha called her sister, Mary. Together they went to the grave. Jesus was sad when He saw everyone crying. The people were saying, 'He loved Lazarus. If He had been here He might have helped him. Then Lazarus might not have died.'

Then Jesus said, 'Open up the grave.' Martha tried to stop them. 'Lord, he has been dead for four days!' Jesus' answer was, 'Martha, didn't I tell you that you will see God's power?' So they opened up the grave. Jesus said, 'Lazarus, come out!' And Lazarus came out of the grave. 'Take him home,' Jesus said.

💡 **Remember:** One day Jesus will raise the dead.

Be prepared and be faithful

Luke 12

"You will be glad if the Lord finds you busy working for Him." (Lk 12:43)

Jesus told another story. Once there was a man who had a large house. He had to go away for a while so he asked one of his servants to look after the place for him. He had to make sure that the other servants had what they needed and he had to check up on them.

What will the owner of the house do when he gets home and finds that the servant he left in charge has done everything he was asked to do? The owner will be very pleased. He will thank the man and treat him well.

But say the owner comes back and finds everything in a mess? The servant he left in charge said to himself, 'The owner is taking too long to come back.' So he started treating the other servants badly. He didn't do his work anymore and got drunk instead. The owner will not like this at all. He'll give the man the sack.

We must be ready when the Lord comes again. That means we must live every day in a way that pleases the Lord.

☀ **Remember:** We must be prepared for Jesus' Second Coming.

Serve the Lord now, before it's too late

Luke 16

"Listen to the Bible." (Lk 16:31)

One day there was a very rich man. A poor man named Lazarus sat at the rich man's back door. There he found pieces of left-over food. He was sick, but the rich man didn't help him.

Then Lazarus died. The angels carried him to heaven. The rich man also died but he landed up in hell. He was doubled up with pain. Then in his misery he saw Lazarus and Abraham in the distance. He shouted, 'Please help me. Send Lazarus with a drop of water. I am so thirsty in these flames.'

Abraham answered, 'During your lifetime on earth you didn't help anybody, including Lazarus. Now it is your turn to suffer.'

The rich man pleaded, 'Please send someone from heaven to warn my father and my five brothers, so that they don't end up in hell.' Abraham said, 'They have the Bible.' The rich man replied, 'But it will be better if someone talks to them from the dead.' But Abraham said, 'If they don't listen to the Bible, they won't listen to anything else.'

The Bible tells us everything we need to know. We must listen!

Remember: The Bible tells us everything we need to know.

The Lord loves us, faults and all

Luke 15

"When his father saw his son in the distance, he ran to him and put his arms around him." (Lk 15:20)

A father had two sons. The youngest said, 'Dad, I want my share of your money now, instead of waiting till you die.'

The boy's father gave him his share. The boy packed all his things and went on a journey to a faraway country. There he went to one wild party after another and wasted all his money. Eventually he didn't even have money for food. He got a job looking after pigs but he was so hungry that he was tempted to eat the food the pigs ate.

Then he thought to himself, 'At home there is enough food. I'll go back home to my father.' So he went back home. He was still far from the house when his father saw him. He ran to his son and took him in his arms. The boy said, 'I'm so sorry, Dad. I know I am not good enough to be called your son anymore.' His father didn't even listen, but told his servants, 'Go and cook the best food. Bring the best clothes. My son was gone but now he is back.'

The Lord is like this father. If we are sorry, He will forgive us.

💡 **Remember:** God is our heavenly Father. He loves us very much.

We must confess our sins

Luke 18

'O God, be merciful to me, for I am a sinner.' (Lk 18:13)

One day Jesus told a story about two men who went to the temple to pray. One of them was an important man who appeared to be very religious. He didn't love the Lord that much, he just wanted to make other people think he was better than them. He prayed, 'Lord, I want to thank You that I am not a sinner like everyone else. I never cheat. I don't lie. I do everything I should.' He went on and on about how good he was.

The other man was a tax collector. Everybody hated tax collectors. He knew he had made mistakes and he was ashamed of them. He didn't dare to lift his eyes to heaven as he prayed, 'O God, I have done bad things. I am a sinner. Please forgive me, even if I don't deserve it.'

Which of these two prayers did the Lord like best? The second one of course. The first man made the mistake of thinking he was very important and that he could do without God. The second man knew he needed the Lord because of all his sins. Only the Lord can forgive sins.

If we have done something wrong, we must tell the Lord we are sorry, and mean what we say. Then we must not do it again.

 Remember: The Lord will forgive us our sins if we confess.

There are wicked people who don't love Jesus

Matthew 21

'The farmer will give the farm to others.' (Mt 21:41)

Once a farmer had a beautiful farm with many fruit trees. He looked after the trees well. Then he had to go away for a long time. He decided to rent out his farm and the tenants agreed to give him a share of the fruit crop.

At harvest time he sent a worker to fetch his share of the fruit. The tenants refused to give it to him. They were rude to the worker, beat him up and chased him off the farm. The owner tried again and sent another worker. The same thing happened to him. Next he sent his son. He thought they wouldn't touch his son. He was wrong – they killed him! They said, 'If the boy is dead, there is no-one to inherit the farm. Then we can keep it.'

What will the owner do when he gets back? He will certainly punish those tenants severely.

God is like the owner who sent His Son to the people. Some of them don't want to be His friend. One day, when God comes again, He will punish them.

-ᆞᄋᆞ- **Remember:** People who don't listen to the Lord, will be punished.

You find evil people everywhere

Matthew 13

'He planted weeds among the good seed.' (Mt 13:25)

There are people all over the world who don't like Jesus. Jesus told this story.

A farmer planted good seed in his field. One night while everyone was asleep, people who didn't like him came to his field. They planted weeds among the good seed. Then they ran away.

The crop began to grow. The weeds looked a lot like the wheat. But one day the farmer's servants told him, 'Sir, the field where you planted that good seed is full of weeds!' He realized the weeds had been planted by his enemies.

'Shall we pull out the weeds?' the servants asked. 'No,' the farmer said, 'you might pull out the wheat together with the weeds. Let both grow together until the harvest. Then we'll be able to tell which is which. We'll burn the weeds and put the wheat in the barn.'

This is the way it is in the world as well. People who love Jesus live among those who don't. When Jesus comes again, those who love Him will go to heaven with Him. The rest will be punished.

Remember: Those who do not love the Lord will be sorry.

To Jerusalem – praise the Lord!

Matthew 21

'Praise Him who is coming. He is our Lord.' (Mt 21:9)

Jesus went to Jerusalem. The time for Him to be crucified was coming closer and He knew it. He said to two of His friends, 'Go to the village over there. You will see a donkey. Bring the donkey here. If anyone asks what you are doing, just say, "The Lord needs him. He will send him back soon."' So they brought Jesus the donkey. In the Old Testament it says Jesus will ride into Jerusalem on a donkey. His friends threw clothes over the donkey's back. Then Jesus climbed onto the donkey and rode towards Jerusalem. Crowds gathered along the roadside. Most of them spread their coats on the road ahead of Jesus. Others cut branches from palm trees and spread them across the road. This was their way of showing how great Jesus was. They treated Him like a king and shouted, 'Praise the Lord. Bless the one who comes in the name of the Lord.'

In Jerusalem everyone came to see what was going on. 'Who is this man?' they asked. And the crowds replied, 'It's Jesus of Nazareth.'

A few days later Jesus was crucified. But when He rose from the dead, He showed that He was indeed King of kings.

☀ **Remember:** Jesus is more important than any worldly ruler.

A woman shows how important Jesus is

John 12

Jesus said, 'Leave her alone. You will always have the poor among you.' (Jn 12:7-8)

A short while before Jesus was crucified, He was invited to dinner by Lazarus and his sisters Mary and Martha. Mary came up to Jesus with a small bottle of very expensive perfume. She rubbed the perfume on Jesus' feet. In those times it was a sign of great respect. Then Mary dried Jesus' feet with her long hair. The lovely smell filled the whole house.

But Judas Iscariot, who looked after the money, was very angry. He said, 'Why waste the perfume like this? We could have sold it and given the money to the poor.' Judas was the one who would, in the end, betray Jesus. He didn't really want the money for the poor – he wanted it for himself.

Then Jesus said, 'She only wanted to show how important I am to her. You will always have the poor among you. There will be enough time to help them. I am going away one of these days. Then it will be too late to do something for Me.' We must make use of every chance we get to do things for the Lord.

Remember: Always try to do something to make Jesus happy.

Jesus celebrates Holy Communion

Matthew 26

Jesus broke the bread and said, 'Take it and eat it, for this is My body.' (Mt 26:26)

The night before Jesus was crucified He wanted to have supper with His friends one last time. 'Where should we have the Passover supper?' His friends wanted to know. 'Go to one of My friends in Jerusalem,' Jesus said. 'Ask him if we can eat the Passover meal at his house.' The disciples did what Jesus said.

As they were eating, Jesus took a loaf of bread and asked God's blessing on it. Then He broke it in pieces and gave each of His friends a piece, saying, 'Take it and eat it. It is My body.' Then He took a cup of wine and gave thanks to God. He said, 'Each of you drink from it. This is My blood poured out so that your sins can be forgiven. Then you will be friends of God again. You must celebrate this last supper with bread and wine until I come back one day. Every time you do it, you must remember Me.' Then they sang a hymn and went to a garden called Gethsemane.

To this day we celebrate this last supper. We call it Holy Communion. Every time we celebrate Holy Communion, we know Jesus loves us and one day will come back to fetch us.

💡 **Remember:** One day, Jesus will come back to fetch us.

Judas the betrayer

Matthew 26

'The truth is, one of you will betray Me,' Jesus said. (Mt 26:21)

The leaders of the Jews didn't like Jesus. They wanted to kill Him. Judas went to them.

'I'll help you,' he said. 'How much will you pay me to betray Jesus?' They paid him thirty pieces of silver.

That night when Jesus and His friends had their last supper together, Judas was there.

Jesus knew what Judas was going to do. While they were eating, Jesus said, 'One of you will betray Me.' Jesus' friends were shocked.

Then Jesus said, 'I will show you. It is the one who dips his bread in the dish with Me.'

Judas made out it wasn't him but later that night he left. He told the soldiers Jesus and His friends would be in the Garden of Gethsemane and that he would show them where to find Jesus.

It was terrible that one of Jesus' friends betrayed Him. It shows us that a person can sit in church and listen to the devil instead of God. It breaks Jesus' heart.

Remember: Don't listen to the devil. Listen to Jesus.

Jesus prays before He is captured

Matthew 26

'Don't do what I want. I want Your will, not Mine,' Jesus said. (Mt 26:39)

Jesus and His friends went to Gethsemane as planned. He asked His friends to wait there. He went on to pray, taking three of His friends with Him. One of them was Peter. 'I am afraid. Stay with Me. Could you stay awake and watch over Me?' Jesus said.

Jesus went on a little farther and prayed. 'My Father! If it is possible, please don't let Me suffer too much. But don't do what I want. Do what You want.' Then Jesus went back to His three friends. They were fast asleep. Jesus woke them up and said, 'Couldn't you stay awake for Me even for a little while?' Then Jesus went back to pray. He said, 'My Father, if I must suffer, then let it be.' When Jesus came back, His three friends were asleep again. He left them to sleep and went back to pray.

Finally He woke His friends and said, 'Let's go. Judas, who will betray Me, is on his way.'

Jesus died on the cross. He died for us. It was not easy for Him to do it but He did it for us.

☼ **Remember:** Jesus died on the cross for us.

Jesus is captured

'He is the One I will greet with a kiss. Grab Him.' Judas said. (Mt 26:48)

After Jesus had prayed, Judas arrived. He brought a mob along with him who were armed with swords and clubs. They brought lights to look for Jesus. Judas identified Jesus. He said to the soldiers, 'He is the One I will greet with a kiss. Grab Him.' So he walked towards Jesus and greeted Him with a kiss. Then the soldiers arrested Jesus.

Peter pulled out his sword. He cut off the high priest's servant's ear. Jesus calmed him down. 'Put away your sword,' He said. 'If you start killing people with your sword, you will soon be killed yourself. I must be captured. If I don't want it to happen, I can ask the angels to help Me. Thousands of them are ready and waiting to do so. But this must happen the way the Bible said it would, a long time ago.'

Then Jesus turned to the soldiers and said, 'Why are you armed with swords and clubs to arrest me? Am I some dangerous criminal? Why didn't you arrest Me when I taught in the temple? I was there every day.'

Then the soldiers took Jesus away and the words of the prophets recorded in the Bible a long time ago, came true.

Remember: A long time ago God prophesied that Jesus would die.

Jesus protects His friends

John 18

Jesus said, 'Let my friends go.' (Jn 18:8)

Just before the soldiers took Jesus away, something happened. All of Jesus' friends were in the Garden of Gethsemane with Him and the soldiers were going to arrest them too. But Jesus would not allow this to happen.

Jesus asked the soldiers who they were looking for. They answered, 'Jesus of Nazareth.'

'I am Jesus of Nazareth,' He said. 'And since I am the one you want, let these others go.'

Then Jesus' friends ran away. One of them ran off in such a hurry that he left some of his clothes behind!

All of Jesus' friends escaped. Some time back Jesus had promised to protect them and He kept His word. The soldiers just looked on as Jesus' friends deserted Him. Although they were there to arrest Jesus, they couldn't do anything He didn't want.

🔅 **Remember:** Jesus will not desert His friends.

Peter denies Jesus

Matthew 26

Peter said, 'I don't even know the man.' (Mt 26:72)

Peter and a friend of his followed the soldiers who had arrested Jesus. They wanted to see what would happen to Him. The soldiers took Jesus to the home of the high priest. He was the most important of all the Jews and had to decide what to do with Jesus.

Peter sat outside in the courtyard. One of the high priest's servants said to him, 'You were one of those with Jesus, weren't you?' But Peter denied it in front of everybody. 'I don't know what you're talking about,' he said.

Someone else noticed him and said, 'Yes, he was with Jesus.' Again Peter denied it, 'I don't know the man!' He even used bad language to show how serious he was. But yet another man said, 'I can tell by your accent that you are one of the men who went round with Jesus.' Now Peter shouted, 'I swear I don't know this man!'

At that moment, Peter heard a cock crow. Suddenly he remembered what Jesus had said to him at the last supper, 'Before the cock crows, you will say three times that you don't know Me.'

Peter walked away crying bitterly.

💡 **Remember:** Never be ashamed of being Jesus' friend.

Jesus on trial before the Jews

Matthew 26

The high priest asked, 'Are You Christ, the Son of God?' (Mt 26:63)

The leader of the Jews was the high priest, Caiaphas. He called all the important Jews together. They were trying to find a reason for killing Jesus. People were saying wicked things about Jesus, but they were lying. One said, 'Jesus said He will destroy the temple.' The high priest asked Jesus, 'What do you say to this?' Jesus said nothing. Then the high priest asked Jesus, 'Are You the One sent specially by God to come and help His people?' Jesus answered, 'Yes, I am. It is true. You will see it is true.'

The high priest called out, 'You are insulting God! We don't need any more witnesses. You have shown us how wicked You are.' Then the high priest pretended to be upset. He asked the others what he should do. 'Guilty!' they shouted. 'He must die!' Then they spat in Jesus' face and hit him with their fists. 'You are the Special One from God,' they mocked Him. 'Come on then, tell us the names of those who are beating You up!'

Then they tied Jesus' hands and sent Him to Pilate, the Roman governor. Only he could pass the death sentence.

💡 **Remember:** Jesus was sent by God to help us.

Jesus' trial before Pilate

Matthew 27

'Crucify Him!' they all shouted. (Mt 27:22)

Very early in the morning Jesus was brought before Pilate. 'Are You the king of the Jews?' Pilate asked Him. 'Yes,' answered Jesus. Pilate talked to Jesus some more but he couldn't find Jesus guilty of anything. He realized Jesus was innocent and he wanted to release Him. Every Passover a prisoner was set free. At this time there was a murderer called Barabbas in jail so Pilate asked the crowd, 'Which of these two do you want me to set free, Jesus or Barabbas?' The crowd shouted, 'Barabbas!' The leaders of the Jews had stirred up the crowd to say this.

Pilate didn't know what to do. Even his wife had dreamt that Jesus was innocent. When the people wanted Barabbas freed, Pilate asked them, 'What should I do with Jesus?' They shouted, 'Crucify Him!' 'Why?' asked Pilate. 'What has He done?' But nobody was listening. They just roared louder, 'Crucify Him!' Pilate saw that nothing would make them change their minds, so he washed his hands in a bowl of water and said, 'You are the ones who want to kill Jesus. I am innocent of His death.' The soldiers took Jesus away to crucify Him.

💡 **Remember:** Jesus was not guilty but He died for our sins.

Judas dies

Matthew 27

'I have done a terrible thing. Jesus was innocent and I betrayed Him.' (Mt 27:4)

Judas betrayed Jesus but when he heard that Jesus was going to be crucified he felt very bad about what he had done. He took the money he'd been paid for betraying Jesus back to the high priest. He said, 'I have done a terrible thing. Jesus was innocent and I betrayed him.' The priests answered, 'That is your problem. What do we care?'

Judas threw the money back at them. Then he went out and hanged himself.

The priests at the temple wondered what to do with the money. They couldn't use it for the temple because it was payment for betrayal. They decided to buy a piece of land with the money. It would be used as a graveyard for people who had no family. That ground is still called the Field of Blood.

We must think before we act. We're often sorry about something we've done and sometimes it's too late to put it right.

-ϙ́- **Remember:** It is better to be safe than sorry.

Jesus is crucified

'This is Jesus, the King of the Jews.' (Mt 27:37)

The soldiers took Jesus away to crucify Him. But first they hurt Him very badly. They put a crown of long, sharp thorns on His head. They made fun of Him and spat in His face. They beat Him on the head with a stick. Then they gave Him His cross. He had to carry it Himself.

Jesus was crucified just outside the city. The place is called Golgotha. It means 'Skull Hill'. After a while Jesus couldn't carry the cross anymore so Simon, who was from Cyrene, helped Him.

At Golgotha the soldiers nailed Jesus to the cross. They divided His clothes among them and fastened a notice to the cross above Jesus' head. It read: 'This is Jesus, the King of the Jews.'

Two criminals were crucified with Jesus, one on either side of Him. One of them made fun of Jesus and mocked Him, but not the other one. Jesus told this man, 'Today you will be with Me in paradise.' The high priest and the other Jews also made fun of Jesus: 'You saved others. Well then, come down from the cross and save yourself.' This is how Jesus suffered on the cross – for each of us.

Remember: Jesus suffered on the cross – for each one of us.

Jesus is the Son of God

Matthew 27

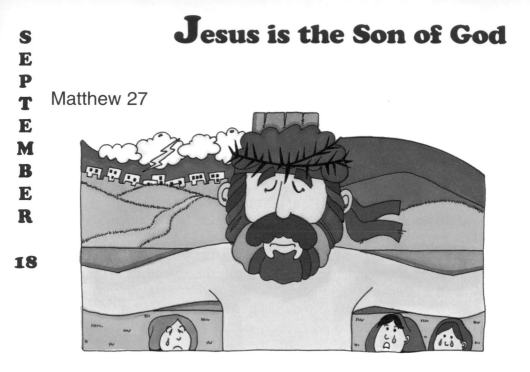

They said, 'Truly, this was the Son of God.' (Mt 27:54)

Jesus was crucified at twelve o'clock, in the middle of the day. Suddenly it became dark and stayed that way until three o'clock. Then Jesus shouted out in a loud voice, 'My God, My God, why have You left Me all alone?' The people standing near the cross couldn't make out exactly what He was saying, so they said, 'Listen, He is calling the prophet Elijah to come and help Him.' One of them filled a sponge with vinegar for Jesus to drink. Then Jesus called out again, 'I have done what I had to.' His head fell forward and He breathed His last.

At that moment the earth shook. Rocks split apart. The curtain in the temple (which kept people out of the holy place of God) was torn in two. Even people who had died came back to life.

The soldiers who were guarding Jesus and the other two saw it all. They were terrified and said, 'Truly, this was the Son of God.'

Jesus' mother and some of her friends were there too. Jesus was dead – but it was not the end of the story.

🔅 **Remember:** Jesus did everything He could for us.

Jesus is buried

Matthew 27

Joseph took Jesus' body and buried it. (Mt 27:59-60)

Late in the afternoon of the day Jesus was crucified, a rich man went to Pilate and asked for Jesus' body. He was one of Jesus' friends. His name was Joseph and he was from Arimathea. He asked Pilate if he could bury the body. Pilate gave his permission.

So Joseph took Jesus' body and prepared to bury it. In those days they wrapped the bodies in a white cloth. On the cloth they put all kinds of sweet-smelling herbs. After doing this Joseph put Jesus in a grave. The grave was like a room carved out of the rock. Joseph rolled a very big stone against the door of this room as he left.

The next day the leaders of the Jews went to Pilate. They said, 'Jesus said He would rise from the dead after three days. We think His friends are going to steal His body. Then they will say He has risen.' So Pilate sent soldiers to guard the grave. If Jesus' disciples wanted to steal His body, they would stop them – but Jesus was only in the grave for three days ...

Remember: Be prepared for Jesus' Second Coming.

Jesus is raised from the dead

Matthew 28

'Jesus isn't here anymore. He has been raised from the dead, just as He said.'
(Mt 28:6)

At daybreak on the Sunday morning after Jesus was crucified, Mary and Mary Magdalene went to see the grave.

Suddenly there was a great earthquake. An angel came down from heaven. He rolled away the stone at the opening of the tomb and sat on it. His face shone like lightning. His clothes were white as snow. The guards shook with fear when they saw him. They were so frightened that they couldn't move. Some of them fainted.

Then the angel spoke to the women, 'Don't be afraid. I know you are looking for Jesus. He is not here anymore. He is alive again. He said it would happen. Come closer. This is where His body lay. See for yourselves, the grave is empty.' Then the angel told the women to tell Jesus' friends what had happened.

As the women turned to go, they saw Jesus standing there. He spoke to them and said, 'Don't be frightened. Go and tell My friends I am on my way to them.'

The women hurried off to tell Jesus' friends.

💡 **Remember:** Jesus' grave was empty. He rose from the dead.

Jesus' friends see Him

Luke 24

They were terribly frightened. They thought they were seeing a ghost. (Lk 24:37)

Jesus' friends talked about everything that had happened. There was the cross, then Jesus was buried, then the grave was empty, then Jesus appeared to the women. So many things had happened in just three days. While they were sitting there, talking, something else happened. Suddenly Jesus was there with them. They were afraid. They thought they were seeing a ghost.

Jesus said to them, 'Why are you frightened? Why do you doubt who I am? Look at My hands. Look at My feet. Touch Me and make sure I am not a ghost, because ghosts don't have bodies.'

Jesus' friends were overjoyed. They couldn't believe their eyes. Jesus was really standing there with them. They could talk to Him again! Then Jesus asked them for something to eat. They gave Him a piece of fish and watched as He ate it. This was no ghost!

Then Jesus talked to them. He helped them to understand the Old Testament which said that all these things would happen. The promises God made then, had come true.

 Remember: Jesus made it clear – God keeps His promises.

Jesus appears to two men

Luke 24

'The Lord has really risen! He appeared to Peter!' (Lk 24:34)

Two men were on their way to Emmaus, a village near Jerusalem. As they walked along, Jesus started walking beside them. They didn't recognize Him. Jesus asked them, 'What are you talking about?' One of the men, Cleopas, replied, 'You must be the only person in Jerusalem who hasn't heard about all the things that have happened the last few days.' 'What things?' Jesus asked.

'The things that happened to Jesus, the man from Nazareth. He preached beautifully. He also did wonderful things. Then the chief priests and rulers arrested Him and He was crucified. We really hoped He was going to help us.'

Jesus said, 'Don't you believe what the Old Testament says? All of these things had to happen to Jesus.' Then Jesus explained to them how God had made all His promises in the Old Testament come true.

It was getting late. While they were having supper together, they suddenly recognized Jesus. They were very excited and they hurried to tell everybody that Jesus really was alive again.

-ᗉ- **Remember:** People hoped that Jesus would help them and He did.

Thomas exclaims, "My Lord and my God"

John 20

Thomas said to Jesus, 'My Lord and my God.' (Jn 20:28)

One night all of Jesus' friends were together, including Thomas who hadn't been with them when they first saw Jesus. They had told Thomas about it but he didn't believe them. How can a dead person come back to life?

That night all the doors were locked. Yet, sudddenly Jesus was there with them. He said, 'Peace be with you.' He looked at Thomas and said, 'Put your finger here and see My hands. Touch them. Come, put your hand here where they put the sword in.' Jesus wanted Thomas to know that He was not a ghost; He had really come back to life.

The last time Thomas had seen Jesus He was nailed to the cross. Now He was standing in front of him, alive. How was it possible? Only God could have done it. All that Thomas could say was, 'My Lord and My God.'

Jesus said to him, 'You believe because you have seen Me. There will be people who will not see Me with their eyes. They will also believe and they will be happy.' We can't see Jesus with our eyes, but we know He is there and it makes us happy.

💡 **Remember:** We cannot see Jesus but we know He is there.

Jesus appears to His friends again

John 21

Then one of Jesus' friends said to Peter, 'It is the Lord!' (Jn 21:7)

"I'm going fishing," Peter said one day. 'We're coming along,' his friends said, so they went out on the lake in their boat. They caught nothing all night.

At sunrise, they saw someone standing on the beach, but they couldn't see who it was. He called out, 'Have you caught any fish?' 'No,' they replied. 'Throw out your net on the other side of the boat, and you'll get plenty of fish!' he said.

They did and they caught so many fish that the net was too heavy to pull into the boat.

One of Jesus' friends then said to Peter, 'That man is the Lord.' Peter jumped into the water straight away and started swimming. They weren't far from the shore. The others followed in the boat. When they got there, Jesus already had a fire burning and was busy cooking fish over it. There was bread as well and His friends brought some of the fish they'd just caught. They had a lovely meal together.

Jesus' friends knew He was alive. He had died, but now He was alive again. It made them so happy.

💡 **Remember:** The Lord lives!

We must love Jesus, that's what He wants

John 21

'Simon, do you love Me?' Jesus asked. (Jn 21:15)

After breakfast Jesus and Peter were talking.

Jesus asked Peter, 'Peter, do you love Me?'

Peter answered Jesus, 'Yes, Lord, You know I love You.' Jesus said, 'Then you must take good care of God's children.'

Jesus asked him a second time, 'Peter, do you love Me?' 'Of course, Lord, You know that I love You,' Peter answered. 'Look after my people,' Jesus said.

A third time Jesus asked Peter, 'Do you love Me?' This made Peter very sad: 'Lord, You know everything. You know I love You.' And again Jesus said, 'Take good care of the children of God.'

Then Jesus went away. But He made sure His friends were not alone. They had to be one another's friends.

Christians must take care of one another. It pleases the Lord.

 Remember: Christians should help one another.

Jesus sends His people to tell everybody about Him

Matthew 28

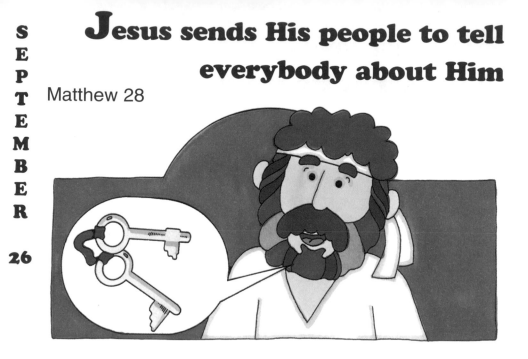

'Go to all people. Tell them about Me and make them My friends.' (Mt 28:19)

Before Jesus went back to heaven, He first told His friends what He wanted them to do.

He said, 'No-one is as poweful as I am. I am the most powerful of all in heaven and on earth. Go to all people. Tell them about Me. Make them My friends.'

'If they believe in Me, you must baptize them. Then you must tell them how to be good Christians. Tell them what makes God happy,' He continued.

Jesus went on talking. He told them, 'You are almost like people who have the keys to heaven. When you tell someone about Me, you unlock heaven's door to him or her. If someone won't listen, you can lock him or her out of heaven. And always remember – I am with you. I will always be with you.'

If we are Jesus' friends, we must tell our friends about Him. Just think how happy Jesus will be if we and all our friends love Him.

🔆 **Remember:** We must tell our friends Jesus wants to be their Friend.

Jesus sends us a special Helper

John 16

'When the Holy Spirit comes, He will help you to do and think what is right.'
(Jn 16:13)

We have heard all about the things Jesus did. Next we hear what happened to His friends after Jesus went to heaven.

Jesus said His friends should tell everybody about Him. We need to do the same if we are His children. Sometimes we feel a little nervous about doing this but Jesus said we should never be afraid. He sends us a special Helper. This is the Holy Spirit. The Holy Spirit is very powerful. The Spirit knows what God wants. That's how He knows how to help us.

We needn't be afraid of the devil. The Holy Spirit is there to help us and to protect us.

If we don't know what to do, we can pray. The Holy Spirit will tell us what to do. We must pray to the Lord every day and ask Him to help us. Remember, we have a special Helper – the Holy Spirit.

We can't see the Holy Spirit, but that doesn't mean He isn't there. The Spirit is in us and that's why He can really help us.

 Remember: God sent the Holy Spirit to be our special Helper.

Jesus is going to get our place in heaven ready

John 14

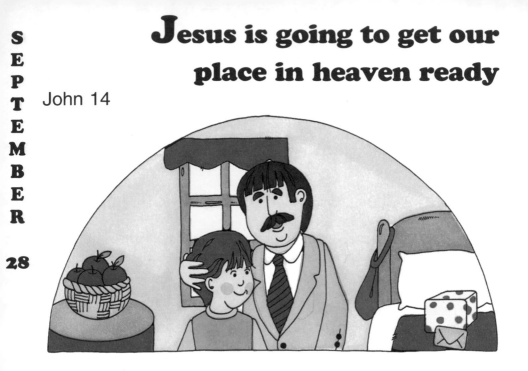

'Trust God, now trust in Me.' (Jn 14:1)

When Jesus was still with His friends on earth, He told them He would one day go back to heaven where His Father is. His friends didn't really understand what He meant so Jesus told them why He was going there.

Say a father's children have been away from home for a very long time but the father knows they are coming home the next day. What does he do? Of course he will see that their beds are made, their rooms are neat, and that there is enough to eat. Everything must be just right.

Jesus says that He will do the same for us. He is going back to His Father's house to get everything ready. All God's children are going to heaven one day. Jesus will make sure that our place is ready for us. If we are God's children, there is room for us to live with Jesus in heaven, the home of God.

We should be happy that Jesus went to heaven and we can be sure our place in heaven is ready.

Remember: Jesus has prepared a special place for us in heaven.

Five girls are ready and five not

Matthew 25

'Be ready. You don't know when the Lord is coming.' (Mt 25:13)

We must always give the Lord only our best. If He comes today, He must be happy with us. Listen to this story.

Once there was a wedding. In the olden days they did things differently. First the men had a party at the groom's house. The women dressed the bride at her home. When the men were ready, they walked from the groom's house to the bride's. The guests waited along the road. When the men came past, they joined them. Everybody had lamps which they carried as they walked together to the bride's house.

Once ten girls were waiting like this for the bridegroom. He took a long time. The lamps of five of the girls went out. They wanted to borrow oil for their lamps from the other girls but the others had only just enough for themselves. So they had to go to a shop for oil. While they were away, the bridegroom came past. The girls who were waiting for him along the road joined him, and together they went to the wedding. The other five arrived at the wedding too late. They were locked out.

We must be ready when the Lord comes for us.

💡 **Remember:** Be sure to be ready if the Lord comes today.

The disciples wait on the Holy Spirit in Jerusalem

SEPTEMBER

30

Acts 1

One day when Jesus and His disciples were having a meal, Jesus told them, 'Do not leave Jerusalem until my Father sends you the heavenly Present He promised you.' (Acts 1:4)

After rising from the dead, Jesus appeared to His disciples from time to time. He talked to them often. Once, while they were all having a meal together, Jesus told the disciples they were to stay on in Jerusalem after He left them. God was going to send His Holy Spirit to come upon them.

The Spirit would give them power to do God's work on earth. From that time on believers would be witnesses for Jesus. They would tell people about Jesus in Jerusalem and everywhere – even to the ends of the earth. The Spirit would take away their shyness and help them say openly that Jesus was their Saviour.

Not long after He said this, Jesus was taken up into the sky. The apostles stood watching as he disappeared into a cloud. As they stood there, wide-eyed, two angels in white clothes suddenly stood there among them. They said, 'Jesus has been taken away from you into heaven. He is now ruling in heaven as Lord of the whole world. And someday, just as you saw Him go, He will return!'

Remember: Jesus is not gone. He is with us always.

A new disciple is chosen

Acts 1

Peter said, 'So now we must choose someone else to take Judas' place. It must be someone who has been with us all the time that we were with the Lord Jesus – from the time He was baptized by John until the day He was taken from us to heaven.' (Acts 1:21-22)

After Jesus went to heaven, the apostles and other believers gathered together in the upstairs room of the house where they were staying in Jerusalem. There were about 120 believers together in the room that day. Among them were Jesus' brothers and some women.

Then Peter stood up and told them that Judas had died. Judas bought himself a piece of ground with the money he was paid for betraying Jesus and hanged himself from a tree in that field.

There had to be twelve apostles, so Peter said they must choose a new one to take Judas' place. It needed to be someone who had been with them all the time they followed Jesus, someone who saw everything Jesus did.

They thought of two men – Barsabbas and Matthias – and they prayed for the right man to be chosen. The Lord then helped them and they chose Matthias.

💡 **Remember:** We should pray to God and listen to Him.

The Holy Spirit comes

Acts 2

Then, what looked like flames or tongues of fire appeared and settled on each of them. And everyone was filled with the Holy Spirit and began speaking in other languages. It was the Holy Spirit who helped them. (Acts 2:3-4)

On the day of Pentecost, an important feast celebrated by the Jews, the believers were gathered together in Jerusalem.

Suddenly, there was a sound from heaven like the roaring of a mighty wind. Then something like flames came down and settled on them. It was the Holy Spirit Who came to fill all the believers with His power. The believers found they could speak in other languages.

Many people in Jerusalem heard this mighty sound and came running to see what was happening. During Pentecost people from many nations came to Jerusalem. They spoke all the different languages under the sun. 'How can this be?' they exclaimed. 'All of us can hear these people speaking in our own languages about the wonderful things God has done.'

The day that the Holy Spirit came to the believers was the beginning of a new time for them. The Spirit now stays in each of us. He helps us with the way we live, so people can see we love Jesus.

☼ **Remember:** The Holy Spirit makes us children of God.

Peter preaches on Pentecost

Acts 2

Peter told the crowd, 'What you see this morning was predicted centuries ago by the prophet Joel: "In the last days," God said, "I will pour out my Spirit upon all people."' (Acts 2:16-17)

The crowd stood listening to the believers with amazement. 'What can this mean?' they asked each other. Others said, 'They're drunk, that's all!' Peter stepped forward. 'It isn't true!' he said and then he explained to them what was happening. The prophet Joel had written in the Old Testament that God would send His Spirit to His children on earth. Old and young, men and women – everybody would be filled with the Holy Spirit.

Joel's words came true on the day of Pentecost. Since that day every Christian shares in the power of the Holy Spirit, including us. We should never think we are too young or not important enough. The Holy Spirit will not pass us by. He lives in our lives and makes us part of the Lord's church. He is the one who helps us love God and other people. He stops us when we want to say or think bad things. Every day the Spirit guides us to do what God tells us. All we need to do is to allow the Spirit into our lives and let Him help us with the way we live, so God can be proud of us.

Remember: The Holy Spirit is with us every day.

A new church in Jerusalem

Acts 2

Those who believed what Peter said were baptized and added to the church. (Acts 2:41)

After Peter preached at Pentecost, the lives of many people changed. Almost three thousand of them started believing in the Lord Jesus that day. They became part of the church in Jerusalem, and what a wonderful church it was! Everybody loved the Lord.

The new believers came to listen to Peter and the other apostles every day. Once a week was not good enough for them. They wanted to learn all about Jesus. They wanted to know exactly what He had done to make them His children.

The Christians cared for one another and shared everything they had. If anyone was having a problem, there was always someone to help. They were like brothers and sisters. They prayed together and had their meals together. Everybody in Jerusalem could tell they believed in Jesus.

When we care for one another as Christians, others notice it. It makes them want to join the church. But if we're always bickering and making trouble, nobody's going to feel like following Jesus. We need to live in such a way that others want to hear more and more about Jesus.

Remember: The Holy Spirit helps us to love other people.

Believers care for one another

Acts 4

All the believers loved one another, and they shared everything they had. (Acts 4:32)

It must have been wonderful to belong to the first church in Jerusalem. They truly loved the Lord and cared for one another. If any Christians were going hungry the others would sell their land or houses and bring the money to the apostles to give to those in need.

For instance, there was Barnabas who was a member of the church. He sold a field he owned and brought the money to the apostles. In this way the Lord looked after them and saw to it that no member of the church went to bed on an empty stomach. There was more than enough for everybody to live on.

If we are the Lord's children we should not keep our money just for ourselves. We should share it with friends who are short of food, or who don't have warm clothes. We need to know right from the start that our money belongs to the Lord and we must give part of it back to Him.

If we are selfish and only want more and more money, toys, and clothes, we upset the Lord. Our lives belong to Him.

 Remember: Our money belongs to the Lord.

Peter heals a lame man

Acts 3

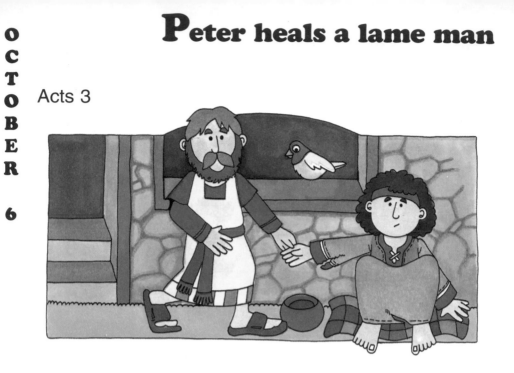

Peter said to the lame man, 'I don't have any money for you. But I'll give you what I have. In the name of Jesus Christ of Nazareth, get up and walk!' (Acts 3:6)

Peter and John went to the temple one afternoon to pray. Just outside the temple, at the gate, they saw a lame man. This man had never walked from the day he was born. Each day his family put him beside the gate, so that he could beg for money.

When Peter and John walked past him, he asked them for money. Peter didn't have any money on him. But he had something far better for the lame man. Peter looked him in the eyes. Then he told the man to get up and walk.

Right there, in front of everybody, Peter took the lame man by the hand and helped him up. And all at once, his legs were healed. He was so happy that he started jumping up and down. Then he walked into the temple with Peter and John, praising the Lord. He knew it was God Who had healed him.

All the people saw him walking and heard him praising the Lord. They recognized him immediately. They couldn't believe this was the same man. God performed a great miracle that day.

🔆 **Remember:** God still heals sick people today.

Peter and John before the Council

Acts 4

The Council called the apostles back in and told them never again to speak or teach about Jesus. But Peter and John replied, 'Do you think God wants us to obey you rather than Him? We cannot stop telling about the wonderful things we have seen and heard.' (Acts 4:18-20)

After Peter had healed the lame man in the name of Jesus, many people came to him in the temple. He started telling them about Jesus. He also told them to stop sinning and to believe in Jesus.

The rulers and elders in the temple were not at all pleased with Peter. They had him and John arrested. The next day the temple guards brought the two apostles before the council of all the leaders and elders of the nation. They told Peter and John to stop telling people about Jesus. They refused. They said they were never going to stop talking about Jesus.

The Council members were angry but they were also worried, because of all the people who had seen the man healed. They let the apostles go.

Jesus still performs miracles to this day. We should never be ashamed to say we are His children. Even if others make fun of us, it doesn't matter, because Jesus is the most important Person in the whole world.

💡 **Remember:** We should not be ashamed to speak about the Lord.

Ananias and Sapphira tell a lie

Acts 5

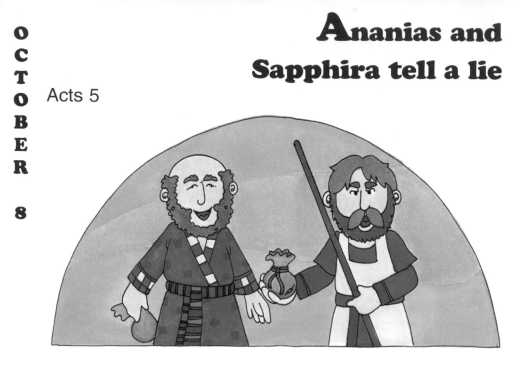

Then Peter said, 'Ananias, why has Satan made you lie? Why did you keep some of the money for yourself? You pretended to give everything to the church.' (Acts 5:3)

This man Ananias and his wife, Sapphira, belonged to the church in Jerusalem. They were dishonest. They sold some property but Ananias gave only part of the money to Peter. He kept some for himself, but he told Peter that he had given him every penny. This was a lie.

Peter was sad that Ananias had lied. He said, 'The property was yours to sell or not to sell, as you wished. The money was yours, and you could do with it as you pleased. So, why lie to the Lord?' As soon as Ananias heard these words he fell down dead.

A little while later his wife came in. She didn't know what had happened. She also lied to Peter and the same thing happened to her. She fell to the floor and died.

The Lord does not like it when we lie. We must tell the truth even if it is not always easy. Sometimes we are tempted to lie to get out of trouble, but we should always tell the truth.

💡 **Remember:** God's children always tell the truth.

Peter and his friends are freed from prison

Acts 5

The Council arrested the apostles and put them in jail. But an angel of the Lord came at night, opened the gates of the jail, and brought them out. (Acts 5:18-19)

The apostles performed a great many miracles and wonders among the people. The sick were being healed by their prayers. More and more people believed and joined the church in Jerusalem. This made the high priest and his friends very jealous. They arrested the apostles and jailed them.

That night the Lord sent an angel to open the doors of the prison and bring the apostles out. The next morning they were back at the temple.

When the Council heard about this they sent soldiers to go and arrest the apostles. 'Didn't we tell you never again to teach in this Man's name?' the high priest demanded. Peter and the apostles told them they would not stop. The Council was furious! But instead of killing the apostles, they had them whipped then they let them go.

Not one of the apostles was embarrassed about believing in Jesus, and neither did they complain about being beaten for talking about Jesus.

Remember: Talk often to others about Jesus.

Stephen is killed

Acts 7

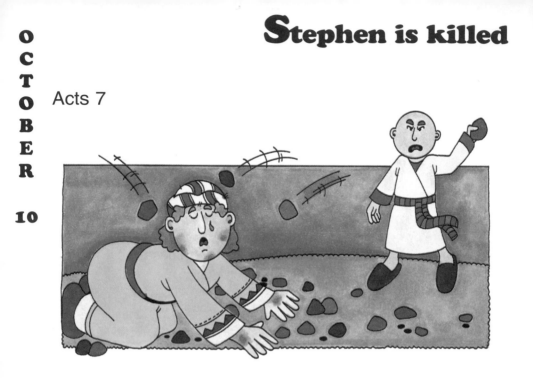

Then Stephen fell to his knees, shouting, 'Lord, don't charge them with this sin!' (Acts 7:60)

The apostles realized that they couldn't do all the work in the church any more, so they chose seven men to look after the poor. One of them was Stephen. Some of the Jews who were not part of the church became very angry with him because he said God didn't live in the temple.

These Jews told lies about Stephen. They said they'd heard him speaking against the temple and mocking Moses. Everyone in the Council was very angry.

Stephen was arrested and brought before the Council. He explained to the Council and the high priest what he believed. In his speech he said that the Jewish leaders were responsible for killing Jesus. This made them furious.

At that moment Stephen could see into heaven. He saw Jesus standing at God's right hand. He told the Jewish leaders this. They were horrified and decided to kill him. They dragged Stephen out of the city and stoned him to death.

As Stephen lay dying he prayed for his killers. He asked the Lord to forgive them. We too should pray for people who don't like us.

💡 **Remember:** Don't speak badly of others.

Simon the magician

Acts 8

The believers who had fled Jerusalem went everywhere preaching the Good News about Jesus. Philip, for example, went to the city of Samaria and told the people there about Christ. (Acts 8:4-5)

After Stephen was killed, the Jewish leaders started throwing Christians in Jerusalem into jail. Many fled. A Christian called Philip went to the city of Samaria where he told the people about Jesus.

There was a well-known sorcerer, or magician, who lived in Samaria, called Simon. When Simon saw how people were starting to believe in Jesus and were being baptized, he himself decided to be baptized.

Some time later Peter and John visited the city. They prayed for these new Christians and the Holy Spirit came upon them. When Simon saw this happen, he offered Peter money to buy this power of the Holy Spirit. Peter was very angry with him. He told Simon to stop his evil ways immediately and pray to the Lord or he'd be punished.

No-one can buy the power of the Lord. His power only works for people whose hearts belong to Him. If we listen to the Lord then His Spirit will work in us.

Remember: Only those who believe in Jesus are children of God.

Philip and the Ethiopian

Acts 8

A very important man from Ethiopia was on his way back home. Sitting in his carriage, he was reading aloud from the book of the prophet Isaiah. The Holy Spirit said to Philip, 'Go over and walk along beside the carriage.' (Acts 8: 28-29)

One day the Lord spoke to Philip. He told him to walk along a quiet road leading from Jerusalem to Gaza. As he did so a carriage passed by. Sitting in the carriage was a very important man from Africa. He was the head of the household of the queen of Ethiopia. This man was reading from the book of Isaiah.

The Holy Spirit told Philip to walk over to the carriage and speak to the man. Philip asked him, 'Do you understand what you are reading?' The man said how could he when there was no-one to explain it to him. So Philip explained what was written in the Bible and told the Ethiopian about Jesus.

The Ethiopian was so happy to hear the good news about Jesus that he asked Philip to baptize him. Afterwards Philip went on his way and, with great joy in his heart, the Ethiopian went back home to Africa.

Remember: The Bible is the Word of God.

Saul's conversion

Acts 9

Saul fell to the ground and heard a voice saying to him, 'Saul! Saul! Why are you persecuting Me?' 'Who are you, Sir?' Saul asked. And the voice replied, 'I am Jesus, the One you are persecuting!' (Acts 9:4-5)

13

A man called Saul lived in Jerusalem. We also know him as Paul. At first he hated the Christians and he was very glad when Stephen was killed. He wanted all the Christians to be wiped out.

When Saul heard that there were many Christians living in the city of Damascus he asked the high priest for a letter which gave him permission to arrest the believers there. Then he set off for Damascus.

On the way there, a brilliant light from heaven suddenly beamed down on him. Saul was frightened and fell to the ground. Then Jesus spoke to Saul. He asked him why he was trying to destroy His followers. When Saul got up he could see nothing. He was blind. The people with him had to take his hand and lead him to Damascus.

There was a believer in Damascus called Ananias. The Lord sent him to pray for Saul in the house where Saul was staying. After Ananias had prayed, Saul regained his sight and he was filled with the Holy Spirit.

 Remember: Nobody is so evil that God cannot save them.

Peter brings Tabitha back to life

Acts 9

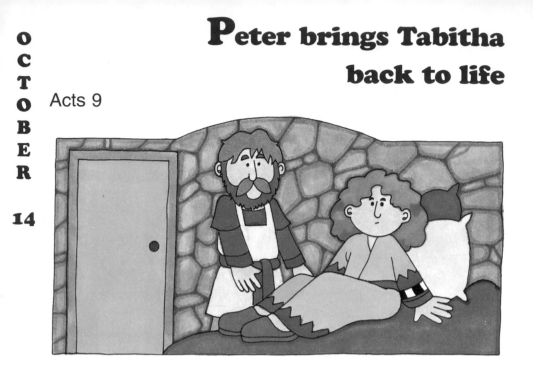

But Peter asked them all to leave the room; then he knelt and prayed. Turning to the body he said, 'Get up, Tabitha.' (Acts 9:40).

Peter travelled from place to place visiting believers. One day he arrived in Lydda. There he healed a man called Aeneas who had been paralyzed for many years.

A believer called Tabitha lived in Joppa, a town nearby. She fell ill and died. Her friends sent for Peter straight away. As soon as he arrived they took him to her room. Everybody was very sad and some were crying. Peter asked them all to leave the room. He knelt down by Tabitha's bed and prayed. Then he turned to the body and told her to get up.

Tabitha opened her eyes. She was alive. It was a miracle! The news spread through the town. Many people started believing in Jesus.

Jesus can raise people from the dead. One day He will bring us back to life again and we will live in heaven with Him forever. Jesus is stronger than death. Jesus overcame death when He came back to life on the third day, so we need never be afraid of death.

·◯· **Remember:** Jesus is stronger than death.

Cornelius' vision

Acts 10

In Caesarea there lived a Roman army officer named Cornelius. He helped the poor and was a man who regularly prayed to God. (Acts 10:1-2)

Cornelius was an important Roman soldier. He was captain of the Italian Regiment. He prayed to God often. One afternoon at about three o'clock he was praying when suddenly he saw an angel of God coming towards him.

'Cornelius!' the angel said. 'The Lord has taken notice of your prayers and gifts to the poor!' The angel told him to send some men down to Joppa to fetch Peter.

The next day Peter went up onto the flat roof of the house in which he was staying. It was about twelve o'clock and as he was praying there he saw something like a sheet coming down from the sky. In the sheet were all sorts of animals that the Jews weren't allowed to eat. Then a voice told him to eat them. 'Never, Lord,' Peter said. The same thing happened three times.

While Peter was still puzzling over the vision, three men sent by Cornelius came looking for him. They told him Cornelius wanted him to go to his house. So he left for Caesarea with the three men the next day.

Remember: It helps to pray. God listens.

Cornelius' whole life changes

Acts 10

Even as Peter was saying these things, the Holy Spirit fell upon all who had heard the message. (Acts 10:44)

When Peter arrived in Caesarea he went straight to Cornelius' house. Cornelius, his relatives and close friends were waiting for him and invited Peter in.

Peter told him that Jewish law forbade him to enter the home of a non-Jew but, since the Lord had sent him there, he would go in.

Cornelius told Peter about the angel who instructed him to send for Peter. At last Peter understood the meaning of the vision of the sheet. It was the Lord showing him not to think of anyone as unclean. He realized that nobody is so bad or sinful that he or she cannot hear God's word.

Peter told everybody gathered together in Cornelius' house about Jesus. As he was talking, the Holy Spirit fell on all who heard the message. Peter was happy to see that God also gave His Spirit to non-Jews. Cornelius and the others were baptized.

We must never think we are better than others. The Lord loves all of us the same. He has no favourites.

💡 **Remember:** The Lord cares about everybody.

Peter in trouble with the church in Jerusalem

Acts 11

When Peter arrived back in Jerusalem, some of the Jewish believers criticized him. 'You went into the home of non-Jews and even ate with them!' they said. (Acts 11:2-3)

The news of the conversion of Cornelius and the others spread like wildfire. Some of the believers in Jerusalem were very angry when they heard about it. They were Jews and they felt it was wrong of Peter to enter the house of a heathen.

When Peter arrived back in Jerusalem, they told him he should not have gone into Cornelius' home, let alone have eaten with him. But he told them exactly how it came about and they were satisfied with his explanation.

Some people think they are better than others who speak a different language or who have a different colour skin. This is a sin in the eyes of the Lord. Some Jewish believers thought they were too good to go into the homes of heathens and talk to them about Jesus. God showed them they were wrong and they listened to Him. We must tell everybody about Jesus.

 Remember: All believers are equally important to the Lord.

Paul works in Antioch

Acts 11

Then Barnabas went on to Tarsus to find Paul. When he found him, he brought him back to Antioch. Both of them stayed there with the church for a full year, teaching many people. (Acts 11:25-26)

Many of the believers who had fled from Jerusalem earlier, were living in Antioch. There they began preaching about Jesus to the people of that city and soon the church there had many members. Jews as well as other people who spoke Greek started believing in Jesus.

When the apostles heard how well the church in Antioch was doing, they sent Barnabas to help them. Barnabas was a good man, full of the Holy Spirit. He taught the believers to do everything the Lord said.

Eventually Barnabas found he couldn't manage all the work of the church on his own any longer so he decided to send for Paul to help him.

During this time someone brought bad news to the Christians in Antioch. The people of the church in Jerusalem were suffering because of a great famine. Those in Antioch started collecting money straight away and Paul and Barnabas took it to the elders of the church in Jerusalem.

:Ö: **Remember:** We should share our money with those in need.

An angel helps Peter escape from prison

Acts 12

Suddenly, there was a bright light in the cell, and an angel of the Lord stood before Peter. The angel tapped him on the side to awaken him and said, 'Quick! Get up!' And the chains fell off his wrists. (Acts 12:7)

King Herod Agrippa did not like the Christians in Jerusalem at all. He had an apostle called James killed, which pleased the Jewish leaders. Then Herod arrested Peter and sent him to jail. Peter was chained between two soldiers while two others guarded the prison gate.

That night when Peter was asleep, with a soldier on either side, an angel suddenly stood before him. The chains fell from his wrists. Then the angel led the way out of the cell. Peter thought he was dreaming. It was only when he was standing outside in the street that he realized what had happened. 'It's really true!' he said to himself.

He went to the home of Mary, John Mark's mother where many believers had gathered to pray. They didn't believe the servant girl when she came running inside crying, 'Peter is standing at the door!' 'You're out of your mind,' they said but in the end they opened the door and were overjoyed to see Peter standing there.

 Remember: No problem is ever too big for the Lord to solve.

Paul and Barnabas' first missionary journey

Acts 13

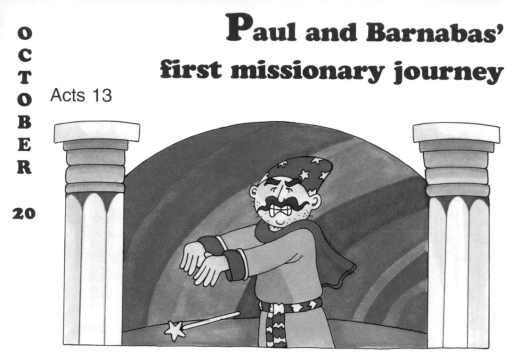

One day believers were worshipping the Lord and fasting in Antioch. Then the Holy Spirit said to them, 'I have special work for Barnabas and Paul. Send them out now to do it.' (Acts 13:2)

One day the believers in Antioch were praying together and fasting when the Holy Spirit showed them that they should send Paul and Barnabas to go and do missionary work.

Paul and Barnabas sailed for the island of Cyprus. They preached from town to town until they finally reached Paphos. There they met a Jewish sorcerer called Elymus. He was with Sergius Paulus, the governor of the island.

The governor had heard of Paul and Barnabas. He invited them to visit him because he wanted to hear them preach. Elymus tried to put a stop to this. Paul turned on him and said God would punish him for trying to stop them. Elymus would be blind for a time. There and then Elymus lost his sight. After this, the governor believed in the Lord.

The Lord does not allow anything to stand in His way. If He wants to save someone, He will do it. We must never think we can run away from Him. The best thing we can ever do is to give our lives to Him.

💡 **Remember:** Every Christian is a witness for the Lord.

Paul heals a lame man

Acts 14

At Lystra there was a man with crippled feet. He had been that way from birth, so he had never walked. He was listening as Paul preached, and Paul noticed him and realized he had faith to be healed. So Paul called to him in a loud voice, 'Stand up!' (Acts 14:8-10)

Paul and Barnabas preached in a city called Iconium. A great number of Jews and Gentiles started believing. This made the Jewish leaders angry and they starting making trouble for the apostles. Eventually Paul and Barnabas had to run for their lives. They moved on to Lystra.

In Lystra, Paul preached again. Among the people listening to him was a man who had been lame from birth. Paul told him to get up and walk. Instantly the man did just that!

When the crowd saw this they thought Paul and Barnabas were Roman gods. This really upset the two apostles. 'Why do you think such a thing?' they cried. 'We work for Jesus. He is the one who performs the miracles.'

Some wicked Jews stirred up the crowds and told them to kill Paul. They stoned Paul, dragged him out of the city and left him there for dead. But the Lord spared Paul's life.

 Remember: Jesus feels sorry for sick people.

Paul talks about God's goodness

Romans 3

All have sinned. All are far away from God. Yet now God in His kindness declares us not guilty. He has done this through Christ Jesus, who has freed us by taking away our sins. (Rom 3:23-24)

Paul preached to many people in many places. He also wrote quite a few letters to different churches. In the letter to the Romans we are told how much God is willing to do so we can become His children. Paul says we are all sinners. Not one of us can become the Lord's child on our own. Even if we try our best to live the way we should and to obey God's laws, we just cannot help sinning.

God thought of a way to save us. He sent Jesus to us and Jesus took all our sins onto His shoulders. He died on the cross in our place.

If we believe in Jesus, our sins don't count anymore because He has already punished Jesus for our sins. We don't need to give God money to save us. It's no use telling Him how good we are. Neither will help us. There is only one way that works. We must tell God we are sorry for all our sins and we must ask Jesus if we can offload our sins onto His shoulders. God will forgive us and we will become His children.

🔆 **Remember:** Jesus died for our sins.

God sent Jesus to die in our place

2 Corinthians 5

God made Christ, who never sinned, to be the offering for our sin. If we belong to Jesus, our sins don't count to God anymore. Then we are free! (2 Cor 5:21)

Paul couldn't stop writing about everything God does to save us. He tells the Christians in Corinth that Jesus never does anything bad. He is not a sinner like we are. But He loves us so much that He was willing to leave His heavenly home and become a human being. There on the cross, Jesus took all our sins, every single one, on Himself. Even our sins that are still to come! He told God He committed all those sins of ours.

When God looked at Jesus on the cross He saw only our sins. Then He became so angry that He punished Jesus with death instead of us. Actually we should have been the ones hanging there. We should have taken our own punishment. But Jesus did it in our place. He died so that God would not punish us.

God loves us so much that He was prepared to let His Son die for us. God doesn't want even one of us to be lost. Believe in Jesus and know that He paid with His blood for all your sins.

 Remember: God is not cross with us any more.

The meeting of the apostles in Jerusalem

Acts 15

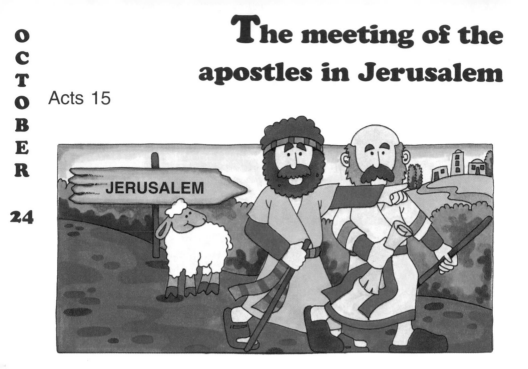

When they arrived in Jerusalem, Paul and Barnabas were welcomed by the whole church, also the apostles and elders. They told them all what God had done through them. But then some of the men who had been Pharisees before, stood up and said, 'All new Christians must be circumcised. They must also obey the law of Moses.' (Acts 15:4-5).

Paul and Barnabas told people who were not Jews about Jesus. Some Jewish believers then said these new Christians had to be circumcised. Paul didn't agree. Then the church in Antioch sent Paul and Barnabas to Jerusalem.

Paul and Barnabas were welcomed in Jerusalem by the apostles. Only a few believers did not agree with Paul. They wanted all Christians to obey Jewish laws. So the leaders of the church held a meeting to decide on the right thing to do. Peter said he didn't think it was necessary for everybody to obey Jewish laws. James, Jesus' brother, felt the same way. Everybody agreed with them.

So the church leaders wrote a letter which they sent to all the churches. In the letter they explained what had been decided at their meeting. Paul and Barnabas were happy, because now they could carry on teaching the non-Jews about Jesus.

Remember: Man-made laws mean nothing in the church.

A jailer tries to kill himself

Acts 16

The chief jailer asked Paul and Silas, 'Sirs, what must I do to be saved?' They replied, 'Believe in the Lord Jesus and you and your household will be saved.' (Acts 16:30-31)

Paul and Barnabas decided to split up. Paul took Timothy and Silas with him to do missionary work.

One day they arrived at a city called Philippi. Just outside the city was a place where people met to pray. There they told the crowd about Jesus.

One day, on their way to that place of prayer again, a slave girl followed them. She was shouting all of the time because she had a demon in her. Paul drove it out and the girl was healed. Her owners grabbed Paul and Silas and dragged them to the marketplace. The two were beaten up and thrown into prison.

Around midnight, Paul and Silas started praying. Suddenly there was an earthquake. The prison doors flew open. The jailer thought all the prisoners had escaped. He wanted to kill himself. Paul stopped him: 'Don't do it! We are all here.' Then he talked to the jailer about Jesus.

The jailer took them home with him. He, and everybody in his house, started believing in God.

 Remember: Nothing is impossible for the Lord.

Believe in the Lord Jesus!

Romans 10

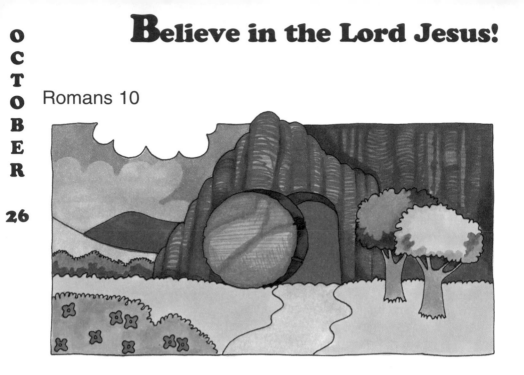

If you say with your mouth that Jesus is Lord and believe in your heart that God raised Him from the dead, you will be saved. (Rom 10:9)

How do we know that someone is a Christian? A Christian is someone who believes Jesus is Lord and was raised from the dead by God. This is what Paul writes in his letter to the Romans.

A Christian knows that Jesus is not lying in a grave somewhere in Jerusalem. He rose from the dead. He is alive! Jesus is in the best and most important place there is. He rules in heaven over everything and everyone here on earth. He is the King of heaven and earth.

If we believe in Jesus, we know that we have been saved by Him. He makes us children of God. He takes away our sins. He takes care of us every day and He will see to it that we go to heaven one day.

Faith is to take Jesus at His word. Faith is believing He does what He says in the Bible. Faith is knowing Jesus' blood washed us as white as snow. He forgives us every bad thing we do. When we tell Him we are sorry for our sins, He won't think of them ever again because He forgives and forgets.

🔆 **Remember:** Because of Jesus we can live forever.

Paul suffers in Thessalonica

Acts 17

Paul explained to the people exactly what is written in the Bible. He showed them that the Bible says Christ had to suffer and rise from the dead. (Acts 17:3)

One day Paul and his helpers came to a city called Thessalonica. They went to the synagogue, where the Jews worshipped, and started telling the people about Jesus.

Some Jews became Christians, others didn't. The Jewish leaders began to get very jealous of Paul when they saw how many people chose to believe in Jesus. They gathered a mob to attack Paul but they couldn't find Paul and Silas in Jason's house where they were staying. They dragged Jason from his home instead and brought him and some of the other believers before the city council. 'Paul and Silas have turned the rest of the world upside down,' they shouted. The people of the city turned against the Christians but Jason promised that they wouldn't make trouble so the city officials allowed them to go. That night after dark, the believers helped Paul and Silas to escape from the city.

 Remember: The Lord protects His children.

The faith of the Thessalonian believers

1 Thessalonians 1

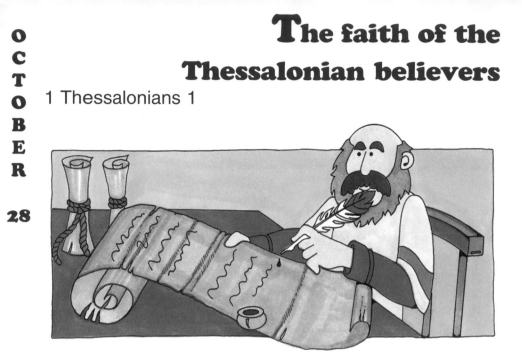

'Just like us, you also started believing in the Lord Jesus. Even though you suffered so much, you gave your life to the Lord. The joy that suddenly came into your lives is from the Holy Spirit.' (1 Thes 1:6).

Paul wrote two letters to the believers in Thessalonica. In the first one he tells them how happy he is that they gave their lives to the Lord. Paul says he cannot thank God enough for this.

Paul writes that the believers in Thessalonica lived like true Christians right from the start. It wasn't easy. People made fun of them and said nasty things about them but they didn't let it worry them. All they wanted to do was what Jesus said and their lives were full of joy. Everybody could see they were brand-new people.

It is really amazing to see how a person's life changes when he or she becomes the Lord's child. We can never be the same once Jesus comes into our lives. We feel, think and behave differently. Jesus makes us new from head to toe.

Can our friends tell by the way we live that we are the Lord's children? Do we like talking about everything Jesus does for us or are we a bit embarrassed? We must never be ashamed to say we're Christians.

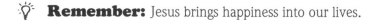 **Remember:** Jesus brings happiness into our lives.

Don't be nasty

1 Thessalonians 5

See that no one pays back evil for evil, but always try to do good to each other and to everyone else. (1 Thes 5:15)

Paul writes to the believers in Thessalonica that Christians do not live like unbelievers. Christians are not always watching others to see if they can catch them doing something wrong. Christians forgive one another and don't bear a grudge if someone has treated them badly. They forget about it quickly.

When Jesus is busy working with our lives, He has a large eraser in His hand. Every day He rubs out all our sins and He wants us to do the same for others. We must make up our minds not to stay angry with people or to pay them back for being unkind or unfriendly to us. We need to tell them we love them even if they treat us badly.

A Christian really cares for others, no matter who they are. We mustn't sit around waiting for others to be friendly with us before we're nice to them. We should be the first to smile and show them we care. If we follow what the Bible tells us we'll be friendly and helpful and we'll never forget to pray for others.

💡 **Remember:** Never emphasize the bad things other people do.

Paul preaches in Athens

Acts 17

When they heard Paul speak of the resurrection of a person who had been dead, some laughed, but others said, 'We want to hear more about this later.'
(Acts 17:32)

One day Paul went to Athens. While he was waiting for his friends he was deeply troubled by all the idols he saw everywhere in the city. Then the people took him to the Areopagus to tell the people there what he believed. The Areopagus was a place where one could go and listen to clever and learned people speak.

Paul told the people of Athens he could see they were very religious. As he was walking around in town he saw their many altars. He even saw one with the words 'To an Unknown God' on it and he said he would like to tell them about this God.

Paul started off by saying that this God doesn't live in man-made temples. He Himself gives life to everything on earth. He gives us what we need. It is because of Him that we live and move and breathe every day.

Then Paul told them that God has appointed Jesus to judge the world. But first He raised Him from the dead. Many laughed when Paul spoke about Jesus coming back to life. Others listened and wanted to know more. Some joined him and became believers.

💡 **Remember:** Because of Him we move and breathe every day.

Paul works in Corinth

Acts 18

One night the Lord spoke to Paul in a vision and told him, 'Don't be afraid! Speak out! Don't be silent! For I am with you, and no-one will harm you because many people here in this city belong to Me.' (Acts 18:9-10)

Paul left Athens and went to Corinth where he stayed with a man called Aquila and his wife, Priscilla. They were tentmakers. Every Sabbath Paul went to the Jewish synagogue to speak to the people about Jesus.

The Jews paid no attention to Paul so he left. Then he went to the house of Titus and preached there.

One night the Lord told Paul not to be afraid. He would take care of him. Paul stayed and worked in Corinth for the next year and a half. When Gallio became the new governor, the Jews tried to bring Paul before him for judgement but Gallio was unimpressed with their accusations and sent them out of the courtroom.

We should ask the Lord every day to protect us and our families and believe that He will. And we should remember to thank Him every night for being with us.

 Remember: Nothing happens unless the Lord knows about it.

God's children should not fight

1 Corinthians 1 & 3

'I beg all of you in the Name of the Lord Jesus Christ to stop arguing among yourselves. Be of one mind, in what you think and believe and do.' (1 Cor 1:10)

Paul wrote a number of letters to the Christians in Corinth. He was worried because they were quarrelling and fighting with one another. Some Corinthian Christians said they liked only Paul. Others said, 'I follow Peter.' Yet others said they weren't interested in what people like Paul or Peter said. They would do only what Christ said.

Soon the people of Corinth divided into different groups and each group thought they were the best Christians. Paul wrote to them and told them to stop quarrelling. He reminded them that Christians should be like one big family.

Even today many people in the church argue about who is right and who is wrong. The church should be like a family in which every member cares for the others. The Lord does not want us to live only for ourselves and always think we are right. We must love one another and take trouble to do things for our friends. We must also try hard to get on with other Christians.

🔅 **Remember:** In God's church we should love one another.

Paul preaches in Ephesus

Acts 19

In Ephesus the message of the Lord spread widely and had a powerful effect. (Acts 19:20)

When Paul left Corinth he went to Ephesus. He stayed there for almost three years. He preached in the Jewish synagogue for three months. Then he left and rented a hall where, for the next two years, he told people about Jesus.

During this time a team of Jews who were not supposed to do it were travelling from town to town casting out evil spirits. When they met a man in Ephesus who had a devil in him, they said, 'I command you in the Name of Jesus to come out.' The spirit attacked them. The story of what happened spread quickly throughout Ephesus. The people were frightened. Magicians burnt all their books on magic. So the word of the Lord changed the lives of many people because He works in many different ways.

Because of Paul's preaching the hand-made gods in the temples were not so popular anymore. The gods in the temple of the goddess Artemis were not selling well at all. The man who made them, Demetrius, and other craftsmen were losing money. Demetrius organized a protest against Paul but it was not successful. The mayor of the city managed to quieten the people.

💡 **Remember:** The devil fears the Lord.

Paul lands up in jail in Ephesus

2 Corinthians 1

I think you ought to know what we went through in the province of Asia. We were treated so badly that we started thinking we would not get out of prison alive. (2 Cor 1:8)

While Paul was working in Ephesus he was sent to prison. There were people in town who were angry with him because he talked to them about Jesus. Paul says this was one of the most difficult times of his life. He was having such a bad time that he started thinking he would never get out of there alive.

The Lord saw Paul's suffering. Just when Paul thought this was the end, God came to the rescue. Paul writes that it was a great miracle. It was like turning around at death's door. After this experience Paul's faith was even stronger than before. He now knew that God would protect him no matter what kind of trouble he was in.

God cares for all of His children. We should never think He is too busy to help us or that He has forgotten about us. Even if it takes some time for God to answer our prayers, He hears everything we ask Him. Just keep on praying. God is listening. He never sleeps.

⋅ф⋅ **Remember:** God can help in every problem we experience.

Paul holds on to the Lord

2 Corinthians 4

We are sometimes pushed around. But we never lose heart. People let us down. But the Lord never leaves us. (2 Cor 4:8)

It is not always easy to be a follower of the Lord. Ask Paul. He was often hunted down by wicked people. He was pushed around and beaten up and they even tried to kill him. Sometimes Paul just didn't know what to do anymore. He was almost like a clay pot which is easily broken.

No matter how much Paul suffered, he never gave up. He went on doing what the Lord said. How did he manage to do this? He gives us the answer himself. He writes that there was a treasure inside of him. This is the Holy Spirit that lived in his heart. Paul also knew that God would never let him down.

Some Christians give up too easily. We mustn't be like them. God is with us. Even if we feel like an old broken clay pot, we are still in the Lord's hands. Even if we don't always know what to do, He cares for us. Believe it. We must hold on to the Lord's hand because there is a precious treasure inside us: the Holy Spirit.

Remember: We are precious to the Lord.

Paul's prayer for the church

Ephesians 3

I pray that you may know how much Christ loves you. His love is so great we will never really understand it. May your whole life be filled with the power that comes from God. (Eph 3:19)

Paul wrote a letter to the Christians in Ephesus where he worked for three years. In this letter he prays that God will give them strength, and that they will make a home for Christ in their hearts.

Paul also asks the Lord to help the Ephesians love others. He prays that they may understand how much God loves them and all His other people.

Jesus' love is too great for us to understand, but there is a way we can see how much He loves us. This happens when we allow His strength to work in our lives. We need to tell God every day that our lives belong to Him. He can steer us any way He wants. Then we will start noticing how powerful and great God is and the way we live will be more like the way He wants it to be.

Paul ends his prayer by giving all the glory to God because He is so good. He says God is far greater than we could ever imagine. He is able to do so much. We cannot even begin to understand how much.

☀ **Remember:** God is far greater than we could ever imagine.

What does a Christian family look like?

Ephesians 5-6

Children, obey your parents because you belong to the Lord. This is the right thing to do. (Eph 6:1)

In his letter to the Ephesians Paul also has a word for mothers and fathers. He tells them how they should treat each other. Paul writes to the children that they should always obey their parents. The Lord expects them to.

Paul tells parents to raise their children the way the Lord wants. If children don't listen, their parents must be strict with them.

Our parents must see to it that we stay on the right way – the Lord's way. That's why they discipline us when we are naughty. Remember, the Lord gave us our parents. We should love them very much and pray for them often. Ask the Lord to take good care of them every day.

We must always listen to our parents. The Lord tells our parents what to do so that we can grow up in the right way. He tells them to take good care of us and He asks us to be good. We must try to make our parents happy by loving them and the Lord.

 Remember: We must pray for our parents every day.

Put on the Lord's armour

Ephesians 6

We are not fighting against people, but against the devil and his evil spirits. (Eph 6:12)

Paul says we have a dangerous enemy. This enemy is the devil. He is always on the look-out for ways to make us do nasty things, but the Lord gives us proper uniforms and weapons to protect us in our fight against the devil.

Our first weapon is a belt of truth. This means we must hold on to Jesus every day. He is the only Truth. The steel plate that covers our breast shows that God is on our side. For shoes, we put on the peace that comes from the good news that Jesus died for our sins. We must tell others, who don't know Jesus, this good news.

In every battle we will need faith as our shield. We must believe in God, all the time. Then the devil cannot harm us. The helmet on our heads is the knowledge that Jesus is our Saviour. Our sword is the Bible. What we learn from the Bible helps us chase the devil away every time he pesters us.

This is the suit of armour which the Lord gives us. We must wear it every day. We must pray for the Lord to make us strong so the devil cannot get a hold on us.

💡 **Remember:** When we wear Jesus' weapons it scares the devil.

Jesus is with us through His Spirit

Ephesians 1

Because you believe in Christ, the Holy Spirit, who is from Him, has put His stamp on you. This shows that you belong to God alone. (Eph 1:13)

The Holy Spirit is very important. He is also God, the same as the Father and the Son. The Holy Spirit lives in every Christian. He is the guarantee God gives us that He will do everything He promised. Without the Holy Spirit we cannot be Christians.

The Holy Spirit must see to it that we listen to God. He must also make sure we get to heaven one day. That is why He is like a stamp or a seal on our lives. Often a certificate has a red seal on it which shows that it is genuine. The certificate belongs to the person to whom it was awarded. In a similar way, the Lord puts a seal on our lives to say we belong to Him. This seal is the Holy Spirit.

The Holy Spirit tells us we are God's children. We are on our way to Him. He puts His stamp on our lives and it won't come off.

🔆 **Remember:** God puts His stamp on our lives. It won't come off.

All Christians are important to God

Galatians 3

When you belong to the Lord it makes no difference what language you speak. It doesn't matter if you are rich or poor, a girl or a boy. All who believe in Jesus are one big family. (Gal 3:28)

Some people think they are more important than others. Some children think they are better than others because they have more money or clothes than them. The Lord doesn't care about such things. He doesn't need to know what we own before He decides to love us. It makes no difference to Him what language we speak, or whether we are a boy or a girl. The Lord loves everybody. He has no favourites.

It's the same in our churches. All Christians are important to the Lord. In Jesus' eyes we are one big family. All of us who believe in Him are one another's brothers and sisters. He is the Head of the family and our Lord. Jesus takes care of us, every day, because He loves us very much.

Jesus doesn't like us to think we are better or cleverer than others. We should not think too much of ourselves but love all the Lord's children.

💡 **Remember:** Other Christians are our brothers and sisters.

The temple of the Holy Spirit

1 Corinthians 6

Don't you know that your body is the temple of the Holy Spirit, who lives in you and was given to you by God? You do not belong to yourselves anymore. (1 Cor 6:19)

A Christian is someone who has been bought at a high price. God bought each one of us and the Lord paid for us with His blood. From head to toe we belong to Him.

After God had bought us He sent the Holy Spirit to each of us. The Holy Spirit lives in us and so our bodies become a temple. The Holy Spirit changes our lives so that we can be a temple for God to live in. We must give our lives to the Holy Spirit, every day. He will do the rest.

When we believe in Jesus we are not our own boss anymore. We belong to Him because He bought us. That's why we must ask the Lord before we say or do something. We can't do or say just what we want, but only what the Lord tells us to.

🔆 **Remember:** Jesus bought us. We are His.

Paul speaks to the Ephesian elders

Acts 20

'Let me speak plainly: it is not my fault if any of you are not saved. Because I have told you exactly how God saves sinners.' (Acts 20:26-27)

Once when Paul was on his way to Jerusalem, he stayed at Troas where he talked to all the believers one Sunday night. Paul spoke for a very long time and a young man named Eutychus fell asleep. He was sitting on a window sill and he fell out of the window which was three storeys up. When they picked him up he was dead. Paul went down, bent over Eutychus, and took him in his arms. Then he said to the people, 'Don't worry, he's alive!' And sure enough, the young man got up and went home, unhurt.

The next part of the journey was by ship. When Paul arrived in Miletus he decided to stay there for a while. He sent a message to the elders in Ephesus to visit him there. When they arrived, Paul told them that they would never see him again. They had to remember every word he taught them about Jesus, and they must have faith in Him. He told the elders to watch over the believers and keep them on the Lord's path.

-ᵧ̣- **Remember:** Keep faith in the Lord.

We must care for one another

'You must remember the words of the Lord Jesus: "It is more blessed to give than to receive."' (Acts 20:35)

Paul reminded the Ephesian elders that he had never taken any money from them. When he stayed with them, he worked with his own two hands. He made tents for a living. Christians should follow his example. They mustn't sit around, expecting others to give them what they need. They must help one another.

Paul says Christians must care for one another and those who have plenty should help those who have very little.

Jesus says it's better to give than to receive. He gave us His life. The least we can do is to share our time, our money and our possessions with others. That will please the Lord.

Selfish Christians who hold on to their possessions without caring for people in need, are not good 'advertisements' for God's love. We should open up our lives to God's goodness and share our blessings with others.

☀ **Remember:** We should never boast about what we have.

We are part of Christ's body on earth

1 Corinthians 12

Now all of you together are Christ's body, and each one of you is a separate and necessary part of it. (1 Cor 12:27)

Paul tells us that we Christians are the Lord's body here on earth. A body is made up of different parts and if one part of our body is not working, we fall ill. When we have a cold, or if we break a limb, our whole body feels it.

Every Christian forms a part of Christ's body. One is the mouth, another is the eyes, yet another is a finger and another the ears. And every Christian, every single little part of Jesus' body, is important because if just one small part does not work, the rest of the body feels it. If one Christian says, 'Oh well, the church doesn't need me,' then the body of Christ doesn't work as well as it should.

We are part of Christ's body here on earth. Jesus wants to use us so the rest of His body can stay healthy and strong. We need to do our bit. We should pray regularly, read our Bible and care for other Christians. In this way we help to keep Christ's body healthy.

$\cdot\!\!\!\!\cdot\!\!\!\!\cdot$ **Remember:** We are an important part of Jesus' body.

Paul is arrested in Jerusalem

Acts 21

Some Jews from the province of Asia saw Paul in the temple and got a mob together. They grabbed Paul, yelling, 'Men of Israel! Help! This is the man who teaches against our people and the temple and the laws of Moses. He has brought people of all nations into our temple. He fills our holy place with sin!' (Acts 21:27-28)

Paul went to Jerusalem to pray in the temple. When he arrived in the city he went first to visit Jesus' brother, James. He and a few elders of the church asked Paul to help out four men who were there for a religious ceremony. Would Paul pay for their offerings?

At the temple a number of Jews recognized him immediately. They were angry when they saw him there and thought he had come just to find fault with them. This was of course not true but they started yelling and stirring up the other Jews so that eventually they all turned on Paul. They dragged him out of the temple in order to kill him outside the city gates.

The commander of the Roman regiment in Jerusalem saw what was happening. He immediately sent his soldiers to arrest Paul and take him to a building next to the temple.

Remember: Trust in the Lord.

Paul defends himself

Acts 22-23

The Lord said to Paul, 'Leave Jerusalem. I am sending you far away. You must go to people who are not Jewish.' (Acts 22:21)

The mob at the temple in Jerusalem was set on killing Paul, but the Roman soldiers saved him. Before they locked him up he asked the commander, 'Please let me talk to these people.'

Paul told the crowd about the day Jesus spoke to him on the road to Damascus and how this had changed his whole life. Then and there he became a Christian. Afterwards he came back to Jerusalem. In the temple he saw a vision of Jesus telling him to get out of Jerusalem. The Lord told Paul that the Jews wouldn't believe him.

The Jewish crowd was furious. They shouted, 'Kill him!' The soldiers locked him up in prison just in time.

The next day Paul was brought before the Jewish high court. When he said he believed in the resurrection of the dead, the people started fighting again. They shouted and started tugging at Paul so he was locked up again. The commander then sent Paul to Caesarea before the Jews could kill him.

💡 **Remember:** The Lord makes us as good as new.

Paul before Felix

Acts 24

Paul said to the Roman governor Felix, 'These men certainly cannot prove the things they accuse me of doing.' (Acts 24:13)

When Paul arrived in Caesarea he was taken to Governor Felix. He stayed in prison until his case was heard. A few days later the Jewish leaders arrived to press charges against Paul. They told Governor Felix that Paul was a danger to other people.

Paul answered that he worshipped the God of his ancestors, just like all Jews. But Felix had him locked up in any case.

Paul was in prison in Caesarea for two years. During this time Felix sent for Paul often. Paul talked to him and his wife about God. He told them we should obey God and must not sin. Paul also warned them that God was coming back to the world one day and sinners would be punished.

Paul was not afraid to witness for Christ, even if it meant sitting in jail for two years. We shouldn't be afraid to talk to our friends about Jesus either or feel embarrassed to say we belong to Jesus. We should talk about Him, no matter what!

 Remember: Christians like to speak about Jesus.

Jesus is the greatest

Philippians 2

At the Name of Jesus every knee will bow, in heaven and on earth. All will say, 'Jesus Christ is Lord! Then God's Name will be glorified.' (Phil 2:10-11).

Jesus is more important than anybody or anything in the whole world. Before He came down to earth, He had the most important position in heaven. All the angels bowed before Him. They worshipped Him all day long. But one day Jesus decided to become an ordinary human being. He took off His heavenly crown and came to live among us.

Jesus knows we are all sinners. It is impossible for us to reach God on our own. That is why Jesus decided to give His life away for our sake.

After the death and resurrection of Jesus, God gave Him the most important place in heaven. Jesus was also given the most important Name in the world. His Name is Lord! Everyone who hears this Name, must bow before Him. Everyone must say Jesus is the Ruler of the whole world.

We who believe in Jesus, bow before Him every day. It's good to know He is our Lord.

Remember: Jesus is our Lord.

Jesus has the whole world in His hands

Colossians 1

Jesus, the Son of God, is the image of the God we cannot see. Jesus is more important than anybody else. He is the ruler over all creation. (Col 1:15)

Paul wrote a beautiful song about the Lord, saying how great and powerful He is. Jesus is the image of God. He is the most important Person in creation. Jesus was there when God created everything. God created, through Him, everything we can see with our eyes, as well as everything we cannot see. Jesus also made all the angels. They are there to serve Him.

Ever since the very beginning, before there was anything or anyone in the world, Jesus was already there. He takes care of the whole world.

We must bow before Jesus every day. He loves us very much. He gave His life for us so that we can be God's children forever. We must serve Him every day and remember that Jesus is the most important Person in the whole world.

Remember: Jesus takes care of our families every day.

Jesus has known us a long time

Romans 6

The prize for sinning is the same for everyone: death! But God gives a wonderful prize to all who believe. He gives us the free gift of everlasting life because we believe Jesus Christ is Lord. (Rom 6:23)

Sin is a terrible thing. It destroys lives. But there is good news. Paul tells us that sinners are given a lousy first prize for their trouble. This prize is death! Those who don't want to listen to God will be in hell forever.

God knew that we could never reach out to Him on our own. We are too wicked for that. We can do nothing to please Him and we must be punished for our sins. But if we believe in Jesus, we will not go to hell. God awards us with His own first prize – everlasting life! All His children will live with Him forever. He takes us directly to Him in heaven.

Only those who believe can win God's prize. Only His children can live with Him forever, because He forgives His children all their sins.

Remember: The first prize awarded to believers is eternal life.

I don't like sin at all

Because you belong to Christ, you have been made new. It is not people who made you new, but Christ. He took away your sinful nature. (Col 2:11)

Jesus came to do something wonderful in our lives. He took our sinful hearts away because we believe in Him. Jesus doesn't save us and then forget all about us. He makes us brand-new people from head to toe.

Paul tells the Christians in Colossae that Jesus performed an operation on us. He cut out our sinful hearts. We don't belong to the devil any more. We are really free because Jesus took all our sins away.

Paul says that Jesus nailed every one of our sins to the cross with Him. Then His blood flowed over them and washed everything clean. He can't see our sins anymore – we are free.

As children of Jesus, we don't like sin so we tell the devil 'no' when he wants us to do or think bad things.

Remember: Jesus has given each one of us a new heart.

Jesus lives in me

Galatians 2

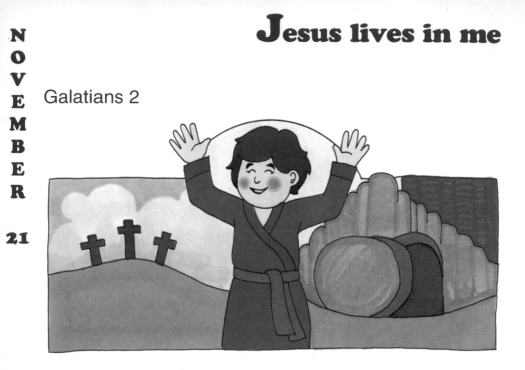

I myself no longer live, but Christ lives in me. So I live my life on earth, trusting in the Son of God. He loves me and gave Himself for me. (Gal 2:20)

When Jesus died on the cross, we died with Him. And when He rose from the dead on the third day, we were raised with Him. We are now dead to sin. The devil can no longer do with us what he wants to.

Paul said that once Jesus lives in us we can no longer do what we want with our lives. We belong to Him so we must listen to Him every day. Jesus decides what we should do and say and think every day.

Jesus loves us very much. He didn't just send a message down from heaven to say He still loves us. He came to us Himself. He died so that we can live forever.

Believing in Jesus is the single most important thing we can ever do. We believe in Jesus because He made us His children. We believe in Him because He died on the cross in our place and gives us everlasting life.

☼ **Remember:** All that we are belongs to Jesus.

Jesus has a place for each of us in heaven

Philippians 3

We are all citizens of heaven, where the Lord Jesus Christ lives. One of these days He will come back to fetch us. (Phil 3:20)

We are citizens of heaven. We are going to live with Jesus forever. Paul wrote that this is the reason why God never stops working in our lives. He will finish His good work in our lives. He will make sure we believe in Him until Jesus comes back to us one day.

We are all citizens of the country we live in. It gives us certain privileges and special rights that citizens of other countries don't have. There is something much more important than being a citizen of our country and that is being a citizen of heaven.

Because we believe in Jesus, we won't end up among the sinners in hell. Jesus will come and fetch us so we can be with Him forever. A child of the Lord is not afraid of death because Jesus is stronger than death. Jesus was the winner and death was the loser.

Every day we must live in such a way that everybody can see we are citizens of heaven. Others should see that we are happy because Jesus has given us everlasting life.

 Remember: Some day we are going to live with Jesus.

Athletes in Jesus' team

1 Corinthians 9

Remember that in a race everyone runs, but only one person can win. He gets the prize. Run for the Lord in such a way that you will win. (1 Cor 9:24)

In a race there can be only one winner. Every athlete runs to win. Paul says the Lord's athletes must also run for first place. The Bible has good news for all athletes in Jesus' team. Everyone who runs flat out for Jesus, is a winner. Everyone who pays attention to what the Bible says, takes first place in the Lord's eyes.

An athlete must train hard to do well. A lazy athlete who does not practise or exercise will never win a medal. We need to train hard if we want to run a good race for the Lord. We must pray often and read our Bible. A good athlete is willing to train hard even when he doesn't feel like it. We should also be willing to work for the Lord even when it's difficult.

We have a very good Trainer – Jesus. He knows exactly how we should run. We just need to do what He tells us and then we'll win an awesome prize – everlasting life!

💡 **Remember:** Run a good race for Jesus.

Be happy – the Lord is with you

Philippians 4

Always be full of joy in the Lord. I say it again – rejoice! (Phil 4:4)

It was not always easy for Paul to be a Christian. Sometimes he landed up in prison. At times people threw stones at him and beat him up, but he never stopped believing. No matter how difficult it was, Paul never gave up. When he wrote to the Philippians, he was in prison for talking to people about Jesus. But being imprisoned couldn't take away his joy.

Paul wrote that Christians must always be joyful. It isn't difficult because ours is a wonderful God. He loves us so much that He sent His only Son to us. But that's not all. God also sent the Holy Spirit to come and live in us. We are never alone and we are going to live forever, with God.

We have many reasons to be joyful every day. The Lord does so much for us. Nothing that happens to us can snatch us from the Lord's hand. Not even the devil is strong enough to steal us from Him.

Let's think of a few reasons for being joyful today, then tell our parents and thank the Lord!

Remember: We should be glad because Jesus is with us.

Talk to the Lord,
He is listening

Philippians 4

Don't worry about anything; instead, pray about everything. Tell God what you need, and thank Him for all He has done. (Phil 4:6)

Prayer is truly amazing. Just think, we can speak to the most important Person in the whole world every day and, best of all, He really listens to us. He hears every word we say. God is never too busy for His children. He makes time to listen to all of our prayers.

We must pray regularly. Paul says we can speak to God about anything under the sun. Nothing in our hearts is too small or too unimportant for Him. We can take everything to Him in prayer.

Prayer is no joke. We don't pray out of habit. Praying is speaking to God Himself and we need to believe that He hears us and will answer our prayers. We must remember to thank Him for taking the time to listen!

Prayer is not just giving God a want-list. Prayer is saying thank you to God for being so great. Prayer should not be all about ourselves, but about God. When we pray like this, then we're not afraid or worried anymore. We believe that God will help us.

🔅 **Remember:** Speak with the Lord every day.

Paul before Festus and Agrippa

Acts 25-26

King Agrippa said to Paul, 'Do you think you can make me a Christian so quickly?' Paul replied, 'Whether quickly or not, I pray that both you and everyone here in this audience might become the same as I am ... ' (Acts 26:28-29)

Paul was in prison in Caesarea for a long time. During that time a new Roman governor took over. His name was Festus. He wanted the Jewish leaders in Jerusalem on his side. So he decided to transfer Paul to Jerusalem for his trial. But Paul refused. He was a Roman citizen and it was his right to be heard by Caesar in Rome.

While Paul was waiting to go to Rome, the Jewish king, Agrippa, arrived in Caesarea. 'I'd like to hear the man speak,' Agrippa said. Many people arrived at the place where Paul was going to talk to King Agrippa about God. Paul told him how he became a Christian. At one stage Paul asked the king, 'King Agrippa, do you believe?' But Agrippa didn't want to become a Christian.

Afterwards Agrippa said to others that Paul was not guilty. He did not deserve to be in prison.

Remember: Pray for somebody who does not believe in Jesus.

Paul on a sinking ship

Acts 27

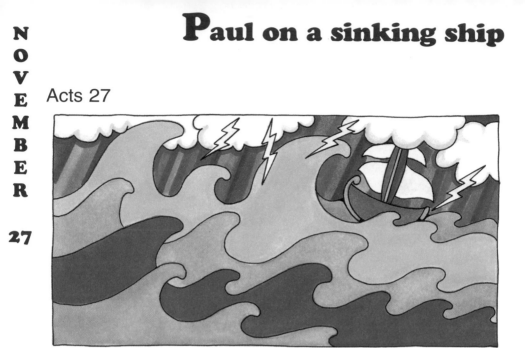

The angel said, 'Don't be afraid, Paul. You will stand trial before Caesar! What's more, because you are on this ship, God will spare the lives of everyone sailing with you.' (Acts 27:24)

Roman soldiers took Paul to Rome on a ship. On the way there Paul warned them that a violent storm was heading their way. He saw trouble ahead if they went on. The ship might be badly damaged.

No-one on the ship paid any attention to Paul. The captain just sailed on. Then the weather changed suddenly. A mighty storm was brewing. The ship was blown off course by the strong wind. Eventually the crew began throwing cargo overboard to make the ship lighter.

Then one night, an angel came to Paul and stood beside him. He told Paul the Lord would spare the lives of everybody on board. God wanted Paul to appear before Caesar in Rome.

After the ship had been drifting on the sea for fourteen days, the sailors saw land. They headed for the shore, but the ship hit some rocks. The ship broke apart but no-one died. Everybody on the ship swam safely ashore!

God keeps His word. He cares for us so much that He holds our lives in His hand. Sometimes He saves us from great danger. We must thank Him often for taking care of us every day.

💡 **Remember:** We must listen to what we are told about the Lord.

Snakebite on the island of Malta

Acts 28

As Paul was putting wood on the fire, a poisonous snake bit him on the hand. The people of the island saw it hanging from Paul's hand and said, 'This man is a murderer. He has just been saved from the sea, but the gods won't stop punishing him.' But Paul shook off the snake into the fire. He was not hurt. (Acts 28:3-5)

Paul and the others were washed up on the island of Malta. It was cold, so they built a fire. A snake hidden in a pile of wood bit Paul on the hand. Paul just shook it off. He was not hurt.

Afterwards Paul visited the chief of the island. His name was Publius. Publius' father was ill with fever. Paul prayed for him and he was healed.

Paul was not ashamed to live for Christ and the Lord used him in many different ways and places. In prisons he led people to Jesus. At sea, when the ship was about to sink, it was because of Paul that the lives of everybody on the ship were spared.

We must never think that the Lord can't use us because we are too young. Age doesn't matter to Him. We can put our hand into His strong hand, and leave the rest to Him.

💡 **Remember:** Pray for other people.

Paul arrives in Rome

Acts 28

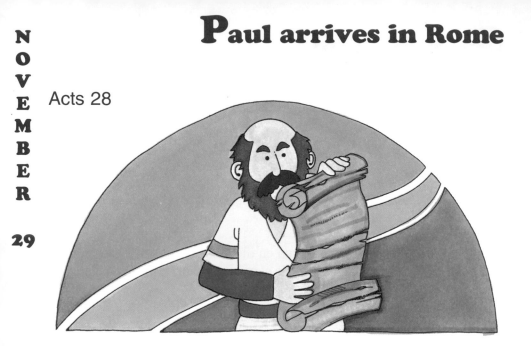

Paul told the people in Rome about God's new world. He taught them all about the Lord Jesus Christ. He did this without fear. And no-one tried to stop him. (Acts 28:31)

After three months on the island of Malta, Paul left for Rome with the Roman soldiers. In Rome the Christians were very glad to see Paul.

The Romans allowed Paul to live in his own rented house. A soldier guarded him. Three days after Paul arrived in Rome, he invited the local Jewish leaders to his home. He talked to them about Jesus but they wouldn't listen to him. Paul told them that's why God sent him to other nations, because his own people, the Jews, were not interested in Jesus.

One person can make a difference! The Lord doesn't need many people to change the world. One person who obeys Him, can do a lot. Take Paul. The Lord used him to tell people all over the world about Jesus. Nothing and nobody could keep him quiet. Even to this day we hear his voice in all the wonderful letters he wrote. If we read them often, we will get to know God well and discover all the wonderful things that Paul wrote about God for ourselves.

-ᜢ- **Remember:** We are important to the Lord. He wants to use us.

The best good news there is

Romans 1

I am not ashamed of this good news about Christ. It is the power of God at work, saving everyone who believes. (Rom 1:16)

In the letter Paul writes to the Christians in Rome, he explains all about the good news. He says God is not an angry God, ready and waiting to punish people. God is on the look-out for sinners but He wants to make them His children. God didn't make people so they'd end up in hell. He wants us all with Him in His heavenly home.

God uses ordinary people to tell others the good news. He doesn't use angels. His agents are people like us. Not some kind of superman, nor adults only. He uses everybody who says Jesus is the Lord of their life.

Every Christian is a witness for the Lord. It is our job to spread the news that God loves sinners. We don't have to pass an exam to do this. We don't need to know the Bible off by heart either. All we need to do is to tell our friends and other people that Jesus loves them. He gives everlasting life to everyone who believes, for free! We should tell Jesus we are sorry for our sins and leave our lives in His hands.

Remember: Tell others about eternal life with Jesus.

God cares

Romans 5

God is not angry with us about our sins anymore, because we now believe in Jesus Christ. So now we have peace with God because of what Jesus Christ our Lord has done for us. (Rom 5:1)

There are people who are afraid of God. They think He is only interested in punishing them for their sins. Paul says, 'Not true!' If we belong to the Lord, He has taken away all our sins. God has already punished Jesus for our sins.

God is not cross with His children anymore because Jesus paid the price for our sins. So that means we are free now. We have peace with God. He is not interested in punishing us.

There is no need for us to be afraid of the Lord. Of course we must have respect for Him, but God is also our Father. He made peace with us and we are His children, no matter what we do. He loves us just the way we are.

The blood of Jesus washed us clean and now God knows us as His children, not as a bunch of sinners. We must thank the Lord every day that we are His children.

💡 **Remember:** The blood of Jesus washed us clean.

Peter also does missionary work

1 Corinthians 9

We have the right to bring our wives along with us when we do missionary work. The other disciples and the Lord's brothers and Peter all do it. (1 Cor 9:5)

Paul wasn't the only person to do missionary work. Many other Christians also brought the good news to people. Before long, people all over the world knew about Jesus. The small group of believers who waited on the Holy Spirit after Jesus' crucifixion soon grew to thousands of people.

Peter started preaching the gospel far outside the borders of Jerusalem. He was head of the church in Jerusalem for a while, but then he decided it was part of his job to preach the gospel in other places as well.

Paul tells us that Peter took his wife along on his missionary journeys. They worked in Corinth and also in Rome. Just like Paul, Peter was not embarrassed to talk about Jesus. His faith was all that mattered to him. Peter travelled many kilometres on foot. He wanted to make sure that as many people as possible would get the chance to hear that Jesus saves them from death.

Remember: We are all missionaries for Christ.

Peter's letters: Live the way Jesus wants you to

1 Peter 1

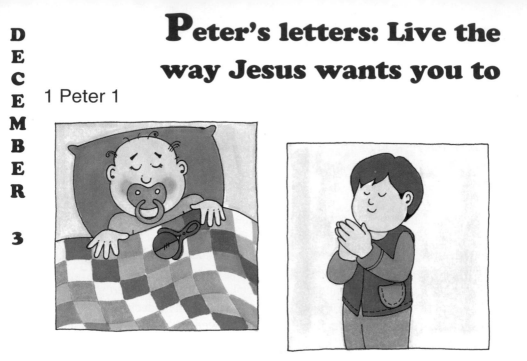

You were born again when you became Christians. But this new life will last forever. (1 Pet 1:23)

Peter wrote a few letters to other Christians. In his first letter he says believers must always listen to God and love one another. This is what God expects us to do.

Peter goes on to say that Christians are born a second time. The first time is when we are brought into the world as babies. The second time is when we become Christians. Then it is just like starting life for the first time.

When we become God's children we are given a new heart – a complete makeover. We are new people, and we must live a new life because we have been changed from head to toe.

We belong to the Lord so we are no longer the slaves of sin. We can tell the devil 'no', we don't want to do bad things. We are going to do what Jesus wants us to, every day.

☀ **Remember:** We are children of God.

We are Jesus' new home

1 Peter 2

You must allow God to use you as living bricks. Let Him build you so that all of you form a new home. You must belong to God only. Like priests you must serve Him. Bring spiritual sacrifices that please him through Jesus Christ. (1 Pet 2:5)

A house is built with bricks, and so is the church of Jesus. There is one difference though – Jesus uses only living bricks. He uses His children. Jesus doesn't live in a church building but in people. He lives in everybody who believes in Him.

Jesus wants us to be living bricks that He can use to put up a great building for God. Christians together must be a temple – one that God can be proud of. For Him to manage this, Jesus asks us to place our lives in His hands every day, so He can use us as He wants.

If we decide for ourselves what God's temple should look like, and try to do the building ourselves, we are never going to please the Lord. But if we are willing to wait until He decides to build us into God's temple where He wants to, then we will please Him. We are like priests who bring offerings that glorify the Name of the Lord.

 Remember: We are a living house for the Lord.

DECEMBER 5

Don't be afraid of suffering

1 Peter 4

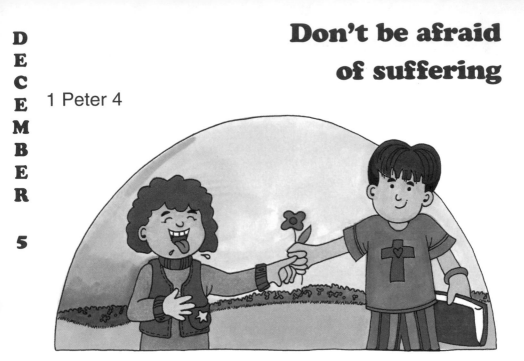

Be happy if you are insulted for being a Christian. This shows that the Holy Spirit of God is with you. (1 Pet 4:14)

Here Peter is writing to Christians who were suffering. People who did not believe in Jesus were giving them a hard time. They were upset. When Peter heard about it, he wrote to them, telling them not to lose heart – Christians sometimes suffer.

Jesus didn't say it would be easy being His children. He knows that wicked people don't like Christians. If others make fun of us because we believe in Jesus, Peter says we should be pleased, because it proves that we are living for Jesus. It shows that the Holy Spirit is working in our lives.

When others make fun of us because we belong to Jesus, we shouldn't try to get them back. That's not what God wants. He wants us to pray for them and to remember what Jesus said – those who believe in Him will sometimes suffer. It pleases the Lord if we take it without complaining. Jesus will keep us safe and fill our lives with His love.

💡 **Remember:** Walk with Jesus – every day.

God is with you, even if others don't like you

Christians who are suffering because it is God's will, must trust their lives to God. He created heaven and earth. He will be with you. Just keep on doing what is right. (1 Pet 4:19)

Peter goes on speaking to Christians who suffer. We must not even think of letting go of God's hand. If we obey God, He will show us the right way, no matter how difficult it might be.

Peter also tells us to remember that when we have problems God is with us, and He is more powerful than anyone or anything in the whole world. Nobody is as great and holy as He is.

When we are suffering we should not sit around and mope and feel sorry for ourselves. We should just carry on living like children of the Lord. We need to go on doing good works for those around us.

Christians who feel sorry for themselves are not much use to Jesus. We must pray for others and help those who are even worse off than us. That will help us forget about our own problems.

 Remember: We must always be kind to our friends.

Believers never think too highly of themselves

DECEMBER 7

1 Peter 5

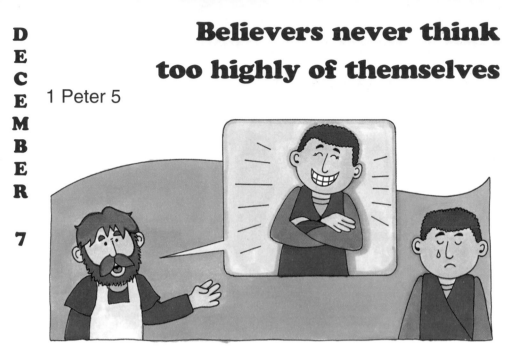

You youngsters, listen to adults. And all of you, old and young, don't think too highly of yourselves. Remember God doesn't like people who think they are better than others. He likes people who are humble. (1 Pet 5:5)

In church children still respect grown-ups, and adults don't consider themselves better than children. Members of a church care for one another. When someone is having a hard time, other Christians reach out to them. Christians are never too busy to lend a helping hand.

Peter says Christians don't think too highly of themselves. At school and in the adult world people always want to be the best and the cleverest and the most successful. But it is different in a church community. There Christians do not brag about themselves. They let the spotlight fall on others.

Our task is to brag about Jesus. We must tell others how great Jesus is. He makes the lives of people brand-new. We must remind our Christian friends how the Lord changed their lives. And we must rejoice with them about this.

The Lord doesn't like people who think they are clever. He wants us to be humble. We must bow before Him and respect others.

💡 **Remember:** Be humble like Jesus.

Don't listen to wicked church members

There have always been false prophets, just as there will be false teachers among you. They will twist the message of the gospel cleverly. They will even turn against their Master Who bought them. They are all on their way to their death. (2 Pet 2:1)

There are people who don't preach the gospel correctly or don't live the way they should. They twist things around to suit themselves. Peter warns us against such people. He says there have always been dishonest people who say they work for God. These people are going to be punished. Their day of reckoning will come.

How do we know when someone is lying about Jesus? We should turn to the Bible and see what it says, and then we'll know what is true and what is false. If someone says something that is not in the Bible, then we'll know he or she is wrong and we must not listen to that person. When people talk about things we can find in the Bible, then we must listen to them.

We must pray every day that people who talk about Jesus in church will speak the whole truth and that no false stories about Jesus will be told.

 Remember: We should read our Bible regularly.

The Lord is coming soon

2 Peter 3

Scoffers will say, 'Jesus promised to come back, didn't He? Then where is He? Why, as far back as I can remember, everything has remained exactly the same since the world was first created.' (2 Pet 3:4)

Peter heard that some people were making fun of Christians. They were saying Christians are lying when they tell people Jesus will come back to us. Nothing has changed. Everything is the same as it has always been. People come and go, but the Lord does not come back.

Peter answered these mockers by saying the Lord is on His way but He wants sinners to repent first before He comes back. Otherwise they will all go to hell, where all wicked people will stay forever. God does not want that to happen. He did not make people so they could go to hell. He made people to go to heaven.

We must invite others to the Lord's banquet. We must tell them how much Jesus loves them and convince them of it. We need to carry on telling people the good news until the day Jesus comes back. We needn't worry about when the Lord will come. We must just keep on inviting people to be ready.

🔆 **Remember:** We must invite our friends to believe in Jesus.

To the Lord a day is like a thousand years

2 Peter 3

You must not forget: a day is like a thousand years to the Lord, and a thousand years is like a day. (2 Pet 3:8)

The Lord's time isn't the same as ours. To Him a full thousand years is like an hour and if He feels like it, He can stretch an hour to a thousand years.

Often we want the Lord to fall in with our plans. We expect Him to give us an answer to our prayers straight away. He must open up heaven when we say so. This is wrong. The Lord doesn't need to make His time fit in with ours. We must fall in with His time. We must learn to wait until the time is right for the Lord.

We needn't be worried because the Second Coming has not taken place yet. The Lord will come back in His own good time. All He asks us to do is to wait patiently. We mustn't start doing wicked things because the Lord wants to wait a while longer before He comes back to earth. His Second Coming will be unexpected. Nobody can tell exactly when it will happen.

We should wait for the Lord every day and learn to be patient until He answers our prayers. We cannot force Him into something just to suit ourselves.

 Remember: Jesus will definitely come back to us again.

God gives us only good things

James 1

Whatever is good and perfect comes to us from God above ... (Jas 1:16)

James, the brother of Jesus, also wrote a letter in the Bible. James says if we get caught up in sin, we have only ourselves to blame. It is not God's fault. Sin is like a tiny seed. If we allow it to start growing in our lives, it can become a giant plant and eventually destroy our lives.

Sin is not from God. The bad things that happen in life do not come from Him. It is people who do wicked things. They steal, kill others and use bad language. God gives us only good things. Life and joy come from God. He opens up His hand and gives us everything that is good.

We dare not allow sin to grow like a plant in our lives. We must stop it in time and never even think of bad things. We should fill our heads with Jesus every day and think about what we read in the Bible. If we pray every day then sin cannot win.

Remember – sin starts in our heads. When we start thinking about bad things we are a step away from doing them. So, we must give our thoughts to the Lord every day.

🔆 **Remember:** God is not responsible for the wrong things we do.

Do what the Lord says

James 2

What's the use of saying you have faith if you don't prove it by what you do? That kind of faith can't save anyone. (Jas 2:14)

Faith is doing. It's not just something we talk about on a Sunday in church. We act out our faith from Monday to Saturday as well as on Sundays. We do what the Lord says seven days a week.

James writes that some churchgoers say they believe, but he sees no sign of it in their lives. They talk a lot, but do nothing.

James gives an example. He says if you see another believer who is hungry or who needs clothes, it is no use saying, 'Well, goodbye and God bless you. Stay warm and eat well.' Faith is doing something about it. Give that person food or clothing. Talk is cheap. It can't take hunger and cold away.

James also uses Abraham as an example. He was willing to offer his son Isaac on the altar when the Lord told him to. It was his faith that made him do whatever God told him.

Faith without deeds is dead. It means nothing to the Lord. Faith which makes us do what the Lord says, is alive.

 Remember: Faith which makes us do what the Lord says, is alive.

God's children say nice things

James 3

The tongue is like a fire. It is full of wickedness that can ruin your whole life. From the beginning to the end of your life, your tongue is dangerous. (Jas 3:6)

James warns us not to speak before thinking. He says our tongues are dangerous. Although the tongue is a small part of our bodies, it can destroy our bodies. It is like the rudder of a huge ship. It steers the ship any way it wants to.

We can hurt people by the words we say. When we make fun of our friends or say nasty things to them, it's like stabbing them with a knife. It's even worse if we say these things behind someone's back.

James says we must watch what we say. We should ask the Lord to set a guard before our mouths. He must stop us from saying things we'll be sorry about later.

We cannot say nice things to God one moment, and the next call somebody else names! We can't have blessing and cursing come pouring out of the same mouth. Our words should make others feel better and they should praise the Lord.

💡 **Remember:** We must take care of what we say every day.

The Lord listens when we pray

James 5

Are any of you suffering? Keep on praying. And those who have reason to be thankful should praise the Lord. (Jas 5:13)

Prayer works. It is speaking to God Himself and we should pray often. If we're having a bad time, we needn't struggle with our problems all by ourselves. We can talk to God about it and ask Him to help us. And when we are happy we should tell the Lord and thank Him.

We should pray when things go wrong and when they go well.

When we're ill we can ask the Lord to make us better and thank Him for making us well again.

There is nothing in our lives that we cannot take to the Lord. No problem is too small. He invites us to pray and He listens when we do.

Remember: We must pray every day.

Watch out for
wicked people

Jude 1

Watch out for wicked people who have wormed their way into your church. They think they can live sinful lives because God forgives them every time. They have turned against our only Master and Lord, Jesus Christ. (Jude 1:4)

Jesus had four brothers. Two of them, James and Jude, wrote letters that are in the Bible. Jude tells us in his letter how wicked people sneak into the church. They try to confuse other Christians. These people tell other believers it's all right to sin. The Lord doesn't mind. He forgives our sins anyway.

Jude warns us to be very careful of these people. They twist what is written in the Bible to suit themselves and the way they live. They don't really do what the Lord says. They even mock the angels and God.

Our God is so good to us. But it doesn't mean we can live however we like. We must say 'no' to sin. And if we have done something wrong, we must tell the Lord we're sorry. We must ask Him to forgive us and we must not do the same thing again.

Sin is like cancer. It keeps on spreading if it is not treated in time. Treat it with the best 'medicine' in the world – the power of the Spirit!

-Ò- **Remember:** Say 'no' to doing wrong.

The Lord will take care of us until the end

Jude 1

And now, all glory to God, who is able to keep you from stumbling. You will stand before Him one day with great joy in your heart. Praise Him, He alone is our God, through Jesus Christ our Lord. Yes, He is powerful, mighty and important. He is the greatest – now, and for evermore. (Jude 1:24-25)

The Lord is a million times more important than the most important person in the world. The Lord has always lived and He will live for ever and ever. He is the most powerful of all, the greatest. There is nobody like Him. **16**

The good news the Bible tells us, is that the Lord cares for us as well. He, who is so great and mighty, takes notice of us. He takes us in His arms and looks after us every single day. He makes sure that we are safe.

The Lord will not allow the devil to take us from Him. He walks alongside us every day. He is with us every step of the way. Isn't this wonderful news? To think that the most important Person in the whole wide world cares for us! To think that He wants us to come and live with Him forever!

 Remember: God keeps us close to Him every day.

Jesus is more important than angels

Hebrews 1

DECEMBER

17

God calls his angels 'messengers as fast as the wind; servants made of flaming fire.' But to His Son He says, 'Your throne, O God, will last forever and ever. You are a fair King.' (Heb 1:7-8)

Angels are very important. They work for the Lord. But Jesus is more important than all the angels put together. Angels were made by the Lord. They worship Him day and night.

Sometimes angels must come down to earth to do certain things for the Lord. They obey the Lord.

Jesus isn't just another important angel. He is the Son of God. Jesus is God Himself. There is a wide gulf between Jesus and the angels. That is why God also calls Jesus God. He is completely different to all the other powers in heaven.

Jesus is King of the whole world. He reigns forever. Jesus has the whole world in His hands. We are alive because Jesus wants us to live. Without Him there can be nothing.

We must worship Jesus because He is the Son of God. He is the King of the whole world for ever and ever.

🔆 **Remember:** We worship Jesus, because He is the Son of God.

Jesus broke the power of the devil

Hebrews 2

D E C E M B E R

Because God's children are human beings, Jesus also became a human being. He did it to destroy the power of the devil. It was only as a human being that He could die, and only by dying could He break the power of the devil, who had the power of death. (Heb 2:14)

The devil is not in charge here on earth anymore. He has been defeated. This **18** happened when Jesus came to the earth. Jesus became a human being because He felt very sorry for all of us. He saw how scared we were of death. That is why He gave His life for us. He came to defeat death. Now death is not our enemy any longer because Jesus is stronger than death. He went straight through death and came out the other side alive.

The day we die, Jesus will be there, waiting for us. He will carry us through death to the house of His Father. That's why Christians aren't afraid of dying anymore.

Jesus knows exactly what we are thinking. He also knows what scares us. That's why He can help us. He takes care of us and stops the devil from getting us into his clutches. Jesus is with us always.

 Remember: Jesus is with us always.

Jesus is our new High Priest

Hebrews 3-4

We have a very important High Priest: Jesus the Son of God, who has gone to heaven. Let us cling to Him and never stop trusting Him. This High Priest of ours understands our weaknesses, because the devil also tempted Him, but He did not sin. (Heb 4:14-15)

In the Old Testament the high priest was the most important priest. It was his job to go into the holiest part of the temple once a year on behalf of the people. The high priest had to bring an offering for the sins of his people.

We read in Hebrews that Jesus is now our new High Priest. He is not like an earthly high priest who must first bring an offering for his own sins. Jesus is without sin. An earthly priest was only allowed in the most holy part of the temple once a year. But Jesus is in heaven where He will live forever. He is in the most important place in the whole world all the time. That is why He can really help us.

Jesus knows how difficult it is to fight sin. He was a human being so He knows how to help us. Jesus is our shelter. We can run to Him any time we are afraid, or don't know what to do.

💡 **Remember:** We can run to Jesus any time we are afraid.

Jesus is our coach

Let us run the race that God has set before us. We must keep our eyes on Jesus all the time. We must not give up. We can depend on Him from start to finish. (Heb 12:1-2)

In any race, athletes must run flat out. An athlete who looks around, is not going to give his best. A good athlete looks straight ahead. He sees the finish and runs flat out to get there first.

We as Christians run for Jesus. Our eyes must be on Him at all times. He is waiting for us at the finish. If we keep on looking around, it will not be long before we slow down and start noticing the wrong things.

Jesus is our Coach. He knows the track on which we are running. He knows exactly what we must do to win. All He asks is that we listen to His voice. We must pray, read the Bible every day and do what the Bible says – then we are good athletes. We run according to God's rules.

We must never take our eyes off Jesus. If we watch Him, we will be good athletes. We will finish the race and win first prize, because Jesus is waiting for us at the finish.

 Remember: Jesus is the best Coach in the whole world.

We must listen only to Jesus

Hebrews 12

Now you have come to Zion, to the city of the living God. Thousands of joyful angels get together here every day. You have come to the place where the Lord's children will live forever. You have come to God Himself, Who is the Judge of all people. You are with people who have been freed from their sins. You have come to Jesus. He gave us God's new covenant. His blood washes us clean from all sin. (Heb 12:22-24)

All of us who believe in Jesus are on our way to a brand-new world. God is there in heaven – the most important of all. All God's angels and all who have been washed clean by the blood of Jesus live there with Him. Jesus lives there and He will make sure we are allowed into heaven.

Only people who believe in Jesus will be allowed into heaven. His blood makes us citizens of heaven. There is no other way to get to Jesus. Trying to live a good life doesn't impress the Lord. There is only one way to God. The Bible tells us that Jesus is the only way to God. We must listen to His voice every day. Then we will be safe and know that a brand-new life is waiting for us.

Remember: Only Jesus can make us children of God.

We will live with Jesus forever

Hebrews 13

Let us praise the Lord. Because we believe in Jesus, our lips must offer our sacrifice of praise to God. Let us glorify His Name. Don't forget to do good and to share what you have with those in need. Such sacrifices please God. (Heb 13:15-16)

We must glorify the name of the Lord. We must be overflowing with joy. Our lips must be like a living sacrifice. Others must hear only good things from our mouths. They must hear that God is more important than anything else in our lives. They must also hear how great and good God is.

We must not bring offerings to the Lord with our lips only. We must also bring offerings with our deeds. The kind of offering the Lord wants from us is to do good deeds for Him. We must not cling to our money. The Bible says what we have we should share with others.

Do we share our money with others or do we spend it all on ourselves? Of course we can buy ourselves nice things. The Lord is not cross with us for doing that, but we must not be blind to the needs of people around us. We must care for them. It's not only grown-ups who should help the needy. Children should do so too.

 Remember: We must serve the Lord with everything we have.

Jesus gives us everlasting life

1 John 5

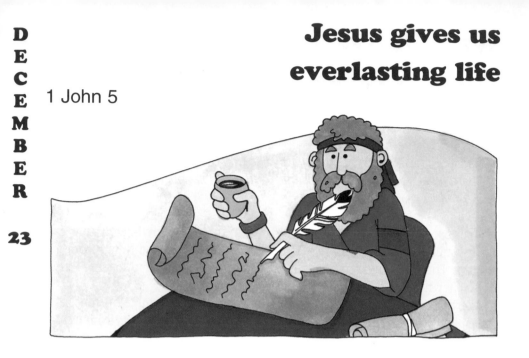

I write this to you who believe in the Son of God, so that you may know you have eternal life. (1 Jn 5:13)

The apostle John wrote a number of letters to believers. In the Bible we can read three of these letters. He explains why he has written the first letter – to tell readers they have everlasting life.

The best words we can ever hear are the words from God's mouth that we belong to Him and that we are going to live forever. John says every human being on earth can hear these words. All we need to do is to put our hand into the hand of Jesus and believe in Him. Then we can have everlasting life. It's as easy as that. We cannot earn everlasting life or buy it with money. We have to believe in Jesus. Faith unlocks the road to life. We need to believe that Jesus died in our place, to pay for all our sins. Then we become God's children forever and He is our Father forever.

Nobody who believes in Jesus will ever be disappointed. God tells us this. He takes care of everyone who belongs to Him. Because His children are very precious to Him, He leads us safely to heaven.

💡 **Remember:** We need to believe that Jesus died for all our sins.

We must ask Jesus to forgive us

1 John 1

If we say we have no sin, we are fooling ourselves. We are not telling the truth. But if we go to the Lord and ask Him to forgive us our sins, He will do it. God never lies. He keeps His promises. He takes away our sins. (1 Jn 1:8-9)

Sin is not obeying the Lord. If we know what the Lord wants us to do and we don't listen, then we are sinning. Sin is going against the Lord's will.

Not even one Christian can say he or she never sins. People who say that are lying. What must we do with our sin? John says we must take it to the Lord. We need to tell Him we are sorry for our sins. We must ask the Lord to forgive us.

If we go to the Lord and say we are sorry, He forgives us our sins. This is a promise. He will never give our sins another thought.

We must not allow our sins to stand between the Lord and us like a brick wall. We must confess our sins and not do those things again. We must ask God to forgive us and then live a new life.

 Remember: We must ask the Lord to forgive our sins.

The Lord's children love one another

**D
E
C
E
M
B
E
R**

25

1 John 3

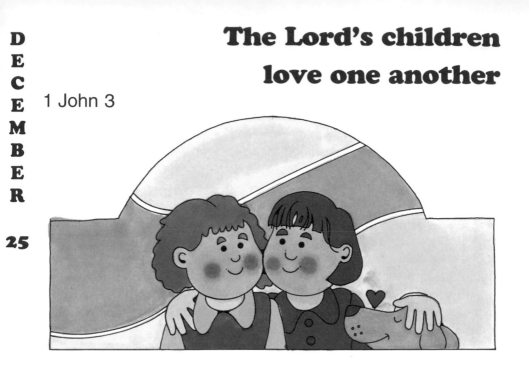

Dear children, let us stop just saying we love each other; let us really show it by our actions. (Jn 3:18).

We cannot say we love God if we hate His children, John says. If we love God, we must love one another. God is love and He loves all of us. That is why we should care for each other.

God shows His love in what He does for us. He let His Son die in our place. God doesn't just say He loves us, He shows it. If we look at Jesus, we can see exactly what love is.

As for us, we can't just say we love other Christians. We must show it with our whole lives. It's no good pretending that we care for others. That's dishonest. We must really care for one another and do kind things for each other. In that way we show others what love is.

We mustn't sit and wait for people to be nice to us. We must love them first and not stop, even if they don't say thank you to us. We mustn't expect thanks. As long as we do what God says, that's all that matters.

🔆 **Remember:** We must care about one another.

God is on His throne

Revelation 4

I was taken to heaven by the Spirit. I saw a throne in heaven. God was sitting on it! (Rev 4:2)

Revelation is a book that is written in picture language. When we read the words, we can form pictures in our mind of what we are reading. It tells us how God and Jesus hold the whole world in Their hands. In chapter 4 John takes us on a journey to heaven and shows us a picture of God sitting on His throne. God rules over everything and everybody. He is so powerful that nothing upsets Him.

In heaven God is surrounded by His church and His creation. John gives us a picture of the church as twenty-four elders, and of creation as four living beings. The Holy Spirit is also in heaven with God.

John sees the members of the Lord's church sitting in a circle around His throne. All of them are the same distance from God. No believer is closer or farther away from Him than the others.

God rules in heaven. Everybody in heaven worships God and bows before Him. In heaven everyone is happy. God is King there.

 Remember: We should thank the Lord that we are His children.

Jesus is the strongest in the whole world

Revelation 5

Then one of the believers in heaven said to me, 'Stop crying. The Lion of the tribe of Judah has won. He alone can open the book in God's right hand.' (Rev 5:5)

While John is in heaven he sees that God is holding a scroll in His hand, but this scroll is sealed. Nobody can open it. This upset John so much that he started crying. John knew that in the book God was holding in His right hand was the plan He had for the world. If nobody could open it, God's plan for the world would not work out.

One of the believers in heaven then told John to stop crying. There is Someone who can open the book in God's hand. He is the Lion, Jesus. When John looked up he saw Jesus standing at the throne of God.

John says that Jesus stood there in heaven like a slaughtered Lamb. He still carried the marks of His earthly struggle on His body. The scars the nails had made where they pierced His hands could still be seen.

Jesus took the book from God's hand. He alone will bring God's plan for the world into operation. Jesus is now in control. The church in heaven was so happy about this that they fell down before Jesus. Everybody worshipped Him.

☼ **Remember:** Jesus is always in control.

Jesus punishes sinners

As I watched, the Lamb broke the first of the seven seals on the scroll. (Rev 6:1)

As John watched, Jesus broke the seals that kept the book shut, one by one. In picture language John tells us that next, different horses each with its own rider, are let loose. They go into the world. The first horse is white. This is John's way of telling us that, right up to the very last day, there will be people who twist the good news.

The colour of the second horse is red. This represented war on earth. Until the day Jesus comes back to earth, people will make war against one another.

The third horse is black. John says this means that there will be a great famine on earth.

The colour of the fourth horse is pale green and Death is the name of its rider. From the time Jesus was taken up to heaven until His Second Coming, death will always be with us.

We must not let these four horses and their riders frighten us. Jesus is there to look after us.

 Remember: God looks after His children.

Everyone before God

Revelation 20

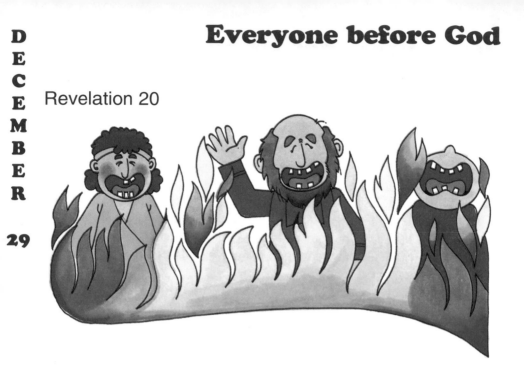

And anyone whose name was not found recorded in the Book of Life was thrown into the lake of fire. (Rev 20:15)

John also tells us in Revelation what is going to happen on the very last day. He sees all the people on earth standing before the throne of God that day – old and young, big and small, the living and the dead. Nobody is left out. Then God opens all His books. In the books all the deeds of people who did not believe in Jesus are written down, every single thing they did. All of these people are doomed. They will be thrown into the pool of fire. There they will stay forever!

But there is another book, the Book of Life. In this book God has written down the names of all His children. They will have everlasting life.

God knows us either by our deeds, or by our names. If He knows us because of what we do, we will spend the rest of our days being punished. But if God knows us by name, He will give us everlasting life.

When we believe in Jesus, He tears all our deeds out of His books.

☀ **Remember:** We are going to live with Jesus one day.

We are going to live in God's new city

Revelation 21

I heard a loud shout from the throne, saying, 'Look, the home of God is now among His people! He will live with them, and they will be His people. God Himself will be with them. He will remove all of their sorrows, and there will be no more death or sorrow or crying or pain. For the old world and its evils are gone forever.' (Rev 21:3-4)

God says in Revelation that He will come and live with us. His new address will be ours.

In God's new city nothing bad will happen. There, nobody will die. Nobody will cry. God Himself will wipe the tears from His children's eyes. Pain and suffering will come to an end. In God's new city people will be safe. There will be no hospitals, because there will be no more sick people.

In God's world everything is brand-new. He keeps it all new Himself, forever. Here, on this earth, everything gets old. It breaks, it doesn't last. Even the strongest people lose their strength and the most active people become old and slow. But with God, none of this is going to happen. When we are with Him we will always have something to celebrate. What a place to look forward to!

 Remember: God made a whole new world for us to live in.

DECEMBER

31

Everybody is safe in God's new streets

Revelation 21-22

No temple could be seen in the city, for the Lord Almighty and the Lamb are its temple. (Rev 21:22)

John gives us a quick peek at our last address. He shows us that God Himself is coming to live in the city. This new city has no temple, because God is there for everybody to see with their own eyes. The sun won't need to shine anymore, because the light coming from God is bright enough.

In God's new city everyone is safe. No crooks or sinners are allowed there. There is enough food for everyone to eat. Nobody will go hungry, ever.

In God's city with its main street made of pure gold and its precious gems, all the people live together happily. No-one fights and there is no quarrelling. Only God matters. Everyone bows before Him and praises Him.

When is God's new city going to be ready for us? We don't know. But Jesus tells us we need to invite Him. We must ask Him to come back to us soon.

The early Christians often used the words 'Marana tha'. It was an invitation to the Lord. It means: 'Come, O Lord! Marana tha' – Come Lord Jesus!

Remember: We must invite Jesus to come back to us soon.